The

MACHINE
KNITTER'S
DICTIONARY

by the same author:

The Craft of Machine Knitting (1978)

The MACHINE KNITTER'S DICTIONARY

Linda Gartshore

Diagrams by Nicholas Leggett

St. Martin's Press, New York

For my Mother and Father with my love

LIBRARY OF CONGRESS CATALOG CARD NUMBER: 83-060726
ISBN 0-312-50221-4

First published in Great Britain by B T Batsford Ltd.

First U.S. Edition

10 9 8 7 6 5 4 3 2 1

Contents

ACKNOWLEDGMENTS

I would like to thank all the knitting machine importers and manufacturers in the United Kingdom for their co-operation, Mr Rheinberg of Rheinbergs Ltd, the International Wool Secretariat, the British Wool Marketing Board, British Celanese Ltd and the International Institute for Cotton for their information and photographs on the raw fibre and its processes. The colour photograph of the author's work on the front jacket of the book was taken by Jan Gordon. Thanks also to Mr Whitlock of Fareham Sewing Machines, who always helps readily with my queries, to Mrs Hardman of Shoreham Knitting Machines, to my Mother for endless hours of typing and finally to my husband for his constant support.

ABBREVIATIONS (see also *Diagram Patterns*). All written knitting patterns are abbreviated and the abbreviations listed here are in most common use. However, it is important to ascertain the actual abbreviations being used before commencing to knit a particular pattern.

M   main colour/yarn
A   1st contrast colour
B   2nd contrast colour
C   3rd contrast colour
D   4th contrast colour
alt   alternate
beg   beginning
carr   carriage
C.O.B.H.   cast on by hand
col   colour
C.O.L   carriage on left
Con. Col.   contrast colour
cont.   continue
C.O.R.   carriage on right
dec   decrease
ev   every
F F   fully fashioned
foll   following
g/grms   grammes
HP   holding position
inc   increase
Ns/Nds.   needles
NWP   non-working position
O   tubular
patt   pattern
pos   position
R   row
rem   remaining
rept   repeat
RC   row counter
R.C.000   reset row counter to zero
R.T.   ribber tension
st   stitch
sts   stitches
St. s   stitch size
St. st.   stocking stitch
T   tension
tog   together
trans   transfer
UWP   upper working position
WP   working position
W.Wl.   waste wool

Needle Arrangements:
/ = needle in working position
● = needle in non-working position
◗ = centre of bed
X = times
K   knit
M   main colour
M.B.   main bed
M/C   machine
MT   main tension
MT-1   one full size finer than main tension
MT-2   two full sizes finer than main tension
MT+1   one full size looser than main tension
MT+2   two full sizes looser than main tension
N/Nd.   needle

ACCESSORIES, FASHION (see also *Edgings, Quilting, Sampling, Swiss Darning*). It is important, when designing an outfit or even a single garment, to consider exactly what will be worn with it. Accessories include hats, scarves, jewellery, gloves, socks, bags and shoes. These can be a combination of machine-knitted and bought accessories, according to the fashion, which will give a total look. It will also enhance the machine-knitted fabric. A bought hat, for example, might have a machine-knitted band to match the main garment. Or an attractive edging might be carried through to an accessory. Alternatively, an area of Swiss darning could be used in this way. A quilted waistcoat and a quilted bag can offset plain knitting. It is the combination of colour and texture, and the clever use of these combinations, that make the fashion outfit complete. Look carefully at fashion magazines to see how top designers team colour and fabric, as a starting point, and develop the best combinations by experimentation.

ACCESSORIES, KNITTING MACHINE (see also *Tools*). Machine accessories vary according to the make and model of the knitting machine. Some are interchangeable while others are specifically for a particular machine. In some countries certain accessories, for example a wool winder and blank cards for punching, are supplied with the machine. The list below is a general list of accessories for various knitting machines. Ask which of these accessories are available for a particular model of knitting machine before purchasing.
Blank cards and pen for electronic machine
Blank graph sheets for charting device and pen
Blank punchcards
Carrying case
Charting device and stitch scales

Clip for fixing instruction book to the yarn tention unit
Colour changer
Electric motor
Garter bar
Garter stitch carriage
Handy punch
Instruction book (various)
Intarsia carriage
Lamp
Linker
Machine knitting stand
Machine knitting table
Needle bed cover
Plating attachment
Punchcard sets
Ratchet punch
Ribber, + extra weights + casting on combs + new table clamps, and close knit bar if applicable
Sets of basic shapes for charting device
Shadow lace transfer tool
Skein winder
Table clamps (see *Clamps*)
Tools can be bought separately, including different coloured nylon cords to help when knitting various sections
Transfer locks/carriage
7 x 1 transfer tool + selection of varying wider transfer tools, over every needle and for rib

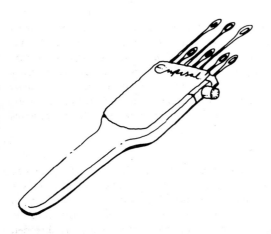

Seven-eyed transfer tool

Weavemaster
Wool winder (ball and cone)
Yarn twister

ACETATE (see also *Fibres, identification, Man-made Fibres, production of, Synthetic Yarns*). This man-made fibre was patented in 1894 and was first spun in England commercially after World War I by British Celanese Ltd. It was first spun in the U.S.A. in 1924 and since then different companies throughout the world have produced the fibre under different trade names. It is made from cellulose base, which is obtained from wood pulp or short cotton fibres and it is known as a regenerated fibre. It dyes before spinning into brilliant colours and drapes well with a lustrous sheen. It is combined with other fibres to produce yarns for machine and hand knitting.

ACRILAN, see *Acrylic*. Trade name for acrylic fibre.

ACRYLIC (see also *Fibres, identification, Iron and Ironing, Man-made Fibres, production of, Yarn Combinations*). Man-made fibre from a combination of minerals, mainly coal, water, petroleum and natural gas, the latter producing a chemical compound. The first acrylic garments were produced by Du Pont under the trade name Orlon, and were for sale in 1951 in American shops. In 1957 Courtaulds in Britain commenced producing the fibre under the trade name Courtelle. Acrylic fibre is strong and very hard wearing and cannot be attacked by moth. It is not very warm, however, and creases badly. It is unsuitable for knitting alone, especially where there are pressure points, for example at the back of skirts and at the knee of trousers. Acrylic yarn stretches easily when damp.

ADJUSTMENTS, see *Pattern Adjustments*.

ADULT EDUCATION (see also *Clubs, knitting*). In many areas machine knitting courses are run by the local Education Authority. Some provide crèche facilities. In London the annual publication *Floodlight* covers all the Adult Education Authority. If no such classes exist in your area and you are interested in starting a course contact your local Education Authority. They will inform you as to your suitability to start such a course. See details at the local library. In U.S.A., contact local outlet for sewing and knitting machines.

AFTERCARE, GARMENT, see *Garment Aftercare*.

ALPACA. Domesticated animal from South American camel family. Soft, fine, lustrous fibre, 20-30 cm (8-12 in) in length. Colour varies from white or reddish brown to black, with silky sheen. Usually mixed with wool or acrylic.

ALPHABET, see *Picture Knitting*.

ANGORA (see also *Pilling, Yarn Combinations*). Soft fluffy yarn from the Angora rabbit, the best quality fibres coming from France, Italy and Japan. It is usually dyed in pale colours and is the softest of all animal fibres. Before knitting this yarn, put it into the refrigerator at least 12 hours before use to stop the fine hairs flying. Never use angora on babies' garments.

ANIMAL FIBRES, see *Alpaca, Angora, Camel, Cashmere, Llama, Mohair, Vicuna, Wool*.

ANTENNA, see *Automatic Yarn Tension Unit*.

ANTENNA SPRING (see also *Automatic Yarn Tension Unit*). Name for the two top wires on the automatic yarn tension unit. These have an eye at the end of each antenna where the yarn is passed through. The pull of the yarn should pull the antenna spring about half way down when knitting. If the antenna is too high the yarn is being fed to the needle too loosely, if it is too low the yarn is being fed too tightly. Adjust the disc tensioner accordingly.

APPLIQUÉ (see also *Blanket Stitch, Renovation*). Cut out fabric shapes that are applied to a garment by sticking, sewing, or embroidery.

ARAN, see *Aran Knitting, History of*.

ARAN WOOL, (see also *Aran Knitting, History of, Iron and Ironing*). A smooth double-knitting wool, originally used in off-white but which can now be bought in other colours. It is extremely warm but cannot be knitted over every needle on the knitting machine. It is best used on weaving in patterns, where it is carried on the surface of the knitting and not knitted in.

ARAN KNITTING, HISTORY OF (see also *Guernsey, history of, History of Knitting, Mock Aran*). This hand knitting originates from the Isle of Aran off the west coast of Ireland. The wool used is an off-white creamy yarn. The Irish name for this thick, home-spun yarn is 'bainin', which means natural. The stitches are grouped together to form pattern blocks but they are not always mathematically designed, for it is not unusual to have an even number of patterns on the front whilst the back ends with half a design. The ground or surface stitch is nearly always plain knitting, but the fabric becomes embossed by the use of cables, crossed stitches and bobble stitches. The patterns are built up from a centre panel with other panels either side of it. It is a combination of cables, bobbles, and cross stitch that form the basis for these intricate and densely textured fabric. The sweater or guernsey from Aran is knitted on two needles and not in rounds. The welt of these sweaters is also patterned. Many Aran stitch patterns originated from the inspiration of the islanders' daily life. The patterns are sometimes from designs taken from Irish crosses and tidy stones, while some of the meanings are biblical: The Tree of Life, The Trinity (Blackberry) stitch, The Ladder of Life, Marriage Lines and The Trellis, are examples. It is not possible to knit true Aran on the knitting machine, but a similar effect can be achieved, called mock Aran.

ARMHOLES (see also *Dolman, Dropped Shoulder, Puff Sleeve, Raglan Shaping, Saddle Shaping, Set-In Shaping*). The armhole and sleeve top should fit quite close to the underarm, but at the same time allowing free movement of the arm. It should not fit so closely that the main body of the garment lifts when the arm is raised. The garment should move with the body and not hide it in bulkiness.

ASTRAKHAN. True astrakhan is the name for a second grade lamb skin from sheep in the Russian province of Astrakhan. It has a lustrous, uneven, (usually) brown, curly texture. Today a mock astrakhan is made in a heavy woven cloth, usually mohair. Mock machine-knitted astrakhan fabric can be produced by knitting a dark brown or black knobbly slub yarn.

AUTOMATIC YARN TENSION UNIT (see also *Antenna Spring, Threading The Machine*). This is common to all machines, sometimes called a yarn break. A stainless steel rod is set vertically into the back of the needle bed. The yarn has to be threaded at four or sometimes five points before it reaches the carriage. Each rod holds at the top two antenna springs. Each spring tensions a different yarn, or yarns. On some machines it is possible to set in at the back of the carriage a second rod, so enabling four separate yarns to be threaded up for use at one time.

BACK STITCH (see also *Casting Off, Making Up*). Used to sew open edges on to closed edges. It is important that the open knitting is pressed first with waste yarn attached. This will stop the open stitches from running so easily. Remember to sew through every stitch otherwise it will run, and then unpick the knitting.

BAGS. Weave and tuck patterns have the firmer structure and are best suited to making knitted bags. Line the bag with either an interesting fabric or a strong lining fabric, made up smaller than the actual size of the bag. The lining will then take the weight of the contents and the bag will retain its shape. Avoid knitting bands for handles as they tend to stretch; plaiting is preferable.

BALBRIGGAN. A small coastal town just north of Dublin, in Ireland, where a lightweight single weft knitted cotton fabric originated. Balbriggan was later the name given to underwear made from this cloth.

BANDANNA (see also *Printing*). Originates from the Hindi word meaning to knot, bind, or tie. It is used to describe Indian resist dyeing.

BANDS (see also *Buttonholes, Making Up*). Bands on the single bed are stocking stitch and mock ribs, and on the double bed are stocking stitch or rib.

Armhole Bands can be knitted in one piece on to the garment. Join the garment at the shoulder seams and pick up the stitches as for a neckband with right side away. Pick up the stitches evenly along the edge stitches of the armhole and knit the required number of rows and cast off. An armhole band can be picked up and knitted in the same way as a V-neck band; the garment is folded lengthwise and the stitches placed for half the band on to the machine. Decrease one stitch on either end of the underarm band, on every alternate row. On a double stocking stitch band increase one stitch at either end on every alternate row. (For rib, see *Neckbands*.)

Buttonbands. To calculate the size of buttonbands always knit the buttonband first and a little too long if in doubt. Make a note of the number of rows knitted and measure the band against the garment; any unravelled rows should be counted. Draw out the band on to paper and mark off for the number of buttonholes required; divide the number of rows for the spaces between each buttonhole. Buttonholes can either be knitted in during knitting as above, or after the garment has been completed. On a ribbed band, knit the band and then mark it for the buttonholes. Cut the thread and unravel enough stitches for the size of the button. Buttonhole stitch around the buttonhole, ensuring that each loose stitch is caught. *For a picot edge or a circular band*, the tension should be slightly tighter than that used for the main garment. A circular hem can be knitted separately by casting on sufficient stitches and knitting the band length. Stitch the band on to the garment by putting right sides together and stitching on; fold over and then stitch on the wrong side.

Cardigan Bands. Ribbed cardigan bands are knitted separately and then sewn on to the garment. If it is a single band, it is cast off with a closed edge cast off. If it is a double band then it is removed on to waste yarn and backstitched down afterwards on to the garment. *For a round neck cardigan band*: with right side facing pick up xx stitches on to the needles from the base of the cardigan front to the top. Knit the band on tension three points tighter than the main garment tension. The fold line is knitted on main tension and the other side of the band is knitted three points tighter. Pass the threaded needle through stitches and remove from the machine, or knit several rows of waste yarn, and then remove. Then stitch sleeves to cardigan back and front. With right side facing, pick up the stitches around the neckline to the centre back and then to the other side of the neckband. Knit the band and remove the knitting as before from the machine. Knit the other side of the band putting in buttonholes if required. Fold the bands and stitch down through each open stitch of the main colour. Finish off the buttonholes where necessary. *For a V-neck cardigan band*, pick up one front, back neck and one sleeve top. For the second band, the other front and sleeve can be picked up. Pick up a few extra stitches where the V-shape starts; this will make the shape of the band more pronounced. Knit the bands as for the round neck. Graft the bands together at the back. If there is difficulty picking up the back neck it can be knitted as a separate band, joining at either side at the back of the neck, rather than the one seam. This difficulty normally occurs only with the larger-sized garments. Fold the bands and stitch down through the open stitches of the first row knitted in the main colour.

To make a separate band cast on with a closed edge the required number of stitches and knit the length to fit all the way round the cardigan. Sew the band to the main garment starting at one edge at the bottom, working upwards and round the neck and then down on the opposite side.

Sewing on the bands: for lengthwise stocking stitch bands finish in mattress stitch. To machine stitch ribbed bands on to cardigans, knit the band with one extra stitch on one edge; the sewing machine stitch is sewn between this ridge. On a round neck cardigan with continental rib attach the neckband carefully, fold in half and slip stitch. Attach front bands, starting at the top of the neckband, fold in half and slip stitch. Sew buttonholes together.

On rib: attach the neckband around the neck using the cast off edge; attach bands from the top of the neckband. On a V-neck cardigan with continental rib attach the band carefully around the neckline, fold it in half and slip stitch. Stitch the buttonholes together. On rib attach the band evenly around the neckline.

Neckbands on the single bed are rectangular and join at the shoulder seam.

For a V-neck band and side selvedges in stocking stitch pick up the stitches as in the diagram. A V-neck jumper is sewn at one shoulder and then folded in half lengthways. With wrong side to the outside pick up the selvedge edge on one half of the neck from the V-neck point to the open shoulder. Armbands can be knitted like this too. Decrease one stitch fully fashioned on every second row using the 2/1 transfer tool, for the V shaping, until the fold line, which should be a looser row.

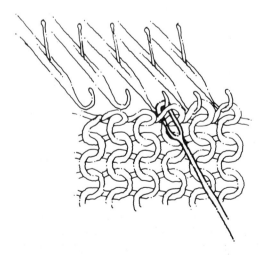

Picking up from the side of the knitting onto the knitting machine for a neckband

Then increase in the same way for the same number of rows fully fashioned. Pass a threaded needle through all the stitches and take the work off the machine. Sew up the V neck and the shoulder and then fold the band and sew through each stitch on the inside of the garment. A V band can also be knitted straight and the two ends overlapped at the V point, one behind the other, on to opposite sides.

For a square neckband the knitting must be completed in several sections and stitched together. The corners are made by decreasing one stitch every other row.

For a round neckband stitch garment pieces together leaving the left side seam open. With wrong side facing, starting at the opening pick up the stitches on to the needles round the neck. Knit one row at main tension. Then use a tighter tension on every second row (about two points) for the band depth. Knit the fold line on main tension and then set the tension so that it is increased by two points every second row, for the same number of rows as for the depth of the band. Pass a threaded needle through all the stitches, or knit several rows of waste yarn and remove from the machine. Fold the band over and sew down through each stitch.

Ribbed welts. If possible leave a garment on the machine at the back and front neck and at the top of raglan sleeves. Use the holding position and waste yarn. Sew up one side of a fitted sleeve or three sides of a raglan and pick up the neckband stitches with right side facing. Knit two rows on the main tension then arrange needles for a 2/1 welt. Knit the welt on an appropriate tension, with the fold line knitted on the main tension plus one number. Having knitted the welt push the empty needles between the welt into working position. Knit two rows on main tension plus one number and then knit several rows of waste yarn and cast off. Stitch the seam of the garment, turn the welt over and backstitch — but not tightly — the knitted loops of the main coloured yarn through the two thicknesses. This is an excellent method for children's garments. For continental rib and rib stitch the neckband around the neck, fold in half and slip stitch.

Ribbed neckbands on the double bed are always knitted separately, and then sewn on to the garment with right sides facing and stitched on the wrong side. It is a difficult task to work out the sizing of bands. If the band is tubular then knit a sample and measure the number of stitches over stocking stitch per 2.5 cm (1 in) and multiply this by the centimetres or inches needed to fit round the neck. Take off 4 cm (1½ in) from this figure and the final result should give a correct fitting band.

Tubular bands are used for a flat, neat finish. Knit the band but increase the stitch size approximately every four rows and this will give the band a curve. Knit the rows required, set the machine for rib and knit about three rows in waste yarn and remove the band from the machine. Press on the round.

A ribbed neckband and armband with tubular or circular rows is knitted by setting the double bed machine for the required rib and knitting the rows for the band. Push up the empty in-between needles to working position, set the knitting machine to tubular knitting, the half pitch lever to H (see *Pitch*) and adjust the stitch size. Knit about 12 rows in the main colour and then using waste yarn and set for rib, re-set to a tighter tension and knit three rows. Take the yarn from the machine and remove the knitting by taking the carriage across. Pull the length of the band and press. Unravel waste rows, pin the top part of the tubular rows on the right side of the main garment piece, overlapping a few rows. Backstitch through the loops of the main yarn. The sewn ends are pulled in to line over the seam on the reverse side. At the seam point put the needle in to each stitch, pull down into line and sew. The garment is caught between the two sections of circular knitting and is therefore an ideal finish for machine shaped garments or cut and sewn necklines.

For a round neck for a plain rib band follow instructions as for the V-neck band. *For rib and tubular* calculate the size of the band by the method given. Push these needles into working position and set for tubular knitting and knit about 12-14 rows, as per pattern. Remove from the machine; when the waste knitting is removed the band will stretch slightly.

For a V neck join the garment at the right shoulder seam. Hold knitting on the left side of the V without pulling up to the needle bed and bring these numbers of needles into working position; bring the same number up on the ribber. Set the needles for rib and knit the rib. Put the stitches from the ribber to the main bed, pick up the garment stitches on to these needles and the band will fit correctly. Bring up the needles for the right-hand side of the V neck and the needles for the back neck (the latter is in the pattern). Bring up needles on ribber too and set for rib, as before. Garments can also be finished with fancy edgings.

Pocket top bands (see also *pockets*). It is a matter of experimentation to decide upon the correct band for a pocket. It is always useful to knit small samples of various pockets and bands and keep them for reference. Knit up to the pocket opening and then knit several rows of waste yarn and remove from the machine. Put the pocket lining on to the empty needles and knit the front of the garment. Pick up the last row knitted in the main yarn at the top of the pocket — the purl side outwards. Put on the end needles at either side of the stitch bar from the main garment which is above the end stitch of the top of the pocket. Knit one row from right to left. Place the bars above the end two stitches of the pocket top and knit another row. Continue doing this until enough rows have been knitted for the pocket top outside. Knit a loose row for the fold line. The pocket top has been knitted to the main garment, therefore avoiding the sewing up of the side seams. *To knit the pocket top and the garment together*, knit up to the pocket opening point. Put all needles into holding position except those for the pocket top. Knit the fold line and the inside of the pocket top and cast off. Put the pocket lining onto the empty needles and knit the remainder of the garment. The inside of the pocket is folded over and stitched into place. *Rib*. Transfer the stitches for the pocket on to the machine from the stitch holder. Rib for approximately 10-12 rows and cast off quite loosely. Stitch the bands down on the sides. For the top, knit approximately 24 rows and cast off loosely, fold the band over and stitch down. Stitch the sides of the bands.

BAR GATE, see *Sinker Gate*.

BAR PUSHER. Known as a needle retaining bar pusher. Its function is to push the bar out at the back of the carriage which holds the needles in place in order to remove a damaged needle.

BASKET STITCH. A fancy knitted block design, mainly hand knitted, achieved by alternating plain and purl in squares. It can be achieved on the knitting machine using the transfer carriage lock, but becomes too long a process done any other way. On Brother machines, to take an example, it is achieved as follows. All stitches are put onto the main bed and the main carriage is at the left. Set the half pitch lever to H. On the ribber push needles in blocks of approximately five into non-working position and five in-between in working position, and knit six rows. Put every other needle in working position on the ribber into upper working position and with the transfer carriage transfer these stitches onto the main bed. Transfer the

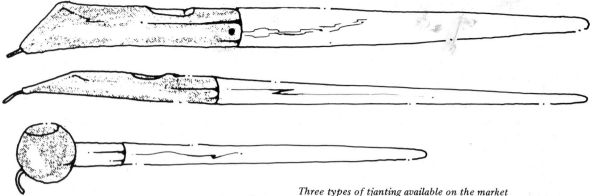

Three types of tjanting available on the market

remaining stitches to the main bed by using the second setting. Repeat these steps to produce a basket weave effect.

BASTING, see *Tacking or Basting*.

BATIK (see also *Printing*). Comes from the word that means to draw and write. Batik is simply fabric, wax, and dye, and is written with a tool called a tjanting. This tool is a copper holder for the hot wax, with a tiny spout and a wooden handle. The larger the outlet spout the thicker the wax line that is drawn. The pattern is drawn directly on to the fabric with molten wax. When the fabric is dyed the waxed areas resist the dye colour. New waxings and different colour dye pots can make an elaborate pattern. The layers of wax are removed when the design is complete. This method can be used to make a complete outfit or a combination of knitted and batiked fabric.

BEADS (see also *Appendix, Insertions, Macramé*). Beads can be sewn on to the knitting after removal

from the machine. They can also be knitted into tiny pockets on the double bed. They may also be knotted or sewn on to a yarn and then knitted across by hand.

BELTS (see also *Beads, Embroidery, Swiss Darning, Welts*). Can be knitted lengthways and widthways. Knit double the required width, fold and seam. Widthways belts are more stable. Make a widthways belt by casting on as for a hem using waste yarn. Knit sufficient rows, pick up the first main yarn row and unravel waste yarn. Cast off the stitches together. Belts can be made by plaiting, macramé, and by twisted cords. Belts can contrast with an outfit as a feature, or match a colour in a toning blouse if wearing a knitted outfit. Belts knitted double, like a welt, the colour on the inside can be different to the colour of the second

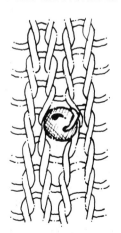

Working beads into a row of knitting

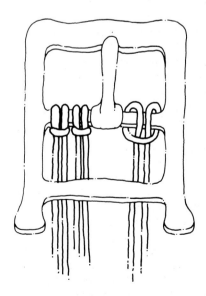

Making a belt by hand. Threads attached to the buckle crossbar

13

half. By transferring holes as for a picot edge, however, the under colour will show through. Sequins can be placed behind the holes in the centre of the belt. The holes can be blanket stitched in a contrasting thread. Belts can be decorated with embroidery, Swiss darning, or they can be all quilted or part quilted. They can also have unusual fastenings or simply knot together. Knitted bobbles as in mock aran can be applied. It is preferable to have the seam line of the belt at the centre of the back and not the edge. Fancy belts can be made by the same method as welts.

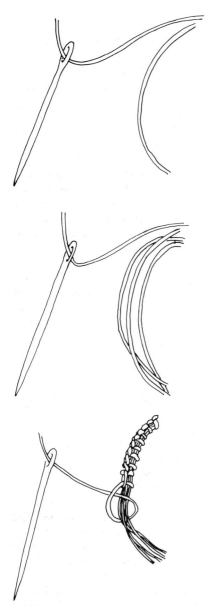

Making a belt carrier

BELT CARRIER (see also *Buttonhole Stitch*). A loop made either side of a garment to hold a belt in place. Thread up needle in main colour. Secure yarn on wrong side through the seam if possible. Allowing for belt width catch a stitch leaving an arch of yarn slightly bigger than the finished carrier should be, further down the seam. Repeat, making these arches three or four times. Work buttonhole stitch over these arches by passing the needle under the arches and through the loop just made. Repeat this until the whole arch is secured with this stitch, then pass the needle through the seam and secure the thread on wrong side of fabric.

BIAS BINDING, see *Skirts*.

BINDING OFF (see also *Casting Off*). Method to remove knitting from the machine.

BIRD'S EYE. A two-colour stitch pattern. Each colour knits a stitch alternately and on every following row, except that the colour order is reversed.

BLANKET STITCH. Similar to buttonhole stitch except that there is space between the stitches. It is used to hold cut edges, and by using different yarn can make an interesting edging or seam. This is the best stitch for appliqué.

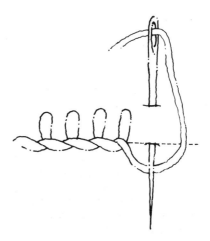

Blanket stitch

BLENDS. Is the combining of two or more fibres in the same yarn or fabric.

BLOCKING (see also *Iron and Ironing*). The pinning out of the knitted fabric pieces for steaming, according to the diagram measurements. This

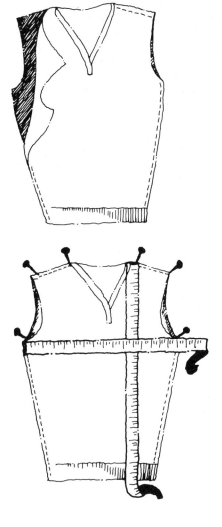

Blocking. (Top) *Two pieces can be tacked together and blocked.* (Bottom) *Pin the garment pieces out to the correct length and width, according to the pattern*

flattens wavy fabric and fixes the stitches. It should not be used on true rib except on button bands; for example, where the band has to remain a particular size. Put the pins in the very edge of the knitting so that they lie flat. Check fabric size with pattern piece if using the cut and sew method. If two pieces for pressing are the same size, when the pins are removed from the first piece of knitting put them into the ironing board where the next piece of knitting must be pinned. This saves measuring from the start. Never pin hems or welts, instead pin along the top where the hem finishes and the main knitting begins.

BLOCKING BOARD, see *Ironing Board*.

BOBBLES (see also *Mock Aran*). Bobbles are knitted in a long strip being separated by waste yarn. They are then removed from the machine, finished by hand and attached to the knitting. Bobbles can also be knitted while knitting the main garment by putting needles to holding position except where a bobble is required. Leave needles in working position according to the width of the bobble. Knit the number of rows for the bobble and then continue knitting over every needle.

BODY BLANKS, see *Cut and Sew*.

BOOKS, INSTRUCTION. Each new machine is supplied with a manual explaining its operation. It is advisable, however, to read other recommended books on machine knitting before starting to knit, as the information in the manuals is not always clear. Any queries arising from the manuals are answered in one of the books in the appendix to this book.

BOTANY WOOL (see also *Wool*). A Merino sheep wool, which comes from Botany Bay, on the east coast of Australia. A fine, wavy wool is now referred to as Merino wool, and the word Botany is used when the final product has been produced. Botany wool is important in the making of worsted suitings.

BOUCLÉ YARN (see also *Yarn Combinations*). A French word to describe a fancy yarn with tiny loops that appear like little bumps on the surface of the yarn.

BRAIDS, see *Edgings, Trims*.

BROTHER KNITTING MACHINES, see *Appendix*.

BRUSHED YARNS (see also *Teasel*). Normally made with a percentage of angora or mohair, although some acrylics are brushed too. The yarn is spun and then the long hairs are teased out with wire brushes to give the furry effect. The surface of a woven or knitted fabric that contains a hairy yarn can be brushed with a wire teasel or brush to make the fabric more bulky and softer. This covers the structure of the fabric. It is important to use weights on the knitted fabric to avoid the yarn building up on the needles and the loops not being formed correctly. Pull down the yarn regularly at the back of the yarn brake to avoid it becoming caught and causing tension problems.

BUCKLES, BELT, see *Belts.*

BUST DARTS, see *Darts.*

BUTT, see *Needlebutt.*

BUTTONS (see also *Fastenings*). Buttons which do not enhance the garment either by shape, tone or yarn can spoil the whole appearance. It is often wiser to cover button moulds with the matching knitting, or a contrast knitting that is also repeated on an edging. The buttons can also

Button covered in hand embroidered knitted fabric

be embroidered, beaded or ordinary buttons painted for extra decoration. Fabric buttons are made by stretching a piece of the knitting over a metal button mould, which holds it in place by the shank at the back. Remember to remove buttons from old garments to keep in a button box for future use, before discarding the garments. Buttons can also be made like bobbles in mock aran, with a bead inside. This looks attractive with loops to fasten the garment, like a Chinese garment.

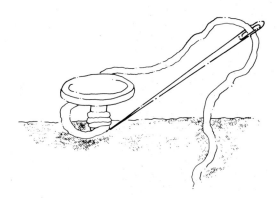

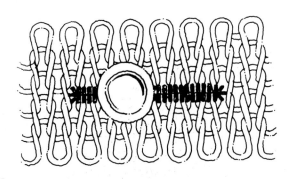

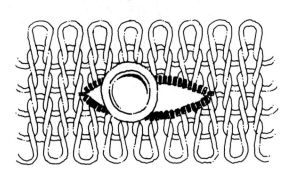

Sewing on a button. The second diagram shows a correct closure, the third diagram shows an incorrect, gaping closure

BUTTONHOLES (see also *Bands*). *Buttonhole bands* are normally knitted in stocking stitch on a slightly tighter tension than the main garment. The band is knitted to double the required width and folded in half lengthways. Buttonholes can be worked in one of the following ways.

For small buttonholes over one needle simply transfer one stitch on to the next needle leaving the needle in working position and continue knitting until the next hole is required.

For hole over two needles transfer two stitches, one to the needle on the left and one on the right. Leave needles in working position and knit one row. Remove yarn from the needle on the right and knit one row. Pick up the yarn that crosses the hole and place on to the needle on the right of the worked needles. Continue knitting. Or put the two needles out of working position and knit two rows. Bring the needles forward to knitting position and place the loops that lie under these needles on to the needles, the lower on to the right-hand needle and the top loop on to the left-hand needle, and continue to knit. *Variation* of this is to knit only one row after transferring stitches, then to place loop over both needles. The loop is wrapped around the needles, as for closed edge cast on, held for two rows and then removed. Follow diagram for small buttonhole over two needles.

For a buttonhole over three or more needles. There are two ways to achieve this (see p. 21):

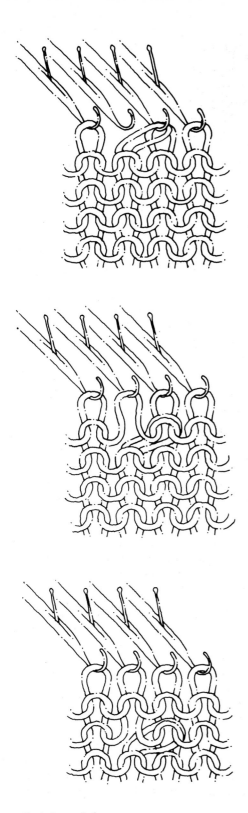

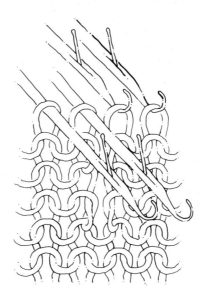

Small vertical buttonhole. Put needles on left of centre forward to holding position and knit for the depth of the buttonhole. Return held needles to working position and put the other needles to hold and knit the same number of rows. Bring held needles into knitting position and continue knitting until the next buttonhole is required

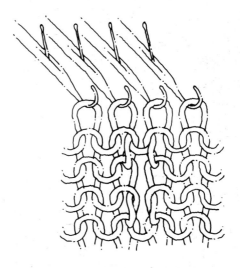

Single buttonhole

BUTTONHOLES

Single buttonhole for a Knit 1 Purl 1 Rib. (1) Place a
single stitch onto the adjacent needle. Continue knitting.
(2) Re-make the stitches with the latch hook

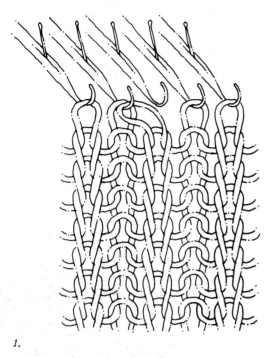

1.

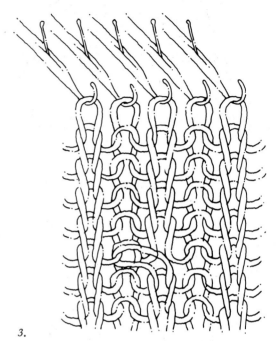

3.

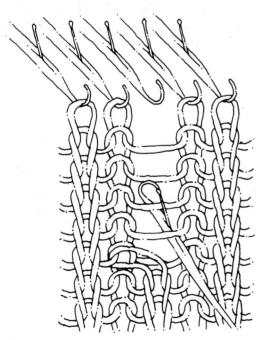

2.

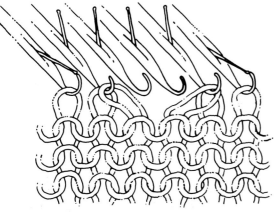

1.

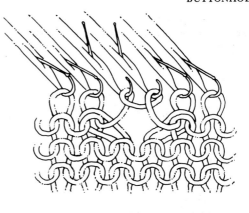

4.

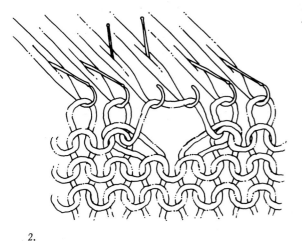

2.

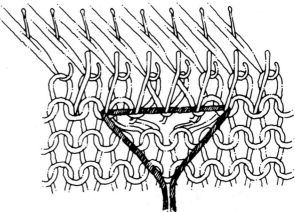

5.

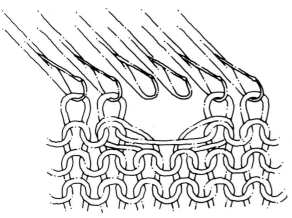

3.

Small buttonhole over two needles. (5) Lay the nylon cord across the new loops and the stitches either side of the two needles, between the needle hooks and the sinker gate. Knit three rows and pull the nylon cord out from the knitting. The buttonhole is then complete

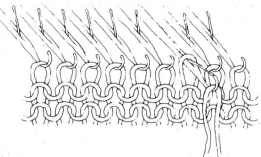

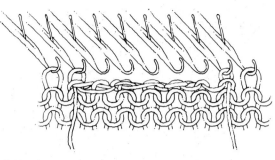

Large single buttonhole. Stages 1-7. 1. Use a loose thread of yarn and follow the steps carefully

5. Use the end of yarn left to make a closed edge cast on over the empty needles

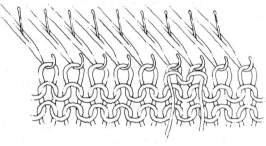

2.

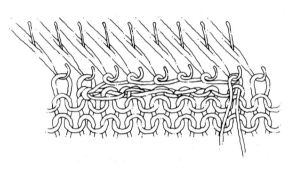

6. Wind the yarn anti-clockwise

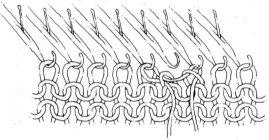

3.

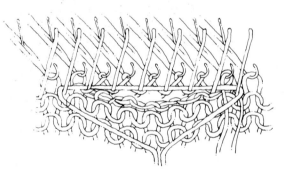

7. Hold down the stitches for at least two rows with the nylon cord, which is placed between the needles and the sinker gate. Remove nylon cord and the buttonhole is complete. This buttonhole can be made to any size according to the number of stitches that are bound off

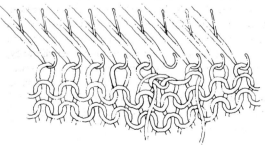

4.

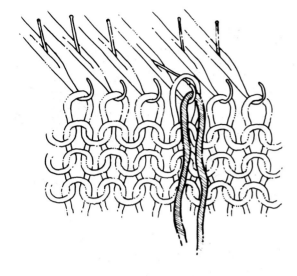

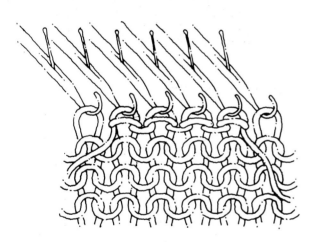

Single buttonhole. Work a piece of contrast yarn across the stitches that are to form the buttonhole. Continue knitting, repeating this wherever a buttonhole is needed. When knitting is complete, remove from machine. Pull out contrast yarn and sew the stitches by hand

1 Use a piece of main yarn leaving a long end on the left. Cast off the required number of stitches to form the right size buttonhole, working from left to right. Push the empty needles to upper working position plus one needle on the left and one on the right. Using the long end of the yarn cast on over these needles as for closed edge cast on and continue knitting.

2 Push the required number of needles to holding position, put stitches behind the latch and lay across a contrast yarn; push needles back to working position one by one so the yarn knits in. Continue knitting. The band is removed from the machine and the contrast thread pulled out and the open loops stitched together neatly by grafting or oversewing.

A double buttonhole band is worked as 2 above, making sure the buttonholes are evenly spaced either side of the centre of the band. The band is then folded in half and the open stitches are sewn together so the hole becomes single. The central needle can be left on non-working position to give a neat fold line for the double band. (All buttonholes are strengthened if worked with a row of buttonhole stitch or blanket stitch.)

A vertical buttonhole is worked by pushing half the needles at opposite end of carriage into holding position and then knitting an even number of rows for the size of the buttonhole required on the remaining needles. Take the carriage to opposite side of needle bed and knit the same number of rows on the held needles putting the other needles into holding position. When complete, continue knitting with all needles in working position.

Buttonholes using the ribber. For a single buttonhole simply transfer one stitch from the ribber to the knitter leaving the needle in working position.

For a double stitch buttonhole. Knitting is worked over every other needle; transfer two stitches on the main bed, one to the left and one to the right. Do the same on the ribber. Push the empty main bed needles into non-working position but leave the ribber needles in working position. Knit one row. Then on main bed push up the two needles and knit one row. Hang the resulting loop on to the main bed on the left-hand needle only, and continue to knit. For a vertical buttonhole, each side of the knitting is worked separately as for the single bed. The double bed is set for a 1/1 rib and the hole is worked with buttonhole stitch.

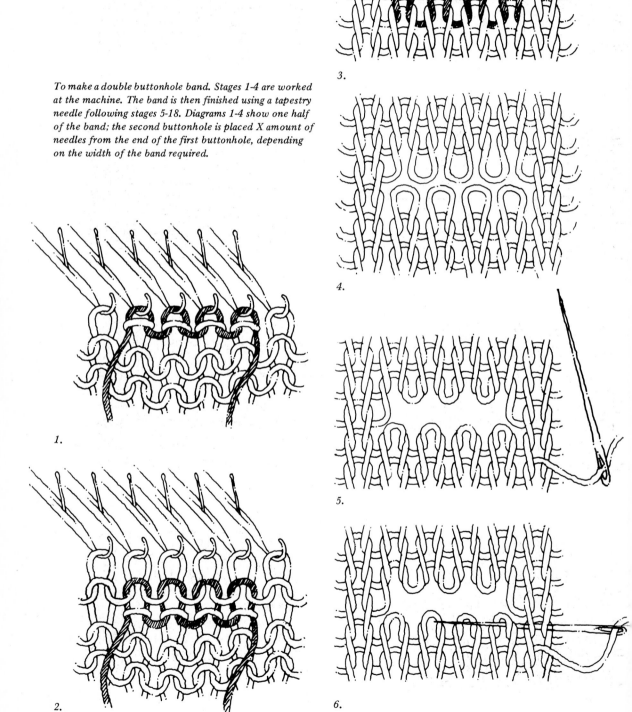

To make a double buttonhole band. Stages 1-4 are worked at the machine. The band is then finished using a tapestry needle following stages 5-18. Diagrams 1-4 show one half of the band; the second buttonhole is placed X amount of needles from the end of the first buttonhole, depending on the width of the band required.

3.

4.

1.

5.

2.

6.

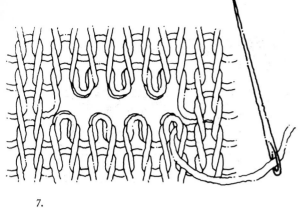

7.

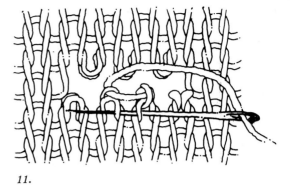

11.

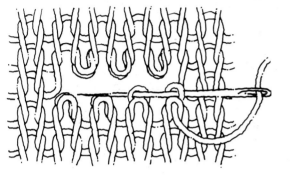

8.

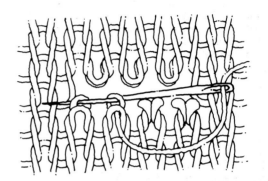

12.

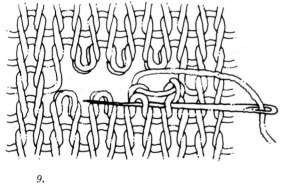

9.

13.

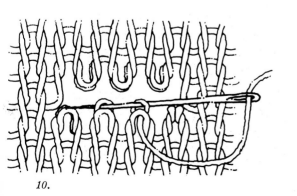

10.

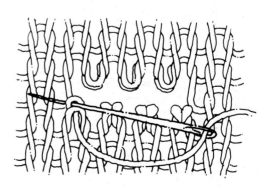

14.

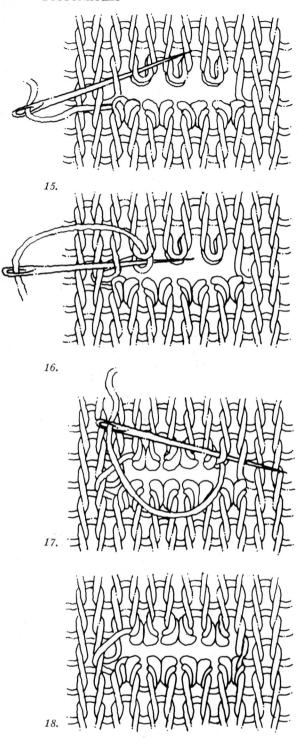

15.

16.

17.

18.

The nylon cord or waste yarn is knitted over the needles
(by hand) required for the buttonhole. This is repeated
for every buttonhole, with knitting in between, according
to the spacing of the buttons. When the band is complete
the nylon cord is pulled out. The band is folded in half
and the buttonholes finished by hand, stages 5-18

Vertical button hole

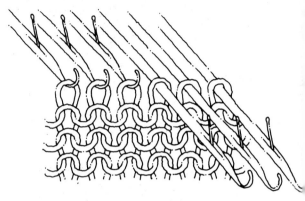

1. *Push up needles on opposite side to the carriage*

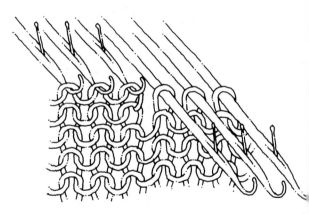

2. *Knit one side of the buttonhole*

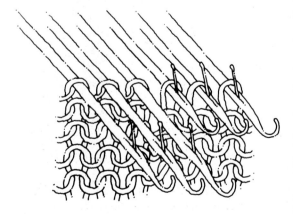

3. *Reverse needle positions*

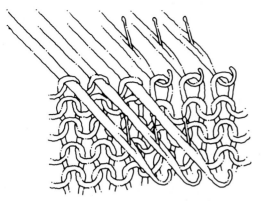

4. Knit the buttonhole depth required

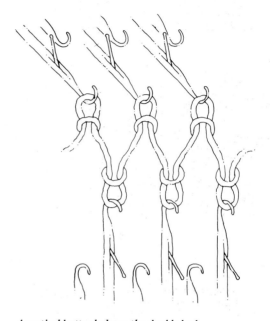

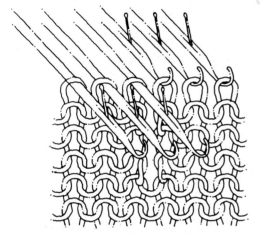

5. Push needles back for knitting in. Use the transfer tool if patterning

A vertical buttonhole on the double bed

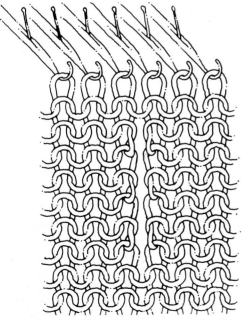

6. Continue knitting until the beginning of the next buttonhole

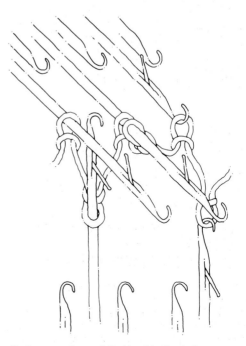

Push up needles on left side of buttonhole

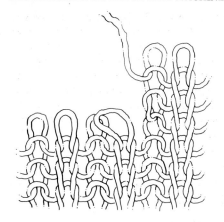

Knit an odd number of rows for the bottonhole

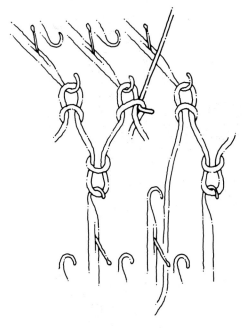

Pick up the loop of the stitch on the previous row and continue knitting.

Push up main bed and ribber needles on the knitted side. Push back other needles and pull down a little of the yarn with the latch hook, for completing the buttonhole later

BUTTONHOLES ON THE SEWING MACHINE (see also *Stable Knits*). A buttonhole attachment can be used on a sewing machine to make buttonholes on knitted fabrics, but it is best suited to stable knits.

BUTTONHOLE LOOP (see also *Belt Carrier, Buttonhole Stitch, Frog Fastenings*). A loop can be used to fasten over buttons on cardigans and at shoulders. They are particularly good for children's garments. They can also be formed by a basic crochet chain stitch. The loops are worked the same as for a belt carrier.

Buttonhole loop fastenings

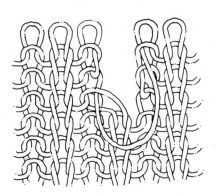

Knit the same number of rows as in the third diagram

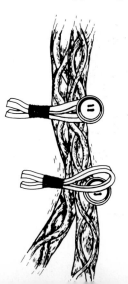

BUTTONHOLE STITCH (see also *Belt Carrier, Blanket Stitch, Buttons*). Sometimes called blanket stitch. Worked by taking yarn threaded on to a tapestry needle and securing end on edge of knitting. Bring needle through knitting but bring needle through the loop made and pull gently so it sits along the edge of the knitting. Take the needle each time from back to front and through the loop. For a more pronounced edge the yarn can be worked double, or a thicker yarn can be used.

Buttonhole stitching using blanket stitch technique on a vertical buttonhole.

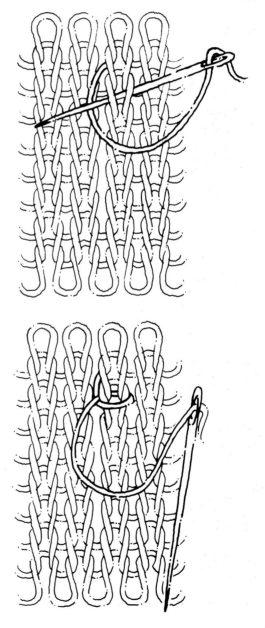

Belt carrier using buttonhole stitch

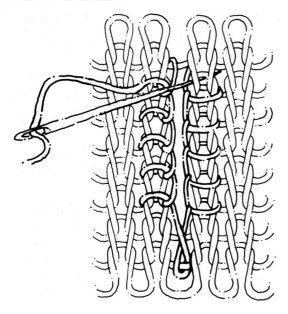

BUYING A MACHINE. Go to a large store or relevant shop to see the various machines. Do not rush the decision as the initial cost of buying a machine can be high. Try the movement of the carriage yourself, as they vary considerably. It is necessary when choosing a machine to understand the performance of the different models and to be able to judge whether the machine will do exactly the job you want it to do. Ask about tuition as it is usual to receive a set number of lessons free. Some firms offer postal tuition. Ask to see the knitted samples that have been produced on the machine. Check which attachments can be added to your machine and whether they offer a guarantee and repair service. Second-hand machines can be found for sale in *Exchange and Mart* (in the U.K.), your local newspaper and in knitting magazines. Check the age of the machine and the name of the model. Then contact the manufacturer and ask if parts and tuition are still available for that particular model. It is better to purchase a second-hand machine with an instruction manual to make sure it is complete. In your area there may be a knitting club or evening class to help you learn.

C

CABLES. Used in Aran knitting as part of an all over pattern. They can also be single cables, for example down either side of a cardigan, on a cardigan band, on pockets, cuffs or welts. Cables can be knitted in a contrast colour to the main knitting; this has a very striking effect. The knitting machine is set for partial knitting in both directions and the contrast yarn is laid on to the needles in holding position. Listed below are six basic cables of which most cable panels are a combination.

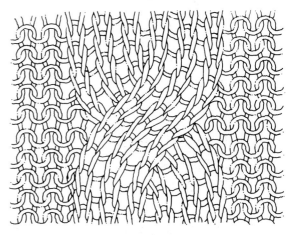

Cabel twist from left to right

1 *Cross stitch 1 under stitch 2.* Lift stitch 2 onto transfer tool and turn it to the right. With another transfer tool move stitch 1 onto the second needle and then stitch 2 onto the first needle.

2 *Cross stitches 1 and 2 under 3 and 4.* Lift stitches 3 and 4 on to the first transfer tool and then turn the tool to the right. With another transfer tool move stitches 1 and 2 on to the third and fourth needles. Place stitches 3 and 4 onto the first and second needles.

3 *Cross stitch 2 under stitch 1,* reverse the procedure for No. 1.

4 *Cross stitches 3 and 4 under stitches 1 and 2.* Reverse procedure for No. 2.

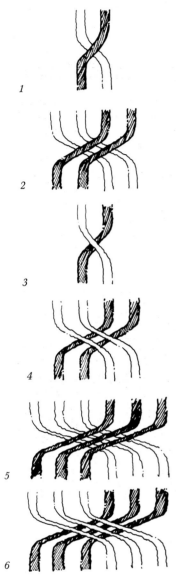

Basic cable stitches

6 under stitches 1, 2 and 3. Knit four rows. Cross the stitches 4, 5 and 6 under 7, 8 and 9 and knit 4 rows. This is one complete pattern; repeat this to the length required.

2 Worked over 8 needles in non-working position. Cross 3 and 4 under 1 and 2. Cross the stitches 5 and 6 under 7 and 8 and knit 4 rows. Repeat this once more and knit 4 rows. *Cross stitches 1 and 2 under stitches 3 and 4, cross stitches 7 and 8 under 5 and 6 and knit 4 rows. Repeat from * once more. These 20 rows are the pattern. Repeat for required length of cable.

3 Worked over 13 stitches between needles in non-working position. Cross stitches 4, 5 and 6 under 1, 2 and 3, cross stitches 8, 9 and 10 under 11, 12 and 13 and knit 1 row. Transfer stitches 6 and 8 on to the 7th needle, leave empty needles in working position and knit 7 rows. These are the 8 rows that form the pattern. Repeat for length of cable.

For a lace cable, knit 1 row by feeding yarn onto each needle by hand, forming a stitch, and pull each needle back to non-working position so long stitches are formed. Insert the cast on comb into the knitting and pull it until the needles are in knitting position. The stitches hang on the hooks. Using the three-needle transfer tool cross the loops as for cables. Put the carriage on the other side of the bed and knit.

CAM BOX (see also *Carriage*). The underside of the carriage.

CAMEL HAIR YARN (see also *Yarn Combinations*). Comes from the two-humped camel which is found in north-west China, Turkey and as far as Siberia. The yarn is usually used undyed and the colour varies from light tan to dark brown. Makes a soft, fine yarn, and is usually bought mixed with a fine quality wool.

CAMS. Operate the needles by their butts emerging from the needlebeds. As the carriage crosses the needlebed the butt connects with a channel on the underneath. The needle slides back and forth and allows the carriage to pass; the butt follows the path of the channel. The walls of the channel are made of sections called cams. Because they are adjustable the butt can be made to follow the desired path to give plain tuck or slip stitch positions. The raising cam and the lowering cam are fixed to cam plates and they connect to the carriage. This is common in hand, circular, flat and automatic machines.

5 *Cross the stitches 1, 2 and 3 under stitches 4, 5 and 6.* Lift stitches 4, 5 and 6 onto the first transfer tool and then turn the tool to the right. With the second transfer tool move stitches 1, 2 and 3 on to the fourth, fifth and sixth needles. Place stitches 4, 5 and 6 on to the first, second and third needles.

6 *Cross stitches 4, 5 and 6 under 1, 2 and 3.* Reverse procedure as for No. 5.

CABLES, DECORATIVE.

1 Worked on stocking stitch with 9 stitches in non-working position. Cross the stitches 4, 5 and

CARDIGAN. A knitted jacket originally in wool. Usually V- or round-necked. Named after Lord Cardigan (1797-1868).

CARDING WOOL. A process whereby wool is teased between wire brushes to separate all the fibres and to remove any impurities. This process is carried out prior to spinning.

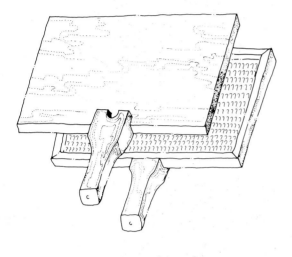

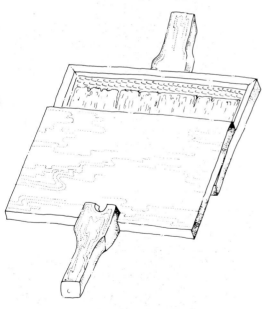

Diagrams show hand carders, which can be used when small quantities of yarn are being prepared. The carders each have a pad of metal hooks and work by placing the yarn on to one crader; the second carder is then placed on top. Then the carders are pulled against each other, which separates the fibres. In industry this process is carried out by machine

CARRIAGE. Sits on top of the needlebed and the movement of the carriage across the needles in action automatically knits each needle in turn, until the end of the row. Once the carriage has been moved across the needles in one direction it cannot be returned until that row has been completed. At the end of each row the carriage clicks and this indicates that the row is complete.

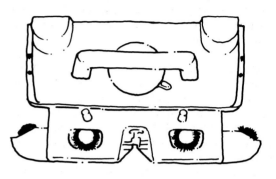

Basic single bed carriage

CARRIAGE BUTTONS/LEVERS. These vary according to the make of the machine. Their function is to set the carriage for various stitch patterns to enable it to knit different stitches.

CARRIAGE JAMS. If the carriage will not move on the needlebed then the cause is either that the carriage is not properly on the track, or the cast on is too tight (i.e. the tension is incorrect), the yarn too tight, or a knot is caught in the yarn feeder. This is corrected by undoing the thumb screws which hold the sinker plate to the carriage and sliding the sinker plate off. Lift the carriage up slightly and slide it back to the beginning of the row. On some machines this is not possible but there is, however, a release lever enabling the carriage to be lifted clear of the needlebed. Unpick the stitches back to the beginning of the row and take the slack back to the ball of wool. Check that the stitches have not been pulled tightly anywhere. Cast on again if necessary, in a higher tension, and check that the ball is wound loosely enough. Check for knots and tangling in the antenna spring and yarn guides. Check that the needles and needle latches are not bent, as this will cause the carriage to jam. The needle butts must be in line. Another possible cause of jamming is insufficient lubrication. If the lace carriage jams then the cause is either tension, taking it across the needles too fast, or that the gate pegs are bent.

CASHMERE (see also *Iron and Ironing, Yarn Combinations*). This hair comes from goats in Kashmir, China, Tibet, Iran and Iraq. The hair is removed by combing when the animal is moulting. A very small part of the fleece is the fine fibre that is used to make very soft, lightweight, but warm garments. Much less yarn is used than normal and it is spun in oil. This is washed out after the garment is complete, and the surface is brushed up on a teazle machine. It is a very expensive fibre as the demand is greater than the supply. It is usually blended with wool. It is used in its undyed state, black, brown, grey, or white.

CASTING OFF. Can be achieved by knitting several rows of waste yarn, removing the yarn from the carriage and taking the carriage across the knitting; it then drops off the bed. This is for joining knitting without a seam, as waste knitting unravels down to main stitches, which are then sewn separately.

Back stitch. This give quite an elastic edge. Taking a tapestry tool threaded with the main yarn and working from the left, insert it into first stitch from front to back. Insert needle from front into second stitch and through the back of the first stitch, coming out to the front. Put needle into third stitch from the front and pull through the second stitch to the front. Repeat this until the row is complete. *To work from the right.* Put needle as before into first stitch and pull out through second stitch front. Insert needle into first stitch and under second stitch and through the third stitch, leaving out the second stitch completely. Put needle into second stitch and pull through the fourth stitch leaving out the third stitch. Keep repeating this until the row is complete.

Using the latch tool. The last row of knitting should be at least 4 numbers higher to give a loose row. Push needle right forward. Working opposite side to carriage, take the first stitch on to the latch tool and push back the needle. Push this stitch behind the latch on the tool. Take the second stitch off its needle by inserting the latch tool and pulling back while at the same time pushing the needle away. The second stitch is drawn through the first and one stitch is left on the latch tool. Place this behind the latch and take the next stitch on to the tool and continue this, pulling the stitches through each one in a chain, until the row is complete. Secure the end by latching the yarn end through it twice.

Using the transfer tool. The most commonly used method. Working from the left, same end as

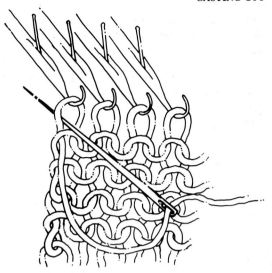

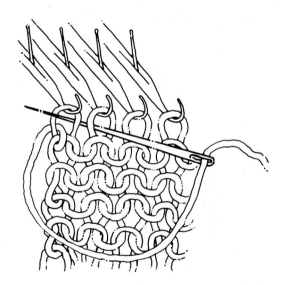

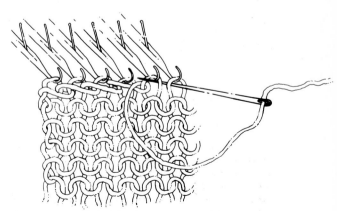

Casting off using back stitch

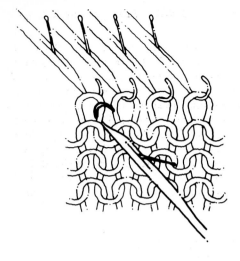

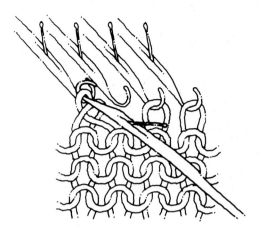

Casting off using the latch hook

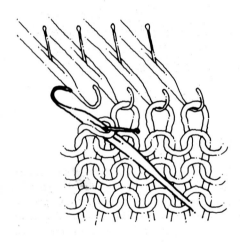

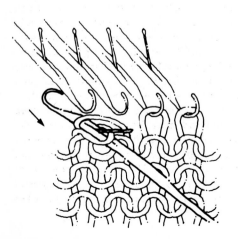

carriage, transfer the first stitch on to the second stitch — and here it varies from the manual — take the stitch on the transfer tool behind the sinker pins and not in front. With a little practice it is just as quick and the knitting sits on the sinker pins, which tension it so it cannot be pulled too tightly. Knit the two stitches together by pushing the needle forward and laying the yarn over the needle hook, then taking the needle back to working position. The two stitches drop off and a new stitch remains on the needle. Take this stitch on to the next needle behind the sinker pins, and repeat as before. Cast off all the stitches in this way until the end of the row; pull the yarn end through the last stitch to cast it off. Lift knitting up and off the needle bed.

Using the transfer tool for chain casting off. Using the transfer tool put the second stitch on to the first needle and then put the two stitches on to the second needle. Push needle forward and the first stitch will go behind the latch, then bring needle back and the first stitch comes off the needle. Transfer third stitch on to second needle, then put stitches on to third needle and continue as before for the remaining stitches. Cast off last stitch by pulling yarn end through the loop.

Straight cast off using needle. A very quick cast off using the end of main yarn in a tapestry needle. Knit last row of knitting on a fairly tight tension. Thread the needle through each stitch and secure at the end. Lift knitting off the needle bed.

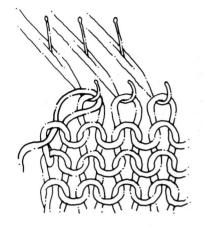

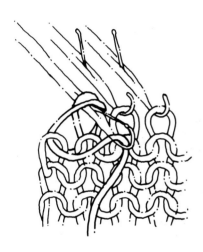

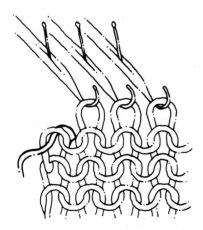

Closed edge cast off. To decrease more than two stitches on the side with yarn, using the transfer tool. Cast off behind the sinker pins

CASTING ON, SINGLE BED (see also *Edgings, Hems*).

1 *Open edge cast on*. This will unravel and is used for sampling and where garment pieces have to be joined or grafted together, at the shoulder, socks, etc. Push required needles to working position and using waste yarn in the carriage move the carriage across the knitting. The yarn is hooked onto each needle and sinker pin alternately. The nylon cord from the tool box is laid across the loops and caught down firmly with one hand. The cast on comb can also be used for larger areas. Knit several rows and then pull out the nylon cord.

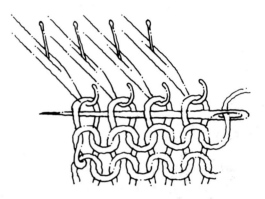

Straight thread cast off

Knit a further 4 or 5 rows and then commence knitting in the main yarn. For hems at this point it is often easier to *knit* in the nylon cord before the main yarn, then when the first row of the main yarn has been picked up for the hem, the nylon cord is instantly pulled out and the waste yarn drops off.

2 *Closed edge cast on*. Bring needles to be knitted to the furthest point from the needlebed. Bring needles forward manually for several rows, should problems arise when knitting. Loop the yarn around each needle from left to right anti-clockwise. The loops must be pushed back on the stems of the needle behind the latch. Hold thumb and finger under the last loop before making another, to tension and control the loops, and make them even and not too tight. Thread the yarn into the feeder and take up any slack by hand. Move the carriage across the needles slowly and evenly and the cast on is complete. If the cast on comb is to be used it is hung on the sinker pins before beginning the cast on and released after the first knitted row.

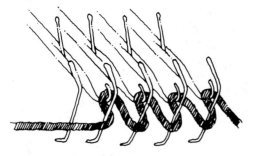

Open edge cast on. Correct

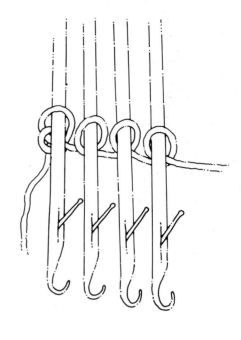

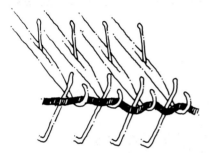

Incorrect

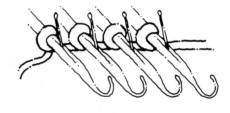

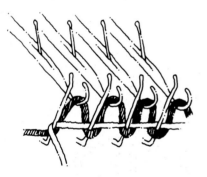

Laying the nylon cord across

3 *Casting on using chain stitch.* Using the latch tool or tappet tool (which looks like a latch needle with a handle) make a chain-like stitch. This is done by pushing needles to be knitted to the furthest point from the needlebed and inserting the latch tool between the first and second needle behind the latch, between the stems. Lay the yarn over the first needle and pull down with the latch tool which already has a loop attached, thus forming a loop. Repeat this procedure across the remaining needles and close the latches. Then thread up the carriage and knit across.

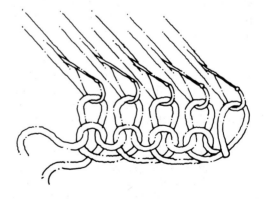

Closed edge cast on

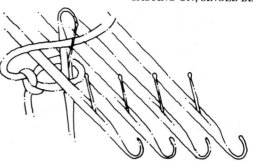

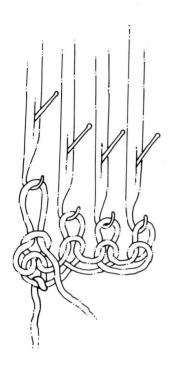

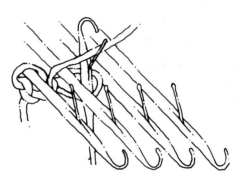

Casting on using the latch hook. Hook the yarn of the last loop over the end needle. Close needle latches. Knit across

Showing how loop is extended by the needle being backward and out of line

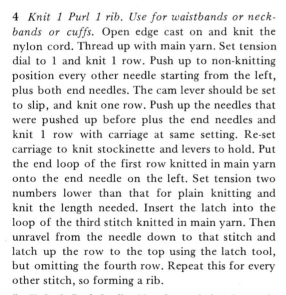

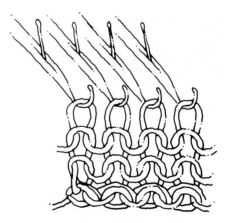

4 *Knit 1 Purl 1 rib. Use for waistbands or neckbands or cuffs.* Open edge cast on and knit the nylon cord. Thread up with main yarn. Set tension dial to 1 and knit 1 row. Push up to non-knitting position every other needle starting from the left, plus both end needles. The cam lever should be set to slip, and knit one row. Push up the needles that were pushed up before plus the end needles and knit 1 row with carriage at same setting. Re-set carriage to knit stockinette and levers to hold. Put the end loop of the first row knitted in main yarn onto the end needle on the left. Set tension two numbers lower than that for plain knitting and knit the length needed. Insert the latch into the loop of the third stitch knitted in main yarn. Then unravel from the needle down to that stitch and latch up the row to the top using the latch tool, but omitting the fourth row. Repeat this for every other stitch, so forming a rib.

5 *Knit 2 Purl 2 rib. Use for waistbands, neckbands and cuffs.* Push up required needles to knitting position, pushing two needles back every second needle to non-working position. Cast on using waste yarn, and knit 12 rows. Knit in the nylon cord. Thread up with main yarn and knit 4 rows with the tension at 0. Push to working position the non-working needle and using the transfer tool pick up the loops *directly above the

nylon cord of the knitting in main yarn and place onto the empty needles. Knit the length needed for the ribbing with machine set for ribbing. Using the transfer tool unravel the loop placed onto the needle at *, and with the tool re-knit the stitch from the front to form a purl stitch and place it on to the empty needle. Do this procedure for all the loops placed on the non-working needles, and the rib is formed.

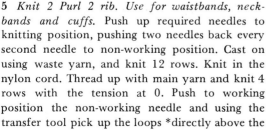

CASTING ON COMB

Mock Rib can be knitted on every needle or 1/1, 2/1, 3/1, 2/2 and variations on this. This type of hem is knitted twice the length and turned up so the centre is a tube. This is the most common way to knit a rib on the single bed.

CASTING ON COMB. A row of hooks attached to a weighted bar. Supplied with some machines, as a method for casting on. Each hook is attached to the yarn, between each needle, and the weight of the bar stops the loops jumping off the needles as the first row is knitted. Weight the knitting evenly to avoid stretching the knitting.

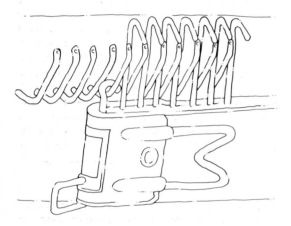

Positioning the casting on comb

CASTING ON, DOUBLE BED (see also *Casting On, single bed*). After knitting 1 row from right to left the fine wire is inserted into the cast on comb over this zigzag row. Both carriages are then set for circular (or it is sometimes called tubular) and 3 rows knitted. Sometimes two rows are sufficient. The row counter is set on 1 as 2 circular rows are one complete row. The machine is then set for ribbing and knitting can continue.

CASTING ON DOUBLE BED WELTS (see also *Racking*). *Fisherman rib.* Simplest form of tuck stitch. Cams are set in both carriages so that each carriage will only tuck in one direction. On one way the main bed collects a loop but the ribber knits normally and this reverses in the opposite direction. Half fisherman rib or English rib is when single row tucking is only on the ribber. This stitch can be changed in appearance by racking with the lever every two rows.

The Singer computer

Tubular hem. This is used when the main part of the garment is to be knitted on both of the beds. The total number of needles are brought into working position, cast on row and 2 circular rows are knitted; stitch size variations then occur so refer to ribber manual.

CELLOPHANE. Strips of cellophane can be used to weave in for interesting experimental textures, either by hand or on the machine — according to its strength.

CHAIN STITCH (see also *Mock Rib*). Embroidery stitch applied to the surface of fabric. A single stitch can be put out of action on the knitting machine or a stitch dropped to create a ladder. This can then be used to create vertical stripes by using a contrast yarn, and use the latchet hook to pick up the row of stitches working a chain stitch.

CHAMOIS CLOTH. A knitted or woven cloth made to imitate chamois skin.

CHARTING BLOCKS AND ALTERATIONS, see *Designing, Diagram Patterns.*

CHARTING DEVICES (see also *Designing, Diagram Patterns, Measurements*). Knitting from a diagram pattern. By tracing over the basic shapes new designs can be made quickly. It is the general rule for machines with a built in charting device that a set of diagram patterns are supplied (not with the knitcopy). If the charting device is bought separately a set is also supplied. Separate sets can be purchased. Where the charting device has plastic sheets a special pen is normally supplied to draw with. Blanks are available for some, but not all, machines. Alterations are made as follows: a V-neck depth is drawn on to the diagram where required, leaving a slight curve towards the shoulder. For round necks redraw the curve being careful that the initial cast off is not too big, resulting in a baggy shape. Square necklines are not drawn square; they slope gently towards the shoulders. Remember to measure the body to check the alterations. Where a diagram pattern is half scale or half garment, to work out the calculations of each pattern piece measure with a ruler and double it. This is then the size of the drawn out garment. See under relevant headings for further information regarding diagram alterations. Each knitting machine manufacturer has a different name for its own particular charting device: Forma — Passap. Half scale; Knitcopy — Juki (Singer). Full scale; Pattern Driver — Juki (Singer). Half scale; Knit-leader — Brother International. Full scale; Knit-radar — Empisal. Half size; Knit tracer — Toyota. Full scale; Pattern Driver — Superba. Half scale.

Stitch scale. The length of these varies according to the charting device. However, the markings on the scale rule represent stitches, so it is very important to select the correct scale from the tension sample/swatch. The stitch scale is in line with the drawn pattern, which shows where to increase and decrease. When the work has to be divided, as for a neckline, a work sheet is necessary to write down neck calculations, the row number from the counter and the pattern card row. Having completed one side, the pattern has to be turned back for the other side of the pattern and reset. When drawing a new pattern it is advisable to use the pen provided with the plastic grid sheets and draw the idea full scale. If the pattern has to be reduced for a half scale device then the squares are simply transferred onto half-scale paper. Most manufacturers are now producing electronic programme computer charting devices. A code number is used instead of a pattern. A sample of knitting is produced and the rows and stitches are programmed into the computer, plus any special length etc. required. For example, the Passap Form Computer (Forma) does not work from a diagram but is supplied with a model book of 40 garments, being produced twice a year, in which the programme for each garment is printed for a variety of sizes. Particular sizes, as people vary considerably, are programmed in (bust, waist, sleeve length, etc.) plus the tension square details. The Form Computer will then indicate a step by step guide to the knitting of the garment. Every time the lock passes along the bed a magnetic switch operates the counter on the device. The Computer shows at first the number of needles to be cast on. Then the number of rows to be knitted are indicated, and each time a row is knitted the figure on the screen decreases until an audible tone is heard signalling that that part of the process is complete. Then it indicates the next process. The Forma will be retained as it is useful for using original designs and for those who prefer working from a drawing instead. The Singer (U.K.) computer is suitable for both hand and machine knitters. The style, shape and size of the garment is selected from the book supplied. Any yarn and pattern stitch can be used. The computer then shows how many stitches to cast on, rows to knit, when to increase and so on. This is extremely useful for the knitter who requires garments other than the standard measurement, and makes for well fitted garments. The computer can be attached to the knitting machine and brackets are supplied for this.

CHEESES. Another name for spool. When yarn is supplied direct form the mill it either comes on cones, cheeses or in hanks.

CHENILLE (see also *Iron and Ironing, Yarn Combinations*). A textured yarn mainly made from cotton, although available in viscose and cotton blends. It is made like a woven fabric; the warp is of fine, strong yarns and the weft of soft, thicker yarns. As it is woven the fine yarns are twisted around each other in pairs. The fabric is then cut into strips about two threads in width warpwise. It is the little fringe that gives the yarn the typical chenille appearance.

CHILDREN'S SIZES. The sizing of children's garments has long been a problem. A child does not develop every part of its body at the same rate. Remember that until about seven years of age children have virtually no waistline. The most usual alteration on a pattern is length. Sizing for babies presents the same problems and no two patterns will have the same measurements. It should also be remembered that all jumpers should have a neck opening to allow for a child's large head. The following chart is a guide to sizing.

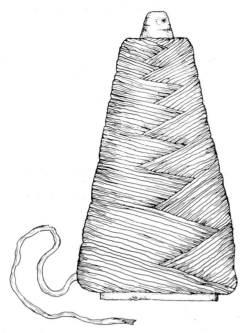

Cone of yarn

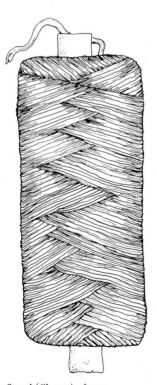

Spool (Cheese) of yarn

Infants' and children's sizes (centimetres)

Chest	46.0	51.0	56.0	61.0	66.0
Length	33.0	34.5	35.5	37.0	39.5
Shoulders (back only)	23.0	25.5	28.0	30.5	33.0
Sleeve length	23.0	25.5	28.0	28.0	32.0
Waist for skirt	45.5	49.5	52.0	56.0	58.5

Girls — teenager

Chest	71.0	76.0	81.5	86.5
Length	42.0	44.5	47.0	49.5
Shoulders (back only)	35.5	38.0	40.5	43.0
Sleeve length	35.5	40.5	43.0	45.5
Waist for skirt	58.5	61.0	63.5	66.0

Boys — teenager

Chest	71.0	76.0	81.5	86.5
Length	45.5	48.0	51.0	53.5
Shoulders (back only)	35.5	38.0	40.5	43.0
Sleeve length	38.0	40.5	44.5	46.0

CIRCULAR KNITTING. Stocking stitch that is knitted on both beds at once. Machine is set so that the carriage moves in one direction on one bed and in the other direction on the other bed. It is literally knitting in the round. This is useful for edgings, garment welts and bands, seamless socks and trousers. Stitch patterns can be knitted on this setting. The setting required for circular knitting to make each carriage inoperative on alternate rows is given in all ribber instruction books.

CLAMPS (see also *Tools*). Used to secure the machine to the table so that it will not move while it is in operation. The machine is angled slightly upwards to help prevent dropped stitches, and so that the right pressure is exerted onto the carriage.

CLAW WEIGHTS (see also *Tools*). Small weights supplied in the tool box, with small metal teeth at the top. They are hooked into the knitting at the edges, which puts the knitting under tension, keeps the stitches from jumping up and dropping off the needles and from being caught under the carriage. Particularly useful with very fine knitting and thick yarns. With the latter it may be necessary to pull the fabric down by hand after each row to ensure that each stitch has knitted. If a stitch has missed, knit it manually by taking the needle forward, placing the loop on to the needle hook and then taking the needle back to working position to form the new stitch. If work has to be left on the machine remove the weights and rest the work on a chair to relieve the strain on the knitting and avoid permanently stretching the row of knitting that is on the needles.

CLEANING AND MAINTENANCE OF KNITTING MACHINE. Brush with brush from tool box after use, between the needles to remove the fluff, having first pushed them right forward. Brush under the carriage and remove any yarn oddments that are caught under the brushes or tied around the table clamp. Clean off old oil on the metal parts by using surgical or methylated spirit on a dry cloth. Use oil provided or any light machine oil on the needlebed, the runners on underside of the carriage and sides of all cams and main cams. Remove excess oil with a tissue or cloth. Keep the brush clean as it is also used for opening the latches. Do not oil every time the machine is used but make sure that the carriage always runs smoothly. Oil machines when manual directs. Never oil the memory drums on punch card machines. Check for any bent needles or needles with latches that do not sit flat back against the needle shaft. Cover the machine with a needle bed cover after use to avoid collecting extra dust.

CLOSE KNIT BAR. Used on certain models of knitting machines when knitting fine yarns, on tension 2 or less. The bar is placed into the space that is between the edge of the needlebed and behind the sinker pins. It protrudes just slightly above the main bed edge. It ensures that pressure is put on the needlehook so that each stitch drops off the needle cleanly. The bar is put into place before casting on and removed only when knitting is completed. Be careful when unpacking a new machine that this bar is not discarded as it is a very narrow plastic strip!

CLUBS, KNITTING. Most towns have a knitting club where people go to learn how to machine knit and pass on news and items of interest to machine knitters. The more experienced knitter is also usually catered for. The knitting machine magazines print lists of knitting clubs.

COLLARS/NECKLINES, TYPE OF. *Collars:* cowl, lapel, middy, polo, rever, roll, sailor, shawl, shirt, stand, tie, yoke. *Necklines:* boat, crew, round, slash, square, U-neck, V-neck, yoke. Other collars or necklines are variations of these shapes.

COLOUR (see also *Sampling, Stripes*). Perhaps the most important element in garment design. Feelings are expressed through colour — blue is cold, red is hot — and this applies to a colour's apparent warmth or coolness. If a warm colour is put next to a cool colour the warm colour will look hotter.

Some diagrams show examples of the working measurements required to produce that particular neckline or collar

Bolero neck. This band is knitted over every stitch and is narrow, approximately 2.5 cm (1 in) wide. From centre front measure 7.5 cm (3 in) down, and it is at this point that the curve is worked

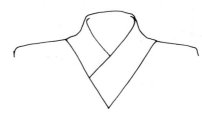

Ribbed lapover V-neck

Ribbed lapover V-neck, rolled

Round neck

Round neck cardigan — lady's

Square neck

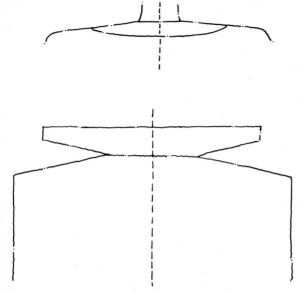

V-neck cardigan — man's

Slash neck. This is a high fitting very neat neck edge. The garment is decreased for the shoulder, then increased at the neckline over approximately 2.7 cm ($1\frac{1}{8}$ in) and then folded over and sewn down. The neck width opening should be at least 26 cm (10¼ in)

V-neck with collar. With this band the collar is knitted at the same time and applied afterwards to the garment. The depth from centre back to base of the V at the centre front measure approximately 20 cm (8 in). The band width is 43 cm (17 in). Knit straight for 2.5 cm (1 in) and then decrease 10 cm (4 in) for the collar at either edge. Knit straight for the collar approximately 7 cm (2¾ in) according to the depth of collar required. The collar depth can compliment the cuff depth

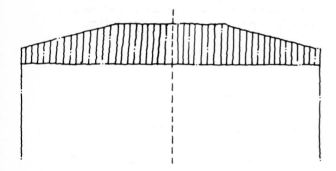

Ribbed Slash neck. This is one variation of the slash neck-line. The ribbing is commenced at the collar bone and decreased for the shoulder shaping. Cast off the remaining stitches at the neckline

V-neck pullover

Yoke

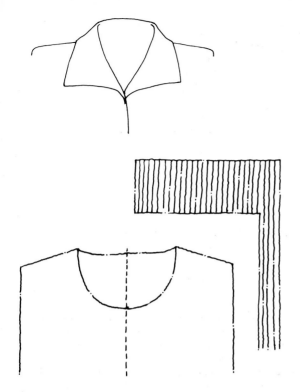

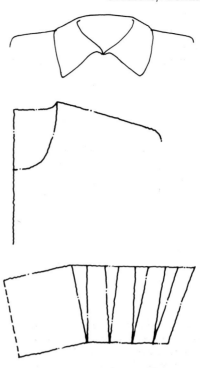

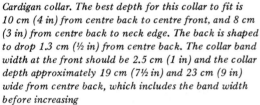

Cardigan collar. The best depth for this collar to fit is 10 cm (4 in) from centre back to centre front, and 8 cm (3 in) from centre back to neck edge. The back is shaped to drop 1.3 cm (½ in) from centre back. The collar band width at the front should be 2.5 cm (1 in) and the collar depth approximately 19 cm (7½ in) and 23 cm (9 in) wide from centre back, which includes the band width before increasing

Fancy fitted collar. This has a slightly higher neck front, measuring approximately 7.5 cm (3 in) from centre back to centre front, allowing a centre back curve of 1.3 cm (½ in) to the shoulder seam. The collar is worked over a width of approximately 10 cm (4 in) and the holding position is used so the short row designing method can be used to achieve a flared collar

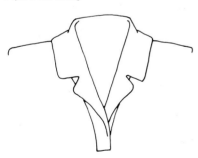

Lapel collar

Polo neck

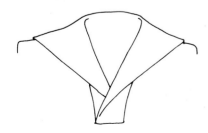

Middy collar

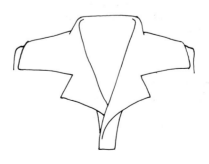

Revers collar

41

Roll collar cardigan — lady's

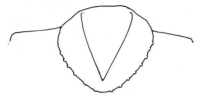

Roll collar with crochet edging

Sailor's type collar

Shirt collar

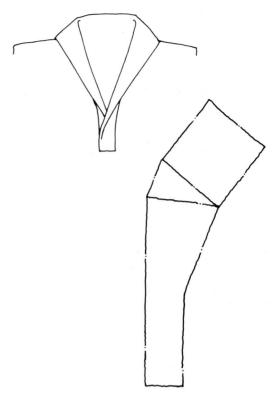

Shawl collar. This collar is worked over an approximate width of 5 cm (2 in) for 14 cm (5½ in) and then gradually increased to a width of 12.5 cm (5 in) over 16.5 cm (6½ in). The curve is then worked over 7.5 cm (3 in) on the one edge, and then a further 10 cm (4 in) is worked

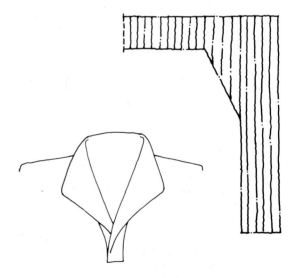

Single rever. This rever is suited to being worked over 5 cm (2 in) for 16.5 cm (6½ in), and then gradually increasing on one side over 12.5 cm (5 in) to a width of 10 cm (4 in). Then increase for the top band having an approximate width of 20 cm (8 in) for 3.7 cm (1½ in)

Square neck with collar

Tie collar

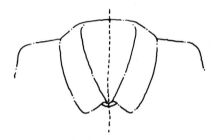

U-neck collar. The narrow collar band is worked separately to the collar. The depth of the neckline from the centre back being 20.5 cm (8 in). Allow a curve from this at centre back of 1.8 cm (¾ in). The width from centre back to neck edge is 7.5 cm (3 in) with a further 10 cm (4 in) to the shoulder point. The band depth is approximately 7.5 cm (3 in) and 28 cm (11 in) wide

Colour is capable of being dramatic, lyrical, harsh brittle or soothing. The energy of a colour can be seen by placing a blue square on a white background and on a black background. The blue on the white seems to expand and on the black to contract. Colour is so complex and so exciting that the need to experiment with yarn, of varying texture and colour, is very important. Use colours so that they work upon each other to become more exciting. The three primary colours that all (or nearly all) colours are mixed from, for dyeing yarns, are red, yellow and blue. These colours can be mixed to form secondary colours: red + yellow = orange, yellow + blue = green, blue + red = purple. Tertiary colours are between any two of these groups of colour. However, a single colour, for example yellow, can be quite a different colour, a lemon yellow or golden yellow. Therefore, when choosing a colour be aware of the range of intensity

between each colour, and the value of the colour, that is, the lightness or darkness. To become aware of colour proportions analyse the colour in a painting or someone else's knitting that you find interesting, and work out the limitations of its colour content. This will help when designing and experimenting with colour. Remember to start with an order and then start to use variations, always returning to the original for comparison. If the starting point is difficult, then impose very strict limitations on either some or all of the basic elements, the shape, size, colour and texture and so on. Work as widely and adventurously within those limits as possible.

COLOUR CHANGER (see also *Simulknit*). An excellent accessory and a very important time-saver, this consists of several arm brakes which enable you to change to another yarn almost automatically. Excellent when knitting stripes, using oddments of yarn. The number of floats are reduced at the back of the fabric by using a colour changer. Check when purchasing your machine how many selections that particular make provides on the colour changer as they vary; four is normal.

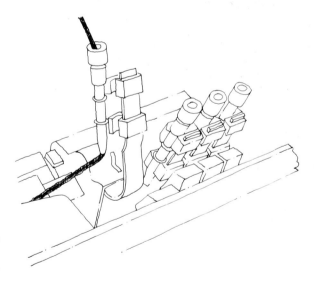

Passap colour changer

Some machines have colour changers for the single and double bed, and sit at different sides of the carriage according to the model. On the double bed the colour changer produces Fair Isle on the face side and a striped stockinet on the reverse. They may be used for pattern as well as plain knitting.

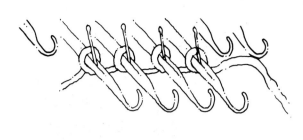

CONES (see also *Cheeses, Cone Winder, Wool Winder*). It is possible to buy yarns direct from some mills, on cones. Some have wider bases and are less likely to topple over when in use. Yarn can fall off cones by slipping down. A circular piece of fabric cut from a pair of tights or stockings can be put over the top of the cone, covering the yarn. This is particularly useful over cotton, rayon, metallic yarns and fine textured yarns. It also helps to stand the cone on a piece of fur fabric to stop the yarn catching on the base of the cone. When buying yarn that has been wound on to second-hand cones, remember that the labels inside the cones are not necessarily referring to the yarn now on the cone.

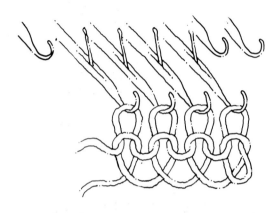

CONTRACTION OF FABRIC (see also *Iron and Ironing*). All knitting has a degree of stretch, and when removed from the machine will contract. However, long lengths of knitting need to be steam pressed before construction, otherwise they will contract when first being washed. Be very careful when pressing acrylics.

CORDS, KNITTED (see also *French Knitting*). *Circular and bought.* Used for a lightweight belt, for mock Aran and to hang a tassel and pompon from. Method: push between 3 and 7 needles furthest forward, carriage at the right, set according to manual. Wind as in diagram around the needles in an anti-clockwise direction as for closed edge cast on, for slipping in one direction and knitting in the other. Move the carriage back and forth across the needle bed, afterwards knitting one row. Push the needles to the furthest forward and move the carriage back and forth three or four times. Hang the claw weights on to the knitting and continue knitting. When length is complete cut off yarn and thread into a tapestry needle. Insert needle through all the stitches and remove cord from machine. These cords can be plaited together or threaded in and out of a row of holes on the centre of a belt, or cuff and collar to make an outstanding feature. French knitting was originally produced on a cotton reel with four nails at the top, and was a children's pastime. The same effect is produced on the machine and is much faster.

CORE SPUN YARN. Yarn that has a central core of either elastomer, rubber, or another yarn, with a covering of a secondary yarn.

CORKSCREW. A fancy yarn which is twisted in an even spiral, wavy shape. One yarn is very fine, like sewing cotton; the second yarn is a bulkier yarn with virtually no twist.

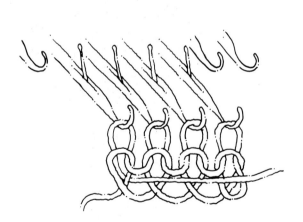

Knitting a cord

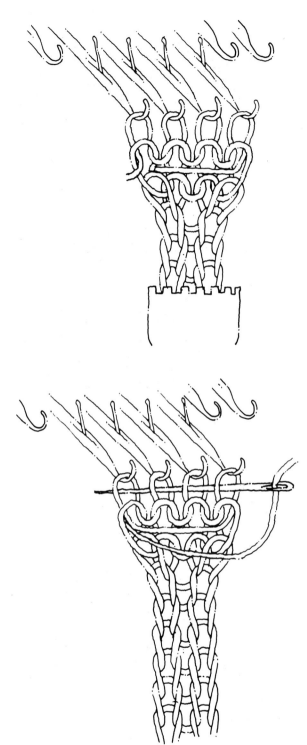

Plaited knitted cords

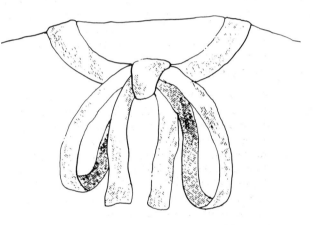

Bought and machine-knitted cords and braids can be used to finish and complement a garment at the neckline

CORNER TURNING. Knitting can be made to turn a corner (e.g. sock heels) by knitting horizontal or vertical darts, as in bust darts. Levers on hold. Carriage at right, bring 3 needles on the left forward and knit 3 rows. Then bringing another 3 needles forward, knit another 3 rows. Continue this until approximately 10 needles are in working position. Carriage at right return holding levers and continue knitting. This shaping can of course be changed by the number of needles selected each time and the number of rows knitted. To make the knitting turn the corner, knit a dart almost over the entire width of the knitting. Several darts will make a curved shape. Vertical darts, in a skirt for example, can be knitted as follows: cast on 24 stitches and knit several rows. Transfer the centre stitch to the needle on its left. With the triple transfer tool move the 3 stitches on the right of centre to the left so that the right-hand needle is empty. Push this into non-working position. Knit 20 rows and repeat, transfering every fourth row.

CORRECTING MISTAKES, see *Mistakes.*

COTTON, HISTORY OF. The word cotton comes from the Arabic, *qutun*. Cotton has been used over the last 5,000 years for textiles. In 2500 B.C. cotton cloths were made in Peru. The Bible refers to cotton. In 445 B.C. Herodotus, the Greek historian, observed in India that wild trees were growing with wool fruit on them. The Romans used cotton around 63 B.C. for awning. The Greeks began growing cotton around A.D. 100, spun the yarn and made it into hairnets. The Moors brought cotton

A cotton plant with closed and open seed pods, showing cotton ready for picking. (International Institute for Cotton)

to Spain in the tenth century and in the thirteenth century an established sailcloth industry was flourishing in Barcelona. Cotton was known about in England in the thirteenth century, although confusion arose about its origins: the English called it cotton wool and the Germans *Baumwolle* — which means tree wool. Christopher Columbus found cotton growing on an island in the Bahamas. Cotton was exported into Britain late in the seventeenth century, and eventually Parliament passed an Act to stop people wearing cotton: a heavy fine of £5 was imposed on those caught wearing it. (This law was eventually repealed as by 1930 cotton was being spun by machine in England). In 1793 an American named Eli Whitney invented the cotton gin, which could separate the cotton fibres from the seeds. Slaves were used in the cotton industry in America and by 1860 four million slaves were working in the cotton fields.

COTTON, PRODUCTION OF. The quality of cotton is determined by the fibre length, how fine it is, its maturity, colour and general conditon. It is mainly white but some is brown. The waxes and the oils are washed out before being processed for different uses as cotton yarn. When the cotton has been carded, combed, drawn out, and been through the roving stage and the spinning, it is then ready for further twisting or doubling. The yarn is then ready for use.

COTTON, TYPES OF (see also *Cones, Fibre Identification*). A vegetable fibre, it is the packing around the seeds in the seed pod. Lacks the elasticity of wool and is therefore harder to knit. The strongest cotton yarns are made from the longest staple fibre, which is Egyptian cotton or Sea Island. American cotton has a medium staple length and strength, and Indian has the poorest quality and the shortest fibre. Mercerised cotton is treated with caustic soda which makes the flat fibres swell and become round. This gives a lustre finish. Mercerised is best for knitting as it is smoother and stronger than the untreated cotton. Cotton can be knitted with any fibre providing the tension is adjusted accordingly and the lack of elasticity is accounted for.

COUNT OF YARN. Yarn is spun thread and ply is the single spun thread of any thickness. This single thread is twisted together with another thread or threads to make a specific thickness of yarn which is referred to as a plied yarn. In the fixed weight system yarn is classified according to its metre per kilo. Therefore with a fine yarn the number is

A modern cotton spinning 'Ring Frame', where the coarse 'rovings' on the bobbins on the top of the frame are being reduced in thickness by the rollers in the middle of the frame and the twist being put into the yarn by the bobbins at the bottom of the frame. (International Institute for Cotton)

higher as there are more metres to the kilo. If the yarn is plied the number of threads is shown alongside the count number, separated by an oblique stroke. The wool system varies in the different wool areas, therefore in some areas there may be slightly more or fewer metres to the kilo. Filament yarn is based on the unit of denier. The number shown is the weight in grams of 9,000 metres of yarn. The higher the number the thicker becomes the yarn. 2/16's is equivalent to a hand-knit 2 ply and used double as a handknit 4 ply. 2/8's gives a handknit 4 ply. 2/24's used double give a handknit 3 ply. 2/32's gives a handknit 1 ply

and can be used with several strands to give the desired ply. This of course will vary slightly according to the texture and the twist of the yarn.

COURSE. Knitting from left to right to left, or right to left to right. In other words across the selected stitches there and back.

COURSES, see *Machine Knitting Courses.*

COURTELLE (see also *Fibres, Synthetic Yarns, Yarn Combinations, Yarn Identification*). Trade name for acrylic fibre, man-made. Close in feel to wool, although lacks elasticity.

COWL NECK (see also *Collars*). A baggy polo neck, the knitting dropping around the neckline in folds. Any basic pullover pattern can be adapted for this type of collar. The inside of the collar fits tighter than the outside.

CRAB STITCH. Backward crochet. One row of double crochet is worked along the edge of the knitting. The work is not turned at the end of the row, but another row of double crochet is worked between the loops of the first crocheted row.

CRAYONS, FABRIC (see also *Printing*). There are two types of crayons available on the market, Pentel pastels and Finart Fabricrayons. The pastels can be drawn directly onto the knitted fabric but Finart have to be transferred from paper by heat. Synthetic fabric has to be used for permanency. Full instructions are on each box. Ideal for small areas of knitting.

CREPE. Type of twist applied to yarn. Makes firmer construction and adult garments usually take at least two to three extra balls.

CREW NECK (see also *Collars*). A high round neck.

CROCHET. A way of making cloth by using a hook-ended needle with either fine or thick yarns. Crochet effects can be knitted on the machine or by hand.

CROCHET EDGINGS. Crochet is used to firm a knitted edge or to finish off an uneven edge where it has been turned up or in. The crochet is worked in a straight line having turned the edge of the knitting to the wrong side and stitched with bias tape in a matching colour. It also gives added weight to the edge and can disguise a zip opening as well as helping to retain its shape.

CROCHET, HISTORY OF. The word crochet comes from the French *croc*, meaning hook. To trace the evolution of crochet is virtually impossible as for centuries it was worked by nuns, who kept the knowledge very much to themselves. It was for this reason that lace and crochet making was for so long called nun's work. The use of the hooked needle to make a network of loops was believed to have been depicted in paintings inside Egyptian temples, but it does not resemble the crochet we know today. The craft of crochet was well established by the sixteenth century and the nuns taught it to their pupils. It became an accomplishment of the high born ladies in society. In Ireland a form of crochet known as Irish crochet developed. The potato famine in Ireland in 1846 and 1847 gave crochet a new importance as people tried in every way to make money to buy a passage to America. The people who managed to do so took the craft with them, and what came to be known as American popcorn crochet was evolved. The Irish nuns made large amounts of crochet lace to sell to rich families, and it soon came about that the lace was being used to trim fashion gowns in London. Queen Victoria wore gifts of this lace and also made it herself. Patterns started appearing in ladies' magazines and it

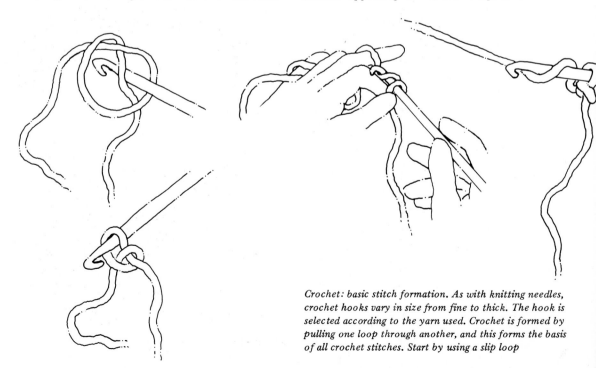

Crochet: basic stitch formation. As with knitting needles, crochet hooks vary in size from fine to thick. The hook is selected according to the yarn used. Crochet is formed by pulling one loop through another, and this forms the basis of all crochet stitches. Start by using a slip loop

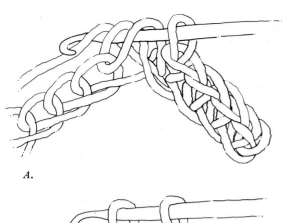

A.

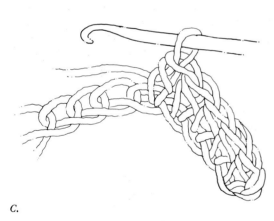

B.

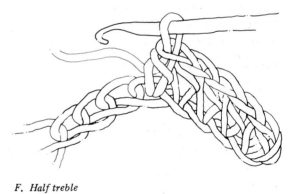

C.

Double crochet   A—C

D.

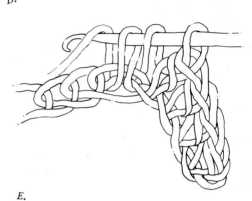

E.

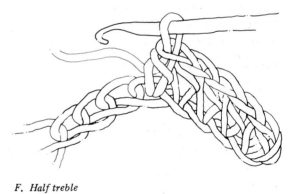

F. *Half treble*

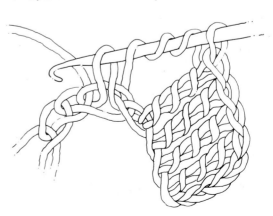

G. *Triple treble*

became tastelessly abused and over-fussy. Because of this it eventually fell into decline and was nearly lost altogether, but in the 1950s interest in America revived the craft. There was little written on its technique and it therefore took some time before crochet basics were put into print. It has now advanced tremendously and high fashion garments can be completely crocheted.

CROCHET/WORK HOOK. For crocheting seams together or for an edge where a zip is to be inserted. The hook is used for catching dropped stitches when knitting. For diagram see *Tools*.

CROSSBRED (see also *Wool*). Crossbred wool comes from sheep that have been mixed bred. They were originally crossed for the meat market but it was quickly realised that the wool was valuable.

CUFFS (see also *Edgings, Hems*). Cuffs, where possible, should match the hem of tops, dresses and jackets.

CUSHIONS (see also *Embroidery, French Knitting, Furnishing, Quilting*). These are ideal to make to practise with unusual yarns and intarsia. They need not be the conventional square shape but can assume all sorts of odd shapes. For example, long tubes with open ends can be stuffed with just a little padding, plaited and then the ends joined together. Children's cushions can take the form of toys or they could take the form of large floor cushions.

CUT AND SEW (see also *Floats, Taping*). Method of constructing knitting that can be carried out in two ways.

1 Fabric can be knitted on the full width of the needlebed to the required length, allowing for shrinkage when pressed, and natural contraction. The fabric is constructed using dressmaking techniques with a paper pattern.

2 Body blanks can be knitted. A body blank is a rectangle with a knitted rib or hem that has the correct height and width of the shape required. The neck, armhole and shoulder shapings are then cut out before construction on the sewing machine or overlocker.
Method of construction. Use a 100% polyester thread or cotton covered polyester thread when stretch is needed. Mercerised or silk thread may be used on more stable knits. Buy dressmaking patterns that are for: 'stretch knits only'. The

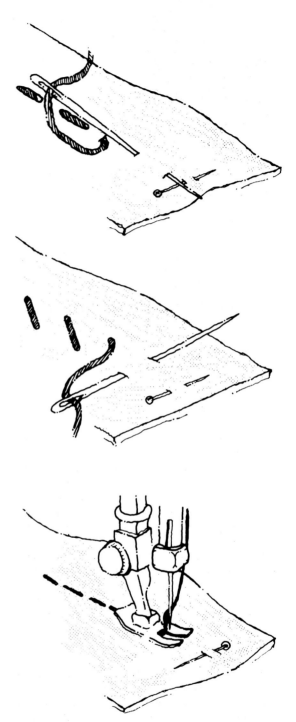

Tacking/basting on the sewing machine

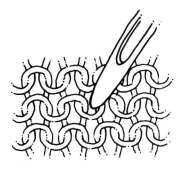

Construction of garment on the sewing machine. The use of the ball point needle

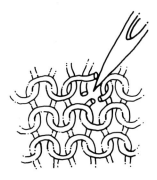

A regular sewing machine needle

Stretch the knitting slightly when sewing. Have little excess on the seams and make sure that the garment is well tacked together before stitching on the machine. The shoulders must always be taped to avoid stretching. Measure the shoulder width on the garment and cut two pieces of narrow tape and either stitch them after the seam has been joined or sew in while overcasting. The tape is always laid on the back of the garment and must be put in before the sleeves. Press the garment as it is being constructed. Raw edges can be zigzagged and trimmed, stable knits can be left unfinished. With edgestitch seams that have a tendency to roll, yarn is used. Bias tape can be stitched on the wrong side to edges that might fray, that are light-weight and may be either turned and caught by hand on the under side, or else top stitch bias edges together on the raw edge.

D

DACRON (see also *Synthetic Yarns*). Polyester is called Dacron in the U.S.A. and Terylene in the U.K. It is a durable fibre which is often blended with wool.

DARNING AND DARNING IN LOOSE ENDS. This is very tedious but important. Instead of using a needle, it is much quicker to use the latch tool in the tool box. It is possible to darn the yarns in while the knitting is on the knitting machine. Lift the loose ends over the end five needles. This method works well for finer yarns but is too bulky for thicker yarns. Ends can also be sewn down when the seam is stitched on a sewing machine and the ends trimmed very carefully.

Renovation. Areas of worn knitting can be repaired by darning. Use yarn of the same colour and weight. If the stitches look too bulky then remove a strand from the yarn. The method of sewing is the same as Swiss darning. If worn patches are caught early it avoids a large darned patch, and looks less unsightly. When knitting garments attach a small knitted square on the inside of the garment where it cannot be seen. This gives instant darning yarn, and should the garment fade slightly with washing, the darning yarn will be the same colour.

pattern states the type of knitting that the pattern is suitable for. Knits are generally classed as either stable or stretchy knits, and the type of garment to be made depends on the amount of stretch in the knitting. Weave and slip stitch are ideal firm fabrics for cut and sew. Having knitted the length of fabric, it must be shrunk either by steaming (see *Iron and Ironing*) or by dry cleaning if it is to be dry cleaned after construction. Any zips or tapes used must also be shrunk. Any alterations to the pattern must be done before cutting. Use heavy weights to keep pattern pieces in place (see *Paper Patterns*). Use the layouts with nap because of the shading. Lay out the pattern and check how many times each piece has to be cut. Use very sharp scissors, keep the fabric flat to the table and cut with steady firm and even slashes, keeping one hand on the pattern to ensure it lies flat. Pin pieces together using ball point pins and use either a straight stitch or a zigzag on the machine. Test a sample first. Or use an overlocker, which trims, overlocks and joins in one process. (See also *Interfacing, Linings, Tailor's Tacks*.) It is advisable to use ball point needles for the machine so that the stitches are not split and do not snag. An even tension is essential otherwise the seams will rip.

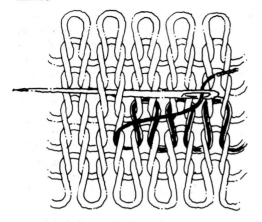

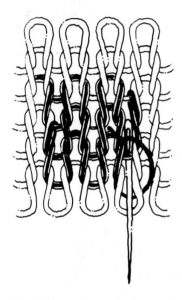

Repairing knitting by darning

DARTS (see also *Corner Turning, Increasing, Short Row Designing*).

Horizontal. A bust dart is seldom used in knitting unless the structure of the fabric is very firm. Because of the elasticity of knitting it conforms to the shape and position the body assumes and therefore generally fits well over the bust. Darts for large busted people are excellent as they reduce bulkiness at the underarm. Yokes may be knitted by making long darts across the width of the knitting to achieve a curved shape. On diagram patterns a dart is shown by a piece cut out of the drawing. When knitting, the stitches are put into holding position and are not cast off. The exception to this is with certain patterns and then the stitches to be held are taken off the needles and replaced when the dart is complete. To work out a dart shaping measure the length from the beginning of the dart to the end and multiply by the number of stitches to 2.5 cm (1 in) and then measure the width of the dart and multiply by the number of rows to 2.5 cm (1 in). By doing this the number of stitches to be held over the number of rows can be calculated.

Vertical. Used on skirts and dresses. The same calculations are done as for a horizontal dart. Then the stitches have to be moved manually on a particular row.

DEALERS, KNITTING MACHINE (see also *Buying a Machine*). Found in most towns. The yellow pages (U.K.) will give details. As a final resort if you are having extreme difficulty the importers of the knitting machines normally have details of outlets of their machines. Dealers advertise in various craft magazines. If the machine is particularly cheap it usually means that tuition is paid for separately.

DECO ATTACHMENT (see also *Accessories*). The Passap knitting machine double bed punchcard system.

DECORATIVE CABLES, see *Cables, decorative.*

DECORATION, SURFACE, see *Cords, knitted, French Knitting, Fringes, Pompon, Sequins, Swiss Darning, Tassel.*

DECREASING. *To decrease a single stitch at either edge* use the single transfer tool. Transfer the end stitch on to the next needle and push the empty needle back to non-working position.

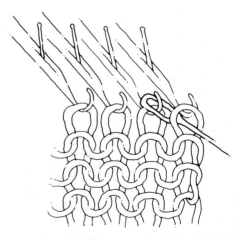

Decreasing a single stitch. The empty needle is pushed back to non-working position

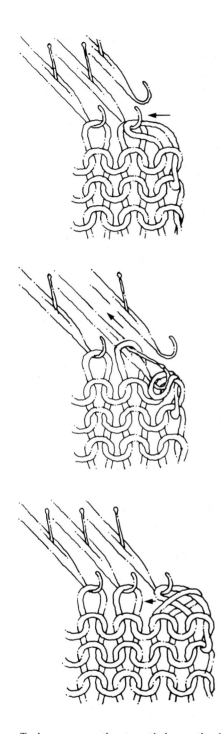

To make a fully fashioned decrease use the 2- or 3-pronged transfer tool. Move the stitches in one needle so that the second or third needle has two stitches and push the empty needle back to non-working position. To decrease more than one stitch at the end of a row use the method as for closed edge cast off using the transfer tool or latch hook. To decrease the number of stitches along a row prior to fitting to narrower part of knitting, the knitting is taken off the machine after knitting several rows of waste yarn. Put the number of needles needed according to the pattern to working position and replace the knitting on to the machine as the pattern states.

To decrease a stitch in the centre of a row, for example where vertical darting is required. Transfer the stitch either to the right or the left where it is required and then transfer all the other stitches up one stitch to fill the gap. Push the needle at the end of the row back to non-working position.

To decrease on the double bed follow diagrams carefully.

Decreasing one stitch fully fashioned.

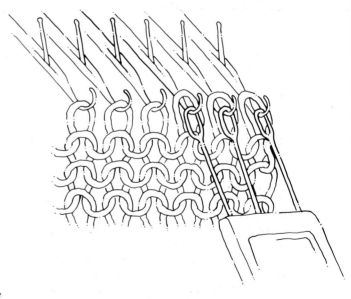

To decrease more than two stitches on the side without yarn. Place end stitch onto next needle hook. Push needle forward so the stitch slips behind the latch. Push needle back and the latch closes over the stitch pulling it through the second stitch. One stitch is then left on the needle hook. Place this stitch onto the next needle hook and repeat procedure. Push empty needle back to non-working position

Using the 3/1 transfer tool, pull the needles forward and then back, so that the latches close and the stitches sit on the transfer tool as in the second diagram.

DECREASING

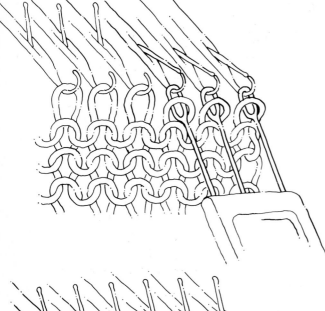

Decreasing on a 1/1 rib.

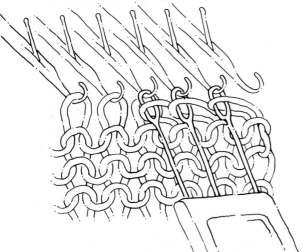

The empty needle is taken back to non-working position

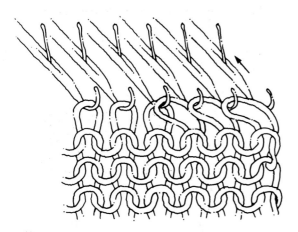

To decrease a single stitch, transfer the stitch from the mainbed to the ribber, pushing the empty needle back into non-working position. Knit across the bed and then transfer the stitch to the mainbed from the ribber as in the second diagram to give the result in the final diagram. Push back the empty needle and continue knitting

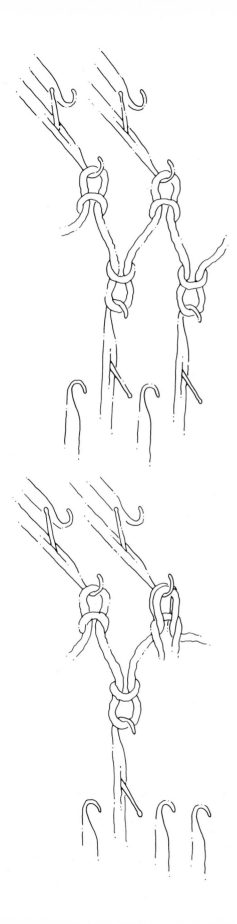

Decreasing on the doublebed, more than one stitch on a 1/1 rib.

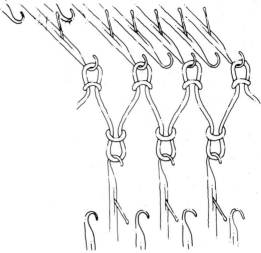

Transfer the number of stitches to be decreased onto the mainbed from the ribber

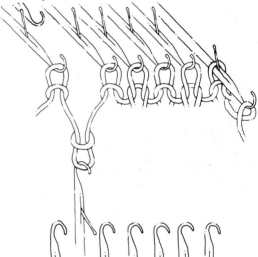

Push empty needles back into non-working position. Cast off the stitches

Put last stitch onto the first needle in knitting position

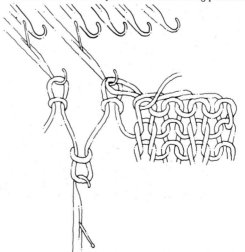

DECREASING

To decrease one stitch on a 2/2 rib. Transfer the end stitch onto the next needle and put the empty needle back into non-working position

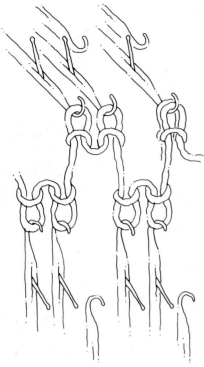

Transfer the end stitch on the mainbed onto the next needle and push the empty needle back into non-working position

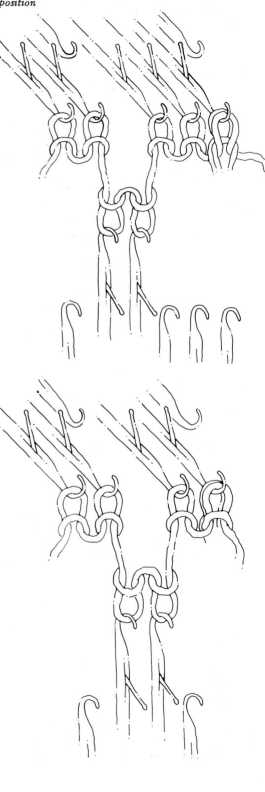

Transfer the end stitch on the mainbed onto the next empty needle. Then transfer the two stitches from the ribber both together onto the mainbed stitch just transferred, so there are three stitches on one needle. Push the empty needle back and continue knitting

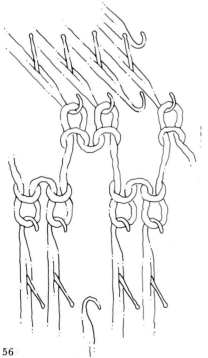

Decreasing on the double bed, more than one stitch on a 2/2 rib. Transfer the stitches onto the adjacent needles on the mainbed from the ribber, pushing the empty needles back to non-working position, as in the next diagram

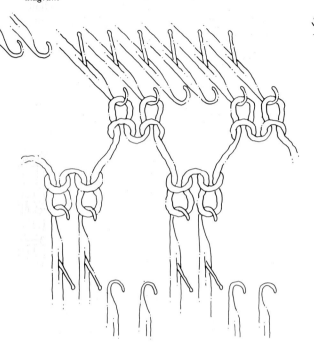 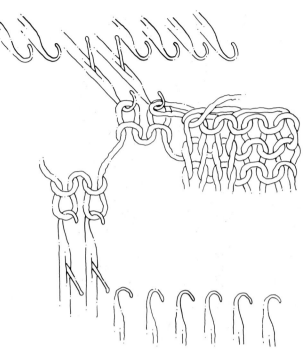

Cast off the stitches, placing the last stitch onto the next needle. Push empty needles to non-working position, as in the final diagram

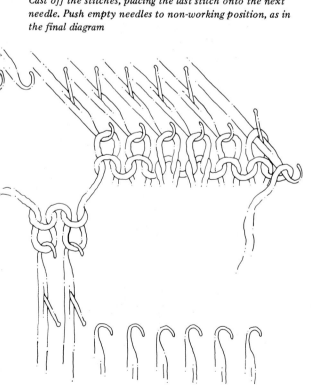

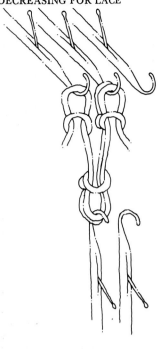

DECREASING FOR LACE. Transfer one stitch at a time on to the adjacent needle. If this needle is in non-working position then bring it to knitting position. Lower the empty needle to non-working position. Continue in this way to decrease further stitches. To decrease more than one stitch, or to cast off, start nearest to the carriage, form chain stitches along the row for every empty needle, catching the knitted loops in the chain.

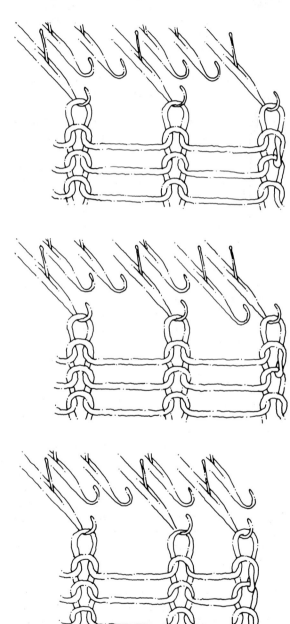

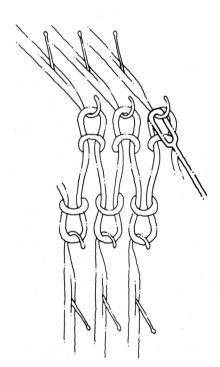

Decreasing on the double bed, on a double rib. To decrease a single stitch transfer the end stitches from the mainbed and the ribber onto their next needle on the inside. Push the empty needles back to non-working position

Decreasing when knitting lace

DECREASING ON RIBBED KNITTING, see *Decreasing*.

DENIER (see also *Count of Yarn*). The size of filament yarn.

DESIGNING, BASIC GARMENTS (see also *Collars/Necklines, Measurements, Sleeves*.) Understanding a good tension and the various yarns available, plus the type of stitch structures that can be achieved, is essential before commencing. Exact measurements are needed. A tolerance allowance of 5 cm (2 in) is essential to allow for ease of movement. Having established the tension and the measurements, then a basic diagram must be drawn with the relevent information beside it. The measurements have to be multiplied by the number of stitches to 2.5 cm (1 in), and calculate the number of rows to be worked to give the required length. The basic patterns drawn on squared paper can be adapted to almost any shape required. However, thinking about a basic garment, the top consists of three basic tube shapes, and can therefore a section is removed on each side of the pieces of knitting, by straight pieces of knitting that can be cut and sewn at the neckline, by slightly shaped pieces, or by straight pieces but with shaping at armholes and neckline. Shoulders have been changed only to fit the body better and there fore a section is removed on each side of the body, creating a slope. For shoulder shaping deduct the number of stitches across back neck, from the total number of stitches and halve the resulting number. For calculations for squared armholes deduct the shoulder width from the body width. For the shoulder shaping deduct the neck stitches from the number of stitches at back after the armhole shaping. For an armhole curve the stitches are calculated the same way as for a squared armhole, but divide these stitches into approximately three equal parts. The shape is then gradually worked in steps by casting off the first group of stitches. The next group is divided up into three smaller parts and the final group is cast off singly. If the garment is to be sleeveless then take off 2.5 cm (1 in) on either side of the armhole. This will leave room for a band to be knitted and fit neatly.

DIAGRAM PATTERNS (see also *Charting Devices, Measurements*). Many patterns are now in the form of a diagram. All the symbols used are at the beginning of the pattern. These symbols vary according to the manufacturer. There is a diagram for each piece of knitting. In general the line in the

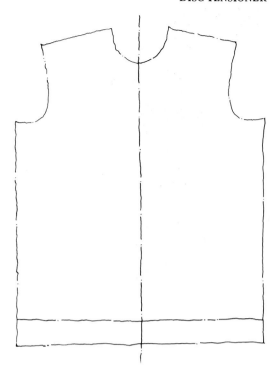

Basic diagram form with details omitted

centre of the diagram represents the centre of the machine. The row numbers on the vertical line at the right of the diagram indicate when to begin shaping. The stitches for casting off, decreasing and increasing are at the right of the centre line. The vertical line shows the length. Always start from the lower edge and work up, unless otherwise directed. Always check finished garment pieces against the measurements given on the blocking diagram. Passap have excellent diagram patterns with every possible detail given to double check the construction. Each part of the garment is subdivided so that, should an error occur, it can easily be remedied within a particular section.

DIP DYED YARN, see *Space Dyed Yarn*.

DISCHARGE PRINTING, see *Printing*.

DISC TENSIONER (see also *Antenna Spring*). The tension at which the yarn will feed into the machine is determined by the unit at the top of the yarn tension unit. The spring discs allow the yarn to pass either easily or tightly through, depending on the yarn. A tight tension is used for thin yarns and a loose tension for thick yarns.

DOLMAN SLEEVE. This shape is made by drawing the body and sleeve of a dropped shoulder pattern together. This makes a large, loose sleeve.

DOUBLE BED (see also *Industrial Machines, Ribbing Attachment*). A machine with two sets of needles set opposite to each other. Produces a double knit or rib fabric. Also know as V bed.

DOUBLE FACE. The back or front of certain fabrics can be used as the face side.

DOUBLE JERSEY. Also known as double knit and if patterned is called double jersey jacquard.

DOUBLE KNIT. Knitting produced on a double bed machine. The knitting appears the same on both sides, except when patterning. It can be used for wrapover skirts, jackets, hoods, cuffs and reversibles.

DOUBLE RIB (see also *Mock Rib, Rib*). A rib is made on the single bed machine by casting on over every needle and then transferring with the latchet hook the needles that are necessary to produce either a 3/1, 2/1, or 1/1 welt.

DRAWSTRING. Cords, plaits, braids, leather strips, ribbons or whatever may be suitable in weight for the garment, may be used as a drawstring. Its length should equal the measurement around the body plus enough length to allow for tying at the side or front of the garment, depending on where the openings for the drawstring are situated.

DRESSMAKER'S DUMMY. A stand the shape of the body, used to pin knitting into shape and so aid in the neat fitting of the garment. It is helpful when using cut and sew facrics. It will also show up, after construction of the garment, any uneven seams or minor shaping faults. It is preferable to use the padded type of dummy that takes pins easily.

DRESSMAKING PATTERNS (see also *Cut and Sew*). Can be used in conjunction with the charting device provided they are for stretchable knits, and they have the 'with nap' layout. Certain charting devices are full size and these patterns are traced on to a graph with a felt tip pen. This only applies to the machines that are supplied with the blank sheets, or where blanks can be bought for a particular machine. To preserve dressmaking patterns press pieces with a warm iron and mount by stapling on to thin card. Never use pins to hold the pattern in place, use several weights. The pattern pieces should be folded neatly and put into a cardboard folder with the instructions and the picture of the garment on the front. The pattern can then be traced off easily and scaled up or down for different sizes.

DRIVE LACE (see also *Lace*). For Empisal machines use a 2-ply yarn and set main bed five numbers higher than the ribber. Main part of knitting is on the ribber. Use special punched cards, which leave every alternate line blank, so that patterning is only selected on every alternate row. Cast on and knit either a full needle rib, a 2 x 2 or a tubular hem. All stitches are transferred onto the ribber. Carriage at right and card inserted and locked on the first row. Take carriage across to set the memory into the machine, and release the card lock. Set lever to slip. Needles on main bed are brought back into working position with the first and last needle on the ribber. Ribber is set to knit normally but the main bed is set to slip with the left hand side lever on the spot and the right hand side on the triangle. The first row is knitted to the right. The ribber knits an ordinary row but the main bed only knits the needles that are in line with a punched hole on the card. A second row is knitted and the ribber knits an ordinary row, but the main bed does not knit as it is the blank row on the punchcard. Place P carriage on right of work and move across all needles in working position. This P carriage is then moved back to the right so that the loops drop from the machine. This is repeated every 2 rows. This P carriage must be moved across the ribber once every row. Count stitches on the ribber only, and calculations can be based on this figure.

DROPPED SHOULDER. Achieved by knitting up at the armhole so that no decreasings take place. The sleeve head is adjusted accordingly.

DROPPED STITCHES (see also *Ladder, Mistakes*). To pick up a dropped stitch insert transfer tool and place the stitch back onto the needle. If the stitch has run several rows down, then catch it with the pointed work hook from the tool box; it is often easier to catch the stitch below. Using the latch hook from the back, work the row of stitches up the knitting and place the loops onto the needle behind the latch. Put the yarn of the dropped stitch into the hook and knit the stitch. If the knitting drops completely off the needles from one end using the transfer tool to place each stitch on to a needle irrespective of which row the stitch is from. It is merely important to catch the stitches quickly. Then unpick several rows until the knitting is looking even again. If following a pattern be sure to reset the row counter and the punchcard.

DRY CLEANING (see also *Garment Aftercare*). Knitting can be dry cleaned. When using the cut and sew method of construction the lengths can be dry cleaned before being cut. The zipper and tape should also be shrunk in the same way.

DYEING, YARN (see also *Yarn Dyeing*). The word used for putting colour into yarns and fibres or fabrics. Some dyes will only take on particular fibres and the process of industrial dyeing is very complex. There are, however, dyes prepared in small quantities for home use.

DYE LOTS. Each batch of yarn that is dyed is given a number and that is the dye lot. Always buy sufficient yarn for each garment from the same dye lot. Yarn from a different dye lot may vary slightly in colour, and may not show up until it has been knitted. Certain dyes can affect the tension of the same yarn.

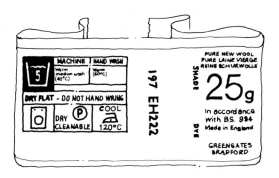

Yarn label that is placed on every ball. It shows the dye batch number, fibre content, where it was processed into yarn and how to wash it

DYES, NATURAL (see also *Dyes, natural, history of, Yarn Dyeing*). Natural dyes are extracted from nature. With natural dyes all parts of plants can be used for the dyeing. Many plants can be used either fresh or dry. It is also possible to buy natural powdered dyes for people who are not quite so anxious to gather their own. Generally the dye is stronger when the plant is fresh and the same plant gives a different shade and sometimes

colour at different times of the year. Natural dyes come in two types, those that give colour directly, like lichen dyes, and mordant dyes. The latter have to have mordants added so that the colour is absorbed properly. The most useful mordants are alum, tin, chrome, and iron.

Alum. Potassium aluminium sulphate, the most commonly used mordant. It is added to cream of tartar and then added to the pot.

Tin. Normally comes as crystals of tin, stannous chloride or muriate of tin. It is excellent for bright shades of yellow and red on silk and wool. It is not suitable for linen and cotton. Tin is also used with cream of tartar, which must be dissolved in the water before adding the tin.

Chrome. Bichromate of potash. It is very light sensitive, so should always be covered to avoid patchy dyeing. Wool after mordanting should not be exposed to the light. Wool becomes soft when mordanted in chrome.

Iron. Ferrous sulphate or copperas, always used with cream of tartar. Iron tends to darken and dull colours. Mordanting with iron is carried out after dyeing, unlike the other mordants.

If wool is being mordanted, do not stir too much as it may felt; three times is sufficient. Natural dyes are broken down into the following: animal, vegetable (nearly all natural dyes originate from plants) and mineral (e.g. iron rust). Roots should be sorted in the autumn, bark too, unless it is resinous, in which case it is better collected in the spring. Seeds and berries are best picked when they are just ripe. Collect lichens in the winter, or after heavy rain for easier removal. Stone lichen gives a better colour than tree lichen. Plants are normally most brilliant when fresh but it is possible to dry them. If, however, they become damp and mould sets in they are completely useless. The time of day that some plants are picked can affect the dye. Plants picked at midnight and the crack of dawn are generally stronger when using alum and chrome. Pick in the middle of the day and when the sun is setting when using iron. Natural dyes can be obtained by using things in the home like tea, coffee, curry powder, anthracite, broad beans, carrots, peas, marrow, cabbage and even lettuce. Fennel, horseradish, mint, parsley marjoram, sage, most soft fruits and many hard skinned fruits and flowers in the garden can also work well. Leaves, walnut shells and some fruits can be deep frozen for storage but they do loose colour.

DYES, NATURAL, HISTORY OF (see also *Dyes, natural*). Hundreds of years ago man worked hard to colour his fabrics, and although many plants gave dye that coloured them earthy yellows and browns, the brighter, more brilliant colours were hard to find and were therefore greatly sought after. 'Royal Purple' was first discovered many centuries before the Christian era by a shepherd, so the story goes, when his dog broke a shellfish in his mouth, resulting in his mouth turning purple. The Tyrians extracted this dyestuff and it was used for weaving. It was very precious and the Tyrians exported it to Rome and other countries. It took more than 8,500 mollusks to obtain one gram of colour! The material dyed from it was so expensive that only royalty could afford it, hence its name. Kermes is the oldest dye on record and it was obtained from insect bodies found on a certain kind of oak tree. A piece of textile found in a neolithic grotto dated 1727 B.C. was believed to be dyed from this dye. In the Old Testament it is called scarlet. Madder was the most common red dyestuff and was used for its rose-red colour, which was very fast and easily available. The Egyptians and East Indians cultivated this plant for centuries and, later, the Europeans. The important chemicals in madder are alizarin and purpurin. The exact chemical equivalent of alizarin can now be made. Spanish conquerers of Mexico found the people dyeing reds with a dyestuff called cochineal, which was made from the bodies of insects that feed on a particular cactus. The Spaniards exported the dye to Europe and it was used for a while to dye fabrics including the fabric for British soldiers' jackets. (This fabric eventually went back to the New World in the eighteenth and nineteenth century, where it was unravelled, respun and then woven by the Navajo Indians for their blankets). The Romans knew of one of the most brilliant yellows, saffron, which was taken from the pistils of the autumn crocus. Indigo has been used for over four thousand years. It is a plant whose leaves contain indigotin, which is the dyestuff. Because it is insoluble in water it is produced by putting the leaves into water until the liquid changes to a yellow slimy substance. It is then beaten, when it changes to blue, formed into a paste and then into bars. It was originally sold in Europe in this form and the dyers at first thought it was a mineral. By 1897 indigo was being made from chemicals. Woad is another plant whose leaves have indigotin, but much less than in the indigo plant. In Europe this plant was grown in the sixthteenth and seventeenth centuries. Dyestuff was extracted from pieces of wood from certain trees: quercitron, logwood, cutch and old fustic. These produce yellows and browns. Weld is a plant from the Mediterranean which produces a very good yellow dyestuff which has been used for thousands of years. Lichens are plants that produce dyestuff, and are well known from their use in Harris tweeds. The lichens produce colours from beige and brown to pink. Because they contain acid they need no mordants in the dye-bath. Some natural dyes need mordants to help the dye penetrate the fibres. Originally the leaves and roots of some plants were used for mordants, as well as urine, as it contains ammonia and uric acid.

DYES, SYNTHETIC, HISTORY OF. Dyes until the middle of the nineteenth century were taken from animal, vegetable or mineral sources. In 1856, at the Royal College of Chemistry in London, William H. Perkin discovered the first artificial dyestuff. By 1859 other colours had been discovered by other chemists; they were all derived from coal tar. In Ludwigshafen in Germany the Badische Anilin und Soda Fabrik began manufacturing dyes. Aniline was eventually replaced by other chemicals as it tended to fade quickly. There are now of course several different types of synthetic dyes that are better for dyeing certain materials or fabric.

DYESTUFFS (see also *Yarn Dyeing*). Vary greatly according to their usage and the fibres/fabric content used.

Acid dyes are used for protein fibres, nylon dyeing and printing.

Azoic dyes are mainly for printing on cotton.

Basic dyes are best used on acrylic fibres for fastness.

Direct dyes are mainly used on cotton. Best for dyeing rather than printing.

Disperse dyes are water-insoluble dyes used for printing on terylene, polyester fibre, cellulose acetate and triacetate.

Mordant dyes are used with a metal salt. Very rarely used commercially.

Premetallised dyes were developed after mordant dyes. Mainly used for dyeing.

Onium dyes called this because they are either sulphonium or ammonium compounds, and are water soluble.

Pigment dyes are insoluble in water. When mixed with a resin binder they are used to print on textile fabrics.

Oxidation dyes are used mainly as hair and fur dyes.

Reactive dyes are so called because they undergo a chemical reaction with cellulose fibres. Used for dyeing and printing with very good washing fastness. Reacts badly on nylon.

Soluble vat dyes, for use on cotton, viscose rayon, silk and wool.

Sulphur dyes give fabrics that have a good washing fastness.

Vat dyes are insoluble in water.

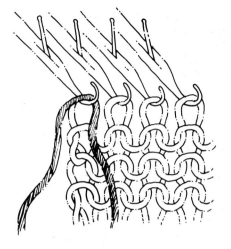

EDGE, MARKING. A contrast piece of yarn is used to mark a particular place on the knitting and then just pulled out later when it has fulfilled its purpose.

EDGINGS (see also *Buttonhole Stitch, Cables, Crochet, Hems, Lace, Picot Edge, Pile Knitting*). Bought edgings can be used, and a fringe or ready made lace can be hooked on to the machine and used as a base for the knitting. Make sure the trim is the right weight for the fabric. These edgings can also be gathered and caught on to the machine, or top stitched by hand on to the knitting having removed it from the machine. Crochet can be used along the edges of garments: at zip openings to keep the edge in shape, and at hemlines where different weight fabrics have been used. The hem is turned up and the crochet worked along a line at the bottom edge. Edgings can either be inserted on the edge of the knitted fabric or put in as insertions between two pieces of knitting. Decorative welts can be varied a great deal, for example a row of holes can be worked along the centre of the cuff or hem. This can have a knitted cord threaded in and out and then gathered to form a small frilled welt. If the hole is quite large, sequins can be set in the middle of the welts so that they shine through the holes. Contrast yarn can be used on the reverse of the welt, and this too will show through the holes. A series of hems can be knitted up the bodice of a garment, and at the base of a skirt to form ridges. Remember to leave sufficient rows in between each hem formation. This idea looks pretty with a contrast yarn on the fold line of each hem. The contrast colour can be graded with each hem formed, either going darker or lighter. Other materials can be used with yarn to make unusual textures, for example plastic, leather,

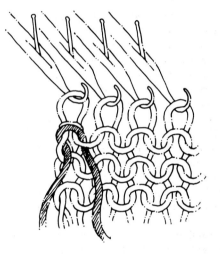

Edge marking with a piece of waste yarn. It is used to mark seam joins, or in the centre of the knitting for marking a sleeve top or a neck edge centre

ribbons, pipe cleaners, braids and other bought trims, felt and wire, sequins, beads, feathers, grasses, shells, etc. If washing the sample provides problems then the garment itself should be dry cleaned.

Cables can be used to make interesting edges. A cable welt can be knitted by pushing up a multiple of 8 plus 2 needles into working position and pushing every following third and eighth needle back to non-working position. Cast on using waste yarn and knit several rows, carriage is at the left. With main yarn but tension two sizes tighter knit approximately 22 rows. Set tension to 1 full size looser than the main tension and knit 1 row. Tension 1 size tighter than the main tension, knit 4 rows and then work the cable. Starting from the right count each set of four stitches, cross the third and the fourth stitches under the first and the second and knit four rows. Repeat the working of the cable three more times. Cross the same stitches and knit 2 rows. Push up the non-working needles to working position, and make a hem by putting the loops of the first main yarn row on to the first, third, fourth, fifth, sixth and eighth needles and every following in that order. A fancy scalloped welt is made by pushing up 6 needles then 3 needles to working position and every fourth and sixth to non-working position. Cast on with waste yarn and knit several rows. Carriage at the left. Tension two sizes tighter than main tension, with main yarn knit the rows for the hem. Tension 1 size looser than main tension and knit 1 row. Tension 2 sizes tighter than main tension, knit the same number of rows as previously. Push up the non-working needles and make the hem by putting the loops of the first row in main yarn on to the first, third, fourth and sixth needles and every following in that order. Steam the welt carefully, pulling down the single ribs with a pin to achieve the wavy edge. The variety of fancy edgings that are possible on the machine are endless; below are various fancy edgings as a starting point. Electronic machine owners should check instruction manuals for setting before starting to knit edging.

Shell edgings are numberous; use a 3-ply yarn for the best result. They are attached to garment by sewing. A single shell set needles as follows:

$$11 . 1 . 11$$
$$0$$

Cast on and knit a few rows, set levers to hold. Push needle in centre to holding position and knit 6 rows. Push the needle back to working position and knit 2 rows. Repeat this for the length necessary.

A tiny shell for babies' garments is knitted the same as above but 4 rows on centre needle is knitted and 2 rows on all needles.

$$1 . 1 . 1$$
$$0$$

Make sure that all edgings knitted on the single bed have weights attached to the knitting.

Fair Isle edgings can be produced by knitting a Fair Isle pattern over a small number of selected needles for the length of the braid required. A Fair Isle band will rouleau scallops can be knitted as follows. Make a close edge cast on over 2 needles and knit a rouleau to the length required. Knit several rows of waste yarn, and remove from the machine. The end can be finished later. For the band set the needles 000011111111 and make a

closed edge cast on over these 8 needles. Put punchcard into place locked on the first row, and knit 1 row. Release the card and set carriage to Fair Isle. Pick up the end stitch of the rouleau onto the first needle at the right. *Now knit 6 rows of the pattern and replace the stitch on the rouleau's 8th row onto the first needle at the right. * Repeat between * until complete.

A lace hem is knitted as follows. Use a 3-ply yarn on tension 8. Cast on with waste yarn and knit several rows. Then thread up with 3-ply yarn and set the tension correctly and knit two rows. Transfer at right every alternate stitch starting on the second, on to its adjacent needle. All needles in working position and knit 2 rows. Knit a further 2 rows and then * push all needles forward, loosen the yarn and lay it across the open latches of the needles. Starting at the right, knit each needle back into non-working position by hand. Take the carriage across to the left side and re-tension the yarn. Carefully push the needles forward to knitting position and starting at the right, cable over set of 6 needles along the row. Then knit 2 rows*, and repeat between *. Set machine to main tension, thread up with thicker yarn, then turn up the hem and knitting can continue.

Decorative braid. This braid is knitted lengthways in a 2-ply yarn. Three colours are needed for the contrast yarn, and any odd lengths of thick yarn can be used. Push up the number of needles for the length required, and make a closed edge cast on and knit 6 rows. With the first contrast yarn and * from the right push up every alternate needle starting with the second, and wind the coloured yarn around the needles anti-clockwise. Knit 1 row, and then at the right push the first needle and then every alternate needle forward. Wind the yarn around the needles clockwise, working from the right to the left and knit 1 row.* With the second coloured yarn repeat between * twice, then with the third coloured yarn repeat between * once. With the fourth coloured yarn repeat between * once. With the third coloured yarn repeat between * once. With the second coloured yarn repeat between * twice. With the first coloured yarn repeat between * once. Then finally knit 6 rows and cast off. The plain knitting is then folded to the back after steaming (depending on yarn content).

A braid with a basic trim on the double bed is knitted by working over eight needles with the lever set to half pitch. Knit several rows in waste yarn.

$$11 . . . 11$$
$$11 \qquad 11$$

Then on the ribber put the two outer stitches on to the needles on the inside. Move the remaining stitch on the left on to the next needle on its right and knit 2 rows in the main yarn.

11 . . . 11

1   1

* **

Bring needle ** to holding position and knit four rows. Push this needle to working position and put the needle * to holding position. Knit 4 rows. Push this needle to working position. Repeat, putting these needles into hold until the braid is long enough.

ELASTIC (see also *Shirring Elastic*). A ribbon with rubber strands that is very springy and stretches easily. Can be used in cuffs at armholes and at the waist or for smocking fine knitting. Many various widths are available according to its intended usage.

ELASTICITY (see also *Cut and Sew*). The main feature of knitting, and it is the degree of stretch and return that puts it into various categories for construction.

ELECTRONIC MACHINES. The latest knitting machines are now computerised and this adds speed and versatility for the knitter to the garments being designed and knitted. It is important to keep these machines scrupulously clean and covered when not in use. Wider motifs are possible which gives more scope to the knitter. The gauge of the needlebed on some electronics does vary from the punchcard machine. If the electronic machine has a wider gauge needlebed then thicker yarn can be used to advantage. It is easier to transfer from rib to stocking stitch on the electronic machine. Some motif cards are designed to travel in both directions, so that the pattern card will knit up or down. The pattern repeat is wider, but narrow patterns can be knitted just as easily. The colours on the pattern and the background are easily reversed. The pattern can be automatically doubled in length. Of course each electronic machine has different features and different accessories and it is advisable to seek various demonstrations of the machines before considering a knitting machine purchase.

EMBROIDERY (see also *Appendix, Swiss Darning*). A method of putting designs on to fabric by hand, using a needle and thread or sewing machine. Embroidery on knitting can be extremely attractive. It can be scattered down the front openings and at the shoulder or it can be used in small areas to make a garment really unusual. It can either

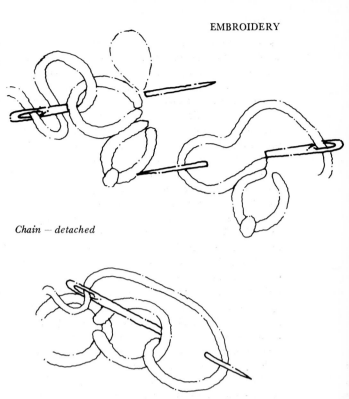

Chain — detached

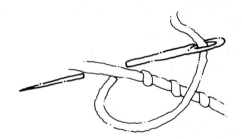

Chain stitch

Couching

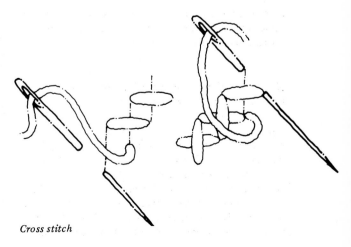

Cross stitch

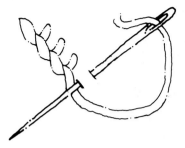

Feather stitch

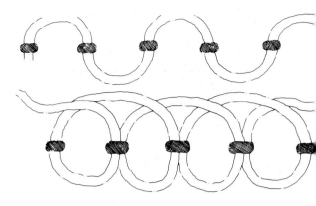

Running stitch with yarn threaded through. Ideal for fancy yarns

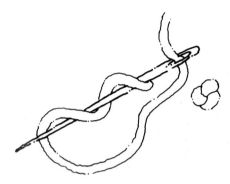

French knot

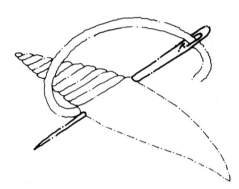

Satin stitch

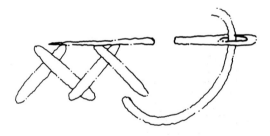

Herringbone stitch

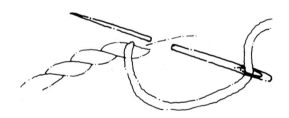

Stem stitch

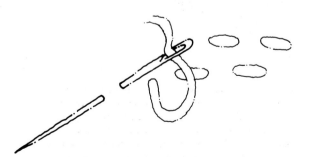

Running stitch (top stitching)

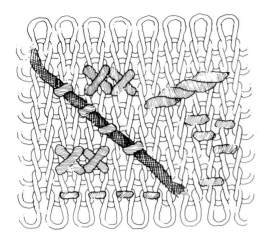

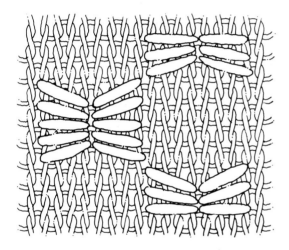

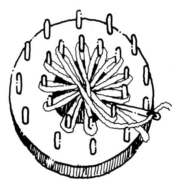

Applying hand embroidery to knitting using contrast yarn. (1) Running stitch with another yarn threaded under the stitches. Cross stitch, and stem stitch. (2) Hand embroidery used to achieve a bow effect

take the form of Swiss darning or completely free embroidery by hand or machine. It is generally better to embroider before construction, but this depends on the amount to be applied. Look at various books for ideas. Beware of using too fine a yarn; use the weight as near as possible to the knitted garment.

EMPISAL/KNITMASTER, see *Appendix.*

ERRORS, see *Mistakes.*

EVENING CLASSES, see *Adult Education.*

EXPERIMENTING, see *Sampling.*

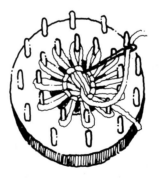

Making fancy flowers in yarn. (1) Secure one yarn end with sticky tape. (2) Thread the other end through a tapestry needle and work across the pegs evenly, and then again twice more. (3) Put the needle into the flower where the original end started, from front to back. Bring the needle back up and down again, working a back stitch. Do this until each petal is secure, pull tightly and sew in end

EXTENSION RAILS. Can be fitted to most knitting machines to facilitate use of the full width of the needlebed.

EYELET HOLES. Little hollow metal rings that are punched through knitted or woven fabric to make holes to take a knitted cord, for example, to lace up a garment. They can be bought in a selection of colours and can be used to make a small feature area on a garment, along with embroidery and Swiss darning, such as on the border of skirts or cuffs. Small holes can be made on a knitting machine by transferring a single stitch where the hole is required, on to the adjacent needle, leaving the empty needle in knitting position. Continue knitting and transfer where the next hole is required.

Punched eyelet holes, lacing up an opening

FABRIC COMBINATIONS (see also *Appliqué, Embroidery, Quilting, Sampling, Stitch Patterns*). Different weights of knitting can be combined to make an outfit, or to make one garment. Bought fabric and home produced fabrics can also be combined. Weight, texture, colour, pattern, quilting and appliqué are all ideas to consider before commencing. A woven fabric, for example, a fine patterned cotton, can be applied to edgings to match a shirt or a quilted waistcoat. The combinations are endless and the various aspects mentioned need careful thought.

FABRIC CRAYONS see *Crayons, fabric, Printing*.

FABRIC QUALITY (see also *Tension Squares, Iron and Ironing*). A good fabric is produced by a correctly tensioned yarn. The knitting should feel firm but not tight. It should stretch and return, but not be floppy. It should drape well. To select the correct tension try sampling with the same yarns over a variety of tensions, writing down each tension carefully. After ironing, feel the fabric; the quality will be apparent, except for yarns that have oil in them, and these need washing first.

FABRIC SOFTENERS. Can be used in the final rinsing water for knitted garments. They also help to avoid pilling and matting.

FACE SIDE. The front of the knitting.

FACINGS, see *Interfacing*.

FAIR ISLE (see also *Floats, Mock Fair Isle, Yarn Feeder*). A patterning of two or more colours, softer to the touch than plain knitting, showing on the face side of the knitting. On the punchcard the holes knit the second colour and the blank spaces the main colour. The number of stitches knitted together should be limited to avoid long floats on the reverse side of the fabric. To achieve Fair Isle on non-punchcard machines the yarn is laid across by hand, and under the needles where they are to float. The reverse side of the Fair Isle can produce some interesting effects, especially if textured yarn is used, and can then be used as a reversible fabric. Yarns of different weights but same colour can be interesting, especially space-dyed yarns. Also yarns of varying texture, for example wool and mohair; the latter can be teasled. If a yarn that has little stretch is knitted with a shirring elastic or a stretchy yarn, when it is washed it will shrink and create a blister effect. If three colours are required to knit Fair Isle then select needles for colour 1 setting the carriage for slip stitch and knit two rows. Select needles for the second colour and knit two rows, then select for the third colour and knit two rows. Two rows of the actual pattern are complete. This is a very slow method and should not be used in large areas. Punch cards normally have to be covered with sticky tape to be adapted for this method. If an impression of colour variety is wanted, then use several fine yarns together in one feeder or use space-dyed yarns. All non-punchcard, punchcard and electronic machine owners should refer to instruction manuals for full setting of machines. The electronic machines offer a wider scope of patterning, double jacquard work is knitted in conjunction with the ribber and colour changer, and knits patterned Fair Isle without floats. The Passap Fair Isle is knitted on the slip setting. Each row of the pattern on the card is knitted twice. Therefore 2 rows of knitting equals four crosses over the needles of the lock (carriage). On the Superba all stitches are transferred to the back bed. Peg the design, and the design width dial is set to the right figure.

FAIR ISLE KNITTING, HISTORY OF (see also *History of Knitting*). Fair Isle is traditional hand knitting which comes from the Scottish island of the same name. The original Fair Isle patterns are knitted in narrow or broad bands of two colours, with a band of white and then natural as the background colour. Soft muted colours are used: reds, blues, and yellows. The same pattern is not repeated but different patterns are knitted throughout the garment. Alternatively, the same pattern can be used but the colour sequence altered. The patterns were believed to have originated from Spain. Possibly one of the ships from the Armada was wrecked on Fair Isle and the local inhabitants copied designs found on the Sailors' jerseys. But Fair Isle knitters say that many of the designs have a more ancient Middle Eastern origin. They believe that the designs were brought to the islands by the Vikings, who practised sprang, an early form of knitting. The Spanish Basque knitters have similar designs to Fair Isle, and they come from the same Celtic stock. They originated in the Middle East and their culture spread as far west as the British Isles and Spain.

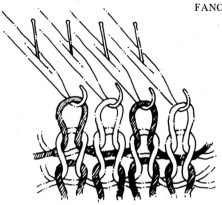

Fair Isle stitch formation

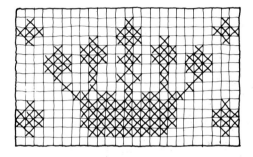

Traditional Fair Isle design: The Crown of Glory

FANCY YARNS (see also *Alpaca, Angora, Bouclé, Camel, Cashmere, Chenille, Corkscrew, Dyeing Yarn, Gimp, Goat Hair Yarn, Knop, Llama, Marl, Mohair and Mohair Loop, Nep Yarn, Rayon, Viscose, Snarl, Yarn Combinations*). Natural or man made and achieved at the spinning or doubling stage of production. A blend is when the colours are mixed when they are fibres, and is normally quite subtle. A mixture is a yarn of two or more different colours that are doubled, and generally referred to as tweeds. Yarns can be space dyed or may be printed on in sections, both giving a random effect. Mohair and angora are spun like other yarns but the long hairs are teased out and create the fluffy surface. Mohair is also used to make loop yarns, and they too vary in thickness; they are sometimes called poodle yarns. Chenille is normally made from cotton although sometimes viscose and cotton are blended together. Use the finest weight on the machine, and the thicker for laying in.

FASHION, HISTORY (see also *History of Knitting*). Knitwear became a fashion item in the 1920s; up until then the garments had been fairly shapeless. Designers gradually refined the shapes. In the sixteenth century, with the rising standard of living of the middle classes, dress became far more elegant, particularly in France and in Italy. Artists played their part in influencing colours. Later in the sixteenth century dress sobered down and people conformed to wearing garments of their trade, such as a lawyer or doctor. Dress became an indication of social class. In Paris in 1791 ready-made clothes were on sale to the public. At the end of Louis XV's time tailoring had started and Paris had more than 1,500 tailors and the same number of dressmakers. The eighteenth century encouraged simple tastes, and Gainsborough brought a naturalness to dress design with bright colours and thin fabrics, and Madame Pompadour in the French Court was quite a dictator of fashion. With ready-made clothes people became well dressed and printed pattern books emerged with the details of the fashionable styles of the time. Tailors copied these and this soon brought about the decline of the traditional or national costume. At the beginning of the nineteenth century Beau Brummel became one of the best dressed men in London — mainly because he inherited £30,000! He had elegant, tasteful garments. Black and grey became the fashionable colours for men to wear. Trousers were worn long and contrasted to the overcoat. They fitted tight to the knee and then widened at the bottom. Women's dresses were more colourful. A man called Leroy was creating fashion ideas early on in the nineteenth century. He copied the shawls and collars of the Mary Stuart period and sent these to the court of Napoleon. It was, however, an English Silk merchant called Worth who started French *haute couture* and he paved the way for others to follow. Paris couturiers started to increase shortly before the First World War, just when fashion was leaping ahead. Names such as Molyneaux and Poiret were among the distinguished women's fashion designers. Chanel started the first fashion revolution by designing the uniform dress and the costume. In the 1930s Elsa Schiaparelli made an impact by producing some of the first designs in synthetic fabrics. Christian Dior gave us examples of line and styles that were adaptable to knitting design. In Paris couturiers show their collections for each season, with samples of their latest ideas. The inspiration from these fashion houses greatly influences the knitting and dressmaking patterns which are offered on sale today.

FASTENINGS (see also *Toggles, Velcro, Zips*). It is advisable, if using bought buttons, to use another button on the reverse side of the fabric where it is likely to have more stress; for example, with the bottom button on a cardigan band, or for smaller buttons. Allow space for the shank when sewing the button to the front of the band; then, when the button has been sewn into place, the yarn is wound around the shank. An alternative to a bottom reinforcing button is to use a piece of cloth underneath. The cloth should be about 5 cm (2 in) larger than the button. Allow space for the shank in the same way. Press studs and hooks and eyes come in plastic and metal, in varying shapes and sizes. According to the weight of yarn used in the knitting they can be stitched directly on to the fabric using the buttonhole stitch. Plastic fastenings will melt under an ironing press. Hooks and eyes can be made to blend with a garment by covering them with a double strand of matching sewing machine thread. Working from the right to the left, place blanket stitches close together over the hook and eye.

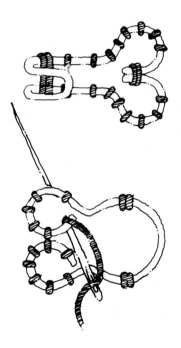

Sewing down a hook and eye

FAULTS, GARMENTS, see *Mistakes*.

FAULTS, MACHINE, see *Mistakes*.

FAULTS, PUNCHARD, see *Mistakes*.

FEATHERS. Can be applied by the sewing machine after knitting, or they can be knotted at intervals to a piece of yarn and hand knitted across the needle bed. Marabou, ostrich, and pheasant are the most attractive and obtainable. If feathers are used from a pheasant or duck and have not been treated it is important to steam them in a pillow case above a saucepan of water; they can then be dried on a tray on a low heat in the oven. This process will clean them and kill any bacteria that may be present.

FELTING (see also *History of Knitting*). A knitted or woven fabric normally made of wool is milled with warm soapy water and this results in a solid, very firm fabric. It is then pounded into shape by being moulded over a solid form. It is used for hats, bags, and berets.

FIBRES. The raw material from which yarns are made, There are two types, staple and filament. Staple is made up from lots of pieces, the length of which depends upon the source. These are spun or twisted to make into yarn. By doing this the length can be extended. Filament is already in a continuous length and can be used as a yarn straight away. Both staple and filament can be natural or man-made.

FIBRES, IDENTIFICATION. This process is for testing fabric for yarn identification only where the fibres have not been blended. Use a match for lighting the sample, preferably over a sink.
  Acrylic. Melts and burns and continues to do so after the flame has been removed. It leaves a hard, brittle, black bead and there is very little smell.
  Acetate. This melts and burns quickly and continues to do so after removal from the flame. It leaves a brittle black bead but smells like vinegar. It will also disintegrate in nail polish remover, which is acetone.
  Cotton (and other plant fibres) and viscose rayon. These burn quickly with a yellow flame, and when the flame is removed they continue to burn and glow. They small like burning paper and leave a soft grey ash.
  Nylon. This fibre will shrink away from a flame. It melts and burns slowly, leaving a hard grey bead and the smell of celery.
  Polyester. This also shrinks away from the flame, melts and burns slowly, but gives off a black smoke, leaves a hard black bead and a sweet smell.
  Wool and silk. They sizzle and go out when removed from the flame, leaving a smell like burning hair or ammonia and a crumbly black ash. If silk contains weighting, a skeleton of ash residue may be left.

FILAMENT YARN, see *Count of Yarn, Fibres*.

FINE KNIT BAR, see *Close Knit Bar*.

FINGERINGS. The name given to knitting yarns up to 4 ply in thickness. They are smooth and plied for strength.

FINISHINGS (see also *Darning and Darning in Loose Ends, Making Up*). All ends should be sewn back into the edge of the knitting so it is invisible on the right side. Thread the end of the yarn through a tapestry needle and oversew along the edge of the knitting. If the knitting is short then insert the needle first into the knitting and then thread the yarn end through the eye of the needle. The yarn can also be sewn along the stitches so that it is unseen on the face side of the knitting.

FISHERMAN'S RIB, see *Rib*.

FLECKED YARNS. Main yarn that has small pieces of another yarn, usually in a contrast colour, speckled along the fibre to create a fine textured yarn.

FLEECE FABRICS. A fleece is the complete woollen coat shorn from a sheep. Mock fleece fabrics are produced in the textile industry, either knitted or woven, heavy or lightweight, but they are all made by attaching wads of fibres to create tufts on a backing cloth. This is often used to line coats.

FLOATS. Produced by a needle or needles not knitting on a row. This gives a float on the fabric because the yarn has floated over the needle to the next stitch. Floats can be cut on certain punchcard patterns where the threads are secure. If a fine, hairy yarn is used for the floats, when cut it can be teasled to achieve a pile effect. There is an iron-on, self-adhesive fabric available on the U.K. market and a spray and a powder to secure the reverse side of the Fair Isle. These can be used when the floats are not being cut. These preparations are useful when using the cut and sew method of construction. Long floats can be a nuisance but can be avoided by adding some holes to a punchcard. If this is unsuitable then the floats must be neatened either by the methods described or with a fusible bonding web like Wundaweb. This can be used on

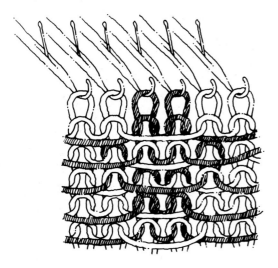

Fair Isle showing floats of yarn on the reverse side of the fabric

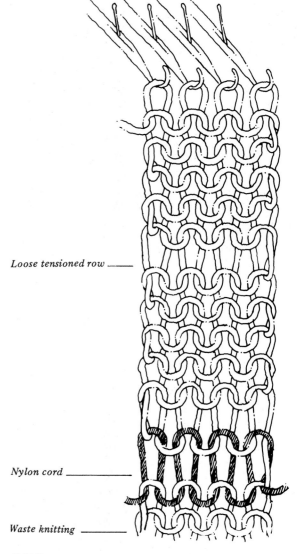

Loose tensioned row _____

Nylon cord _____

Waste knitting _____

Fold line

wool and yarns that can withstand the heat necessary to fuse the fabrics together. A lining can also be used of either a fine knit or a lining fabric, depending on the weight and stretchability of the garment. Another method of solving the problems of the floats is to use a transfer tool to hook the thread in the middle of the float when it appears on the knitting, on to the needle hook above it. This method is suitable for machines that do not bring forward from the needlebed selected needles. For machines that do bring needles forward, push the needle a little out of line, hook on the float and then return the needle to the correct position. These last two methods are not suitable where complete contrast yarns are used, as the picked up floats tend to show through the knitting. On more recent machines with a ribber attachment the Fair Isle floats are now knitted in.

FLUTE. The same as a mock rib. It is made by leaving one or sometimes more needles out of action and knitting several rows. The bars formed where the stitch should be are called rungs.

FOLD. Another word for ply (e.g. two-fold).

FOLD LINE. The row of knitting that forms the centre line of the hem, belt, border or waistband when knitting is doubled up, creating an edge line. A vertical foldline is used for pleats and borders. The knit side is the right side. Select where the

line is to be and remove the stitch onto the latchet hook (it looks like a needle from the bed), push empty needle back to non-working position. Leave the latchet tool hanging and knit approximately 15 rows. Take the hook from the back of the knitting and catch the bar of the knitting above, form a knitted loop by taking the tool back and forward. Continue forming new stitches until the last row. Knit more rows and latch up the stitches until the required length and then place the stitch from the tool onto the empty needle. If the purl side is the right side then take the stitch from the start of the fold line and proceed as above, but knit up the stitch from the front of the knitting. A

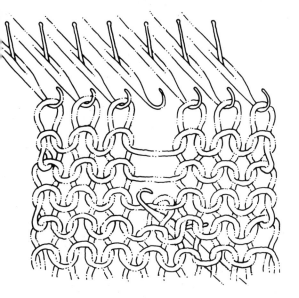

Working the purl side for a vertical pleat

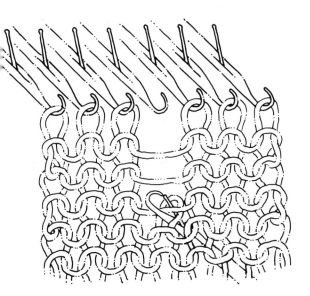

Vertical fold line on the knit side of the fabric. Insert the latch hook at the back into the stitch and let it hang from the knitting, where the fold is to begin. Continue knitting, having put the empty needle into non-working position. Then re-work the stitches from the back on to the empty needle, which has been brought forward to knitting position. This can also be worked on the purl side but the latch hook is worked from the front, as in Mock Rib. A horizontal row can be worked across the needlebed by re-working the stitches sitting on the needle hooks

horizontal line is used for pleats, borders and double cuffs. Knit the fold line row two numbers lower than the main tension. Using the latchet hook, the stitches are reformed one at a time to knit stitches. (See *Garter Stitch*). Use method for a single row of garter stitch. Reset the tension dial and continue knitting. A simpler fold line is achieved by setting the stitch size 2 numbers higher when the knit side is the right side. Knit one row, reset dial and continue knitting. When the purl side is the right side the tension dial should be set 2 numbers lower than the main tension for the fold line. Knit one row, reset tension dial and continue knitting. A very neat fold line is achieved by knitting a row of fine cotton on the fold line and then returning to the main yarn.

FORMA, PASSAP, see *Charting Device*.

FREE MOVE. This is when carriage moves over needles in working position without knitting them. Refer to instruction manual. Free move is used when the carriage is on the wrong side of the needlebed or when shaping a garment.

FRENCH KNITTING, see *Cords*.

FRENCH KNOTS (see also *Embroidery*). Made on knitting with embroidery thread. Catch yarn on reverse side and bring needle through knitting to the front. Wind the base of the yarn around the needle several times and put the needle through to

French knitting. Take the yarn, threaded through the tapestry needle, down through the centre of the reel

Wind yarn from the left to the right around each nail

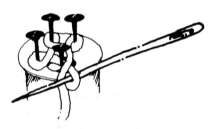

Using a tapestry needle or crochet hook, pull the lower loop over the top loop and over the nail. Continue this process to make a cord.

To cast off, put each loop over the adjacent clockwise needle until one stitch remains. Take the end of yarn through the centre of this stitch and pull it tightly. Darn in the end of yarn

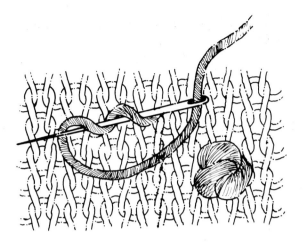

French knots. On the left, working a french knot. On the right, a completed french knot

the reverse side of the knitting, and a french knot is then formed.

FRILLS (see also *Partial Knitting*). For single bed cast on over the required number of needles for the depth of the frill as it is knitted sideways. Knit several rows. Set machine for hold and put 2 needles at the left into holding position and knit 2 rows. The little holes that form are decorative and are a result of not taking the yarn around the end needle. Continue holding and knitting until there are 2 needles in working position. Push the first 2 needles into position so that they knit in and knit 2 rows. Continue this until all the needles are in knitting position. Then knit approximately 8 rows to give the required fullness. Repeat the whole process until the frill is the desired length.

FRINGES (see also *Plaiting*).
1 For the length of fringes bring out one needle ninth to eleventh from main knitting at the opposite side to the carriage. Operating the carriage twice across the needle will catch the yarn. Take the carriage twice more across the knitting and then remove the stitches from the needle and tie at the edge of the knitting to avoid being caught in the carriage. Repeat process until sufficient fringes have been made.
2 A pile fabric or loop fabric can be made by using a cast on comb or pressing bar. Cast on and knit several rows, then select alternate needles, take the secondary yarn and hold the comb approximately 5 cm (2 in) – depending on the length of pile wanted – from the needle bed. Do

Machine knitted fringe. In the first diagram the carriage is at left

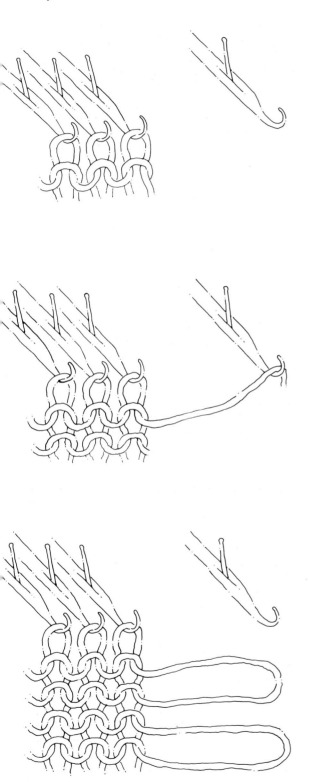

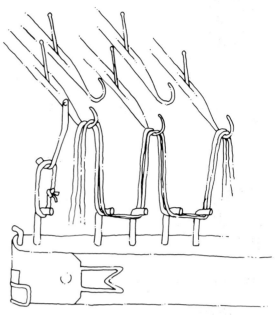

To make a pile fabric using the cast on comb

remember to keep it taut otherwise the loops will vary in size. Take this yarn over the first selected needle onto its hook and under the hook opposite on the comb. Continue back to the next needle etc. until the end of the row. Knit one row in main yarn, and the secondary colour is knitted in with it. This pile can be pulled so the loops become uneven – to make the fabric more stable the secondary yarn should be wound around the needle hook once before going under the hook of the comb. For a more open pile vary the number of rows between loops. The secondary yarn can be varied in texture and length so the pile can be undulating. Fringes can also be made like tassels (*q.v.*).

3 Fringes can be put on scarves by cutting lengths of yarn a little longer than twice the desired length of the fringe. Fold the cut lengths in half. Insert crochet hook from the back of the knitting and catch the fringe in the centre. Pull it through the knitting about half way to make a loop. Slip ends through the loop to make a knot, pull firmly and repeat for each fringe required. Having completed the fringes trim altogether to an even length. They can then be plaited if so desired. The latest Empisal ribbing attachments have a useful accessory which now makes it possible to produce a punch pile. Fringes can also be made by macramé.

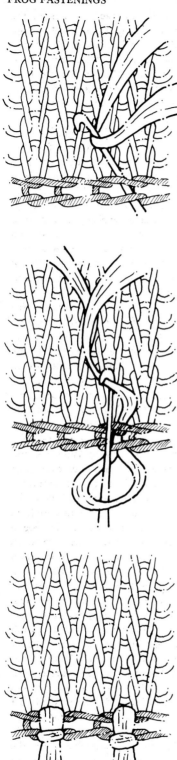

Making fringes using the crochet hook

Macramé fringes

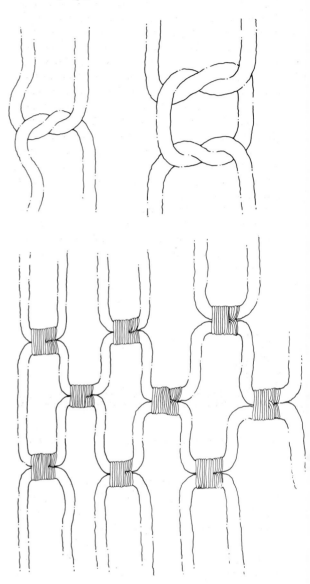

FROG FASTENINGS. Frog fastenings work on the same principle as toggles for jacket or cardigan openings but are more ornamental and made of a corded ribbon. They are fastened either by a loop over a button on the opposite side, press studs, or else a hook and eye can be used concealed under the fabric.

FULLY FASHIONED (see also *Increasing*). Used when shaping is required and fully fashioning points will show. Best used on plain fabrics using the three-by-one transfer tool. Use for shaping shoulders, skirts, V-necks, socks, sleeves, yokes, etc.

76

FURNISHING FABRICS (see also *Colour, Cushions, Felting, Sampling, Yarn Combinations*). Can be produced on the knitting machine with careful choice of yarn and pattern selection. Use slip or weave fabrics where stability is required. These can be hung sideways for curtains where possible. For rugs use the fringe technique or knit a pattern where the floats can be suitably cut. Use cotton where there is likely to be regular washing. Wool can be felted after knitting. Be very careful about the choice of weight for furnishings. Choose colour according to the room; for example, never use red in the bedroom in any quantity as it is unrestful. Machine stitching rows at regular intervals will increase stability. Lace stitch in cotton, shaped by darting, is ideal for lampshades, but the fabric should only be used over a plain stable lampshade, due to the risk of fire. Seats can be made and stuffed with foam or can be re-covered to match the bedcovering.

GARMENT ADJUSTMENTS, see *Pattern Adjustments.*

GARMENT AFTERCARE. It is important that garments retain their original shape and texture. Nearly every garment should be hand washed, unless machine washable wool has been used or dry cleaning is preferred. Superwash wool is the name given to wool where the fibres have been treated with a plastic film to make them shrink resistant and machine washable. Never allow knitted garments to become excessively soiled. When hand washing, turn the garment inside out and wash carefully in warm, soapy water, having checked on the fibre content of the garment. Wool can be washed in cold water with Woolite, which is excellent for mohair and angora too. Rinse the garment very well and finish with a fabric conditioner if required. Do not spin garments, and it is also not advisable to put them in the tumble dryer. However, a few minutes on a cool setting on the tumble dryer when the garment is virtually dry is acceptable. The best way to dry your garment is naturally. It should be laid on a flat surface which

has been covered with newspaper to absorb the moisture, and then put a clean white towel on top. The garment should be pulled gently into shape and left until the newspaper and the towel have absorbed most of the water. The garment can then be placed over a line or an airer in such a way that the weight is supported and it cannot drop. Press lightly if required.

Stain removal (for pure wool garments). If the garment is washable immediately rinse before the stain has time to set. Always rinse the stained area in cold water as hot water can set the stain into the fabric. Then the garment should be washed in the normal way. Milk, tea, white coffee, gravy, blood etc. may benefit from washing in biological washing powder, but they should not be soaked because it can affect the colour of the garment and it may weaken the fibres. For a beer stain, dab the area with a solution of one part of acetic acid (vinegar) to four parts of water. Then be sure to rinse the garment thoroughly. For butter, ice cream and grease scrape off as much of the excess fat as possible and then treat with a solvent. Put the garment out in the air and then wash in the normal way. Solvents are trichlorethylene (which is sold under different trade names), turpentine, acetone, and white methylated spirits. When using solvents make sure that windows and doors are open. Never use near a naked flame or on any article which has a content of acetate fibres. For crayons blot the area with a solvent, rinse well and then wash. Eyebrow pencil can be removed with solvent; afterwards several drops of ammonia should be blotted on to the area and then the garment rinsed in clean water. Fruit stains are hard to remove but a weak solution of hydrogen peroxide (one part of ten-volume hydrogen peroxide to six parts of water) can be sponged on to the area. Rinse well and then wash in the usual way. This also applies to dyes, but be careful that the original colour of the garment is not removed. Grass stains should be removed by saturating the area with white methylated spirits. Rinse and wash the garment. Ink and rust stains are virtually impossible to remove and should be taken to a dry cleaner for advice. Lipstick can be treated with neat liquid detergent; rub it very gently, rinse and wash. Emulsion paint should be washed off immediately, never let it dry. For oil paint sponge with solvent or white spirit and then wash well. For tar, remove as much as possible from the surface. Apply butter or margarine over the area which will soften it, and then wipe off with a cloth. Remove any remaining stains with a solvent. For ball-point ink blot the area with white methylated spirit. Leave to air and then wash according to the fabric.

GARMENT, DISTORTION (see also *Acrylic, Linings*). Garments can distort easily by using the wrong type of yarn and the wrong tension. The most common distortion is in the seating of skirts. Too tight a fitting garment or badly sewn seams can also cause distortion. It is therefore vitally important that measurements are accurate and sampling of yarn and tension squares are completed before knitting a garment. A lining should be used where there is likely to be extra strain on a garment.

GARTER BAR. Enables the knitting to be reversed quickly and easily whatever the width and so achieve purl stitch effect. If the garter bar is used for turning several rows on a garment it can be rather slow. It should be used for isolated rows. A garter carriage is available for some machines for doing garter stitch. The yarns are held and tensioned by the garter bar. It is for use on single bed or on the main bed when the ribber is in the lowered position. It cannot be used on the Passap and Superba. The needle stoppers are used to hold the needles rigid in their correct position so that the eyes of the needle bar can be placed on to all the needle hooks in one go. (The needle bar looks like a very long series of transfer tools.) The work can be turned with the garter bar; it can be used to form a garter stitch ridge, so that the work is turned every so many rows or on the base of a hem. It can be used to pattern baby garments and for taking work off the machine, or to hold stitches for partial knitting, during necklines for example and for shoulder shaping in the holding position. It is also useful for picot edge, eyelet rows and cable panels where the stitches are removed on to the bar and replaced in the order for the appropriate result.

GARTER STITCH (see also *Garter Bar, Hems*). This is the simplest form of hand knitting and is made up of plain knit stitches only. It stretches sideways and was given its name originally as it was used for garters and the top of stockings. It is formed by making the same stitch all the time and the knitting is turned at the end of each row. On the knitting machine the stitches are formed at the same side so the basic stitch is stocking stitch. Knit two rows with the tension two numbers lower than normal. Using the latchet hook insert it into the row below the hooked row and push the needle forward and then back, so releasing the

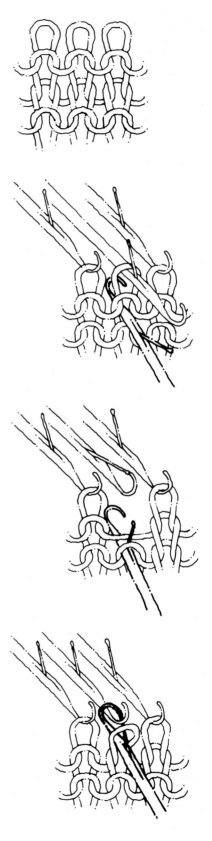

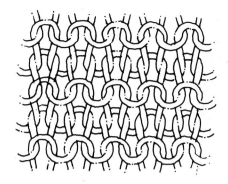

Forming a garter stitch

stitch and then knit up the stitch by hand so that the tool forms a purl stitch. Place stitch on to the needle and repeat procedure along the row. Knit two rows of stocking stitch and repeat the reforming of the stitches every second row as before.

GATE PEGS, see *Sinker Gate.*

GATHERS. Can be achieved by the short row designing method. Remember to take the yarn under the first needle that is forward before knitting from left to right. If needles are held on the left and the right it will result in the centre stitches forming puckers, which can be large or small depending on yarn and the number of needles working. Gathers are best used on light-weight fabrics.

GAUGE. This is the number of needles per 2.5 cm (1 in). Most single bed machines have two hundred and are 6 gauge. However, there is an increasing tendency towards the manufacture of different gauge machines and some wide gauge machines for use with thick yarns are available. With coarse gauge machines the hook of the needle is large to take thick heavy yarns. On fine gauge machines the needle hook is small for fine yarns. The gauge of the machine will effect the tension of the fabric and therefore when working from a pattern check that it is for that particular gauge machine. If the gauge is different then the tension swatch should be adapted accordingly. Tools are not interchangeable when the gauge varies.

GAUGE SCALE. Can be used to measure a tension swatch. Thirty-five stitches are cast on either side of the centre 0 in waste yarn, and several rows are knitted. Two rows are then knitted in a contrast yarn. With main yarn knit 30 rows and mark the twenty-first stitch either side of the centre 0 with a contrast yarn, then knit a further 30 rows. Knit

2 rows of the contrast yarn, several rows of waste yarn and then remove knitting from machine. Leave the swatch to relax. Place scale with S side facing, putting the left end touching the contrast stitch. Measure to the point of the other contrast stitch and the number which corresponds with this stitch is the number of stitches in 10 cm (4 in) on the swatch. For the number of rows place the gauge scale with the R side facing between the rows of contrast yarn. Measure this length and the number on the scale is the number of rows to 10 cm (4 in). Read the scale in the direction of the arrow.

GIMP YARN. A fine fancy yarn with elasticity, usually made with silk, worsted or cotton twisted around a central cord core. Gimp yarns dip-dye well. If the yarn is thick then it should be used on a weave pattern, as the thicker parts may become caught on the needles. Be careful of the fabric becoming harsh. Creates an interesting surface quality.

GOAT HAIR YARN (see also *Cashmere, Mohair/ Mohair Loop, Yarn Combinations*). A very fine, brown, hairy yarn, quite rough to the touch. It can be mixed with any yarn but will always show up on the reverse side of the fabric. Do not knit this yarn on its own. Produces a very unusual fabric.

GRAFTING (see also *Making Up*). A method for joining two raw edges together. It is important that several rows of waste yarn are knitted before removing the work from the machine. Having steamed the knitting, unravel the waste yarn until you have two rows of loops for grafting, or leave the waste yarn on the knitting until grafting is complete. This is an invisible way of seaming and looks like another row of knitting when completed. This method can also be used to join an open edge to a closed edge. Hold the two pieces of knitting so that they are edge to edge. Starting at the right, follow diagrams carefully (see p. 80). Continue across the knitting, pulling gently so that the loops of the knitting match the main knitting, until the row is complete.

GREEN RULER, see *Gauge Scale.*

GREY GOODS. Sometimes known as Griege Goods. A knitted or woven fabric that is undyed, or unfinished in any way.

GUERNSEY KNITTING, HISTORY OF. In the United Kingdom, while people were learning to

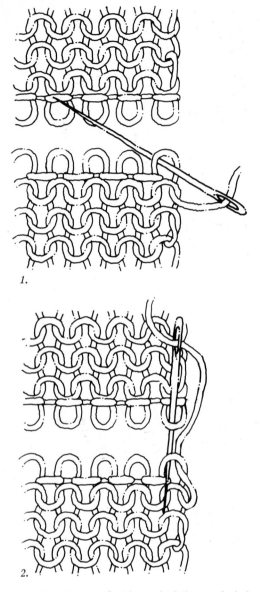

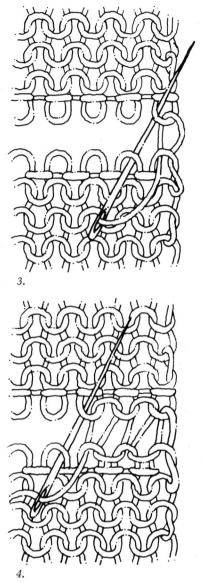

Grafting methods. Grafting purl stitch to purl stitch

knit silk stockings and shirts, nearly every fishing port around the coastline was developing a completely different type of knitting for its fishermen. It originated in Jersey and Guernsey, in the Channel Islands, which eventually were the names given to these garments. The garments were originally identical in shape, with dropped shoulder lines and square armholes. Guernseys were, however, normally knitted in thick dark blue yarn while Jerseys were knitted in a thinner yarn in a variety of colours. The traditional Guernsey is still being made today, but mostly by machine. Also known

as gansey, its appearance has altered very little and it is still very tough and practical. Jerseys have, however, changed and a jersey now simply means a fashion garment of virtually any shape. These garments for fishermen were knitted in the round on very fine needles, using a yarn that was spun in oil, which made it virtually wind- and weatherproof. (In the final rinsing water when washing a Guernsey add a little pure oil to the water so that the weatherproofing is maintained.) As this knitting spread around the ports, each part of the country developed its own patterns. The patterns had a brocade appearance because of the closeness of the knitting. It was important that each coastal town had its own pattern. If an accident occurred

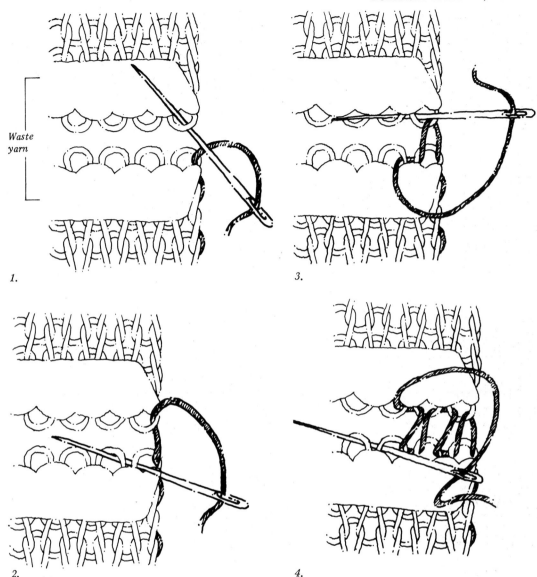

Waste yarn

1.

2.

3.

4.

To graft knit stitch to knit stitch

at sea and a drowned fisherman was washed ashore, it was possible to identify the port from which he came by the pattern on his sweater. (In Scotland they used finer, slightly softer yarn and this spread to the Aran Islands, where the Aran patterns that are known now were developed.) Although most of the Guernsey stitches varied according to the area, they were named after things in a fisherman's every day life. For example ropes are worked as cables. The mesh in a fishing net is worked as diamonds, and there are combinations of zigzag and flag patterns, honeycomb and herringbone stitches. A well known knitter living around Filey had a stitch named after her — Betty Martin. The flag or kilt pattern, as it is known in Scotland, is used everywhere. The basic pattern is a triangular shape of the flag but it varies in width and depth. The tree of life is based on the shapes of fern or pine cones. (This pattern is also used in two-colour traditional Fair Isle patterns.) The gusset underarm of the Guernsey is achieved on the machine by increasing sharply about 5 cm (2 in) below the armhole on the back, front and sleeves using the seven-eyed transfer tool. At the armhole put the extra seven or eight stitches on to waste yarn, which is grafted later. Continue to work up to the shoulder with virtually no shaping.

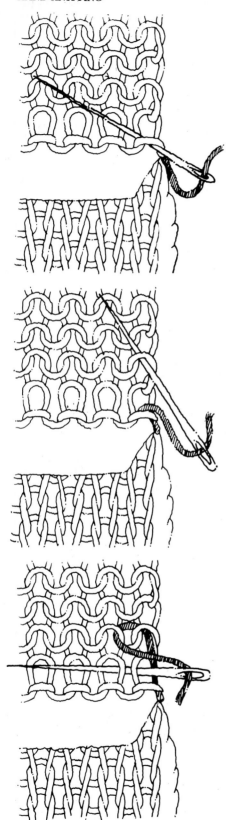

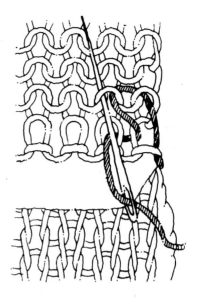

Grafting a hem

HAND KNITTING. Sometimes machine knitters like to add sections of hand knitting to their machine or to machine knitted fabrics. Below are the needle sizings for hand knitting. Machine knitting is very even and the character of hand knitting is its slight unevenness.

Needle sizes

AMERICAN	METRIC	BRITISH
00	2	14
0	2¼	13
1	2¾	12
2	3	11
3	3¼	10
4	3¾	9
5	4	8
6	4½	7
7	5	6
8	5½	5
9	6	4
10	6½	3
10½	7	2
11	7½	1
12	8	0
13	9	00
15	10	000

Two needle casting on

Single needle casting on

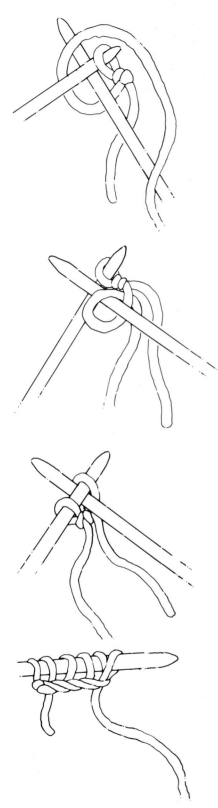

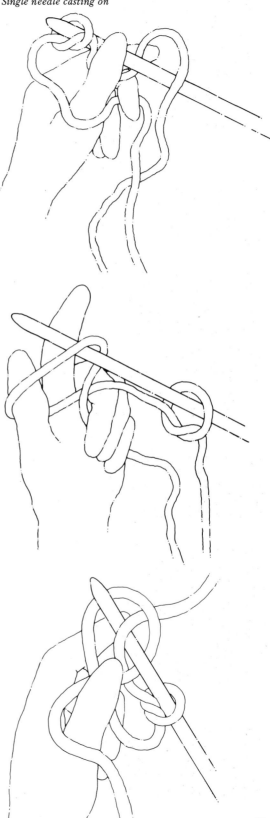

HAND KNITTING

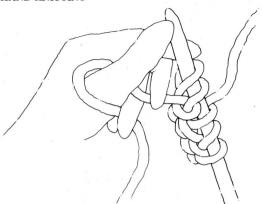

Knit stitch

Purl stitch

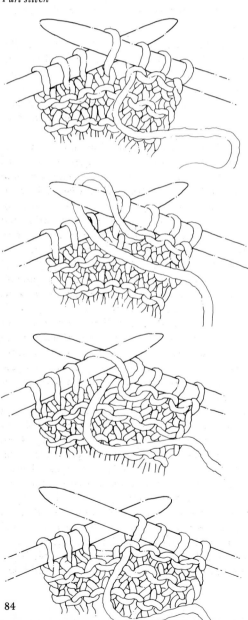

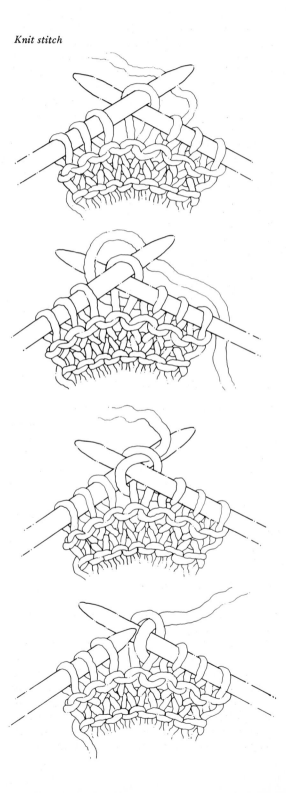

HAND SELECTION (see also *Intarsia, Picture Knitting*). The selection by hand of the required needles.

HANK (see also *Cheese*). A hank of yarn is yarn that has been wound circularly on a hank or skein winder. Some yarn is bought in a hank and it can be cheaper this way. Yarn is also wound into a hank for dyeing, to allow the dye to penetrate evenly through the strands of yarn. By placing both hands inside the hank and pulling against each other, any uneven threads are pulled into the hank shape. Jumpers can be unravelled, so the yarn can be re-used. The yarn is wound into hanks for steaming and this removes the crimpiness of the yarn which would affect the tension of the knitting.

Hank of yarn tied at intervals in a figure-of-eight

HANK DYEING. Use a skein winder or the back of two chairs spaced apart. Wind the yarn around, securing the first end to the first circle of yarn. The end of the hank is tied through the hank in a figure-of-eight and secured to itself. The hank is then tied at intervals with pieces of the same yarn in a figure-of-eight through the hank. Do not tie tightly or the dye will not take at these points, and a tie and dye effect will occur. Do not use a thread of a different colour to tie the hank, otherwise the colour might bleed into the hank in the dye bath.

HANK WINDER, see *Skein Winder*.

HEMS (see also *Casting On, Edgings, Grafting, Making Up, Rib*).
Plain hem. Cast on and knit several rows over required number of needles; using waste yarn knit in the nylon cord. Set tension dial one number lower than for main knitting. Knit required number of rows for hem depth, in main colour, re-set tension dial to main tension and knit the same number of rows. Using the single transfer tool pick up the knitted row of loops from the first row of

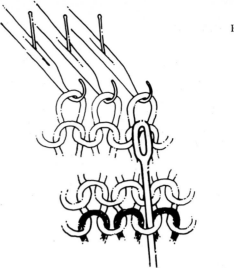

Picking up the stitches for a hem on the first row above the nylon cord

the main colour, placing the loops on to the corresponding needles. Set tension dial two numbers higher than main tension and knit one row. Pull out the nylon cord to remove the waste knitting. Set tension dial to main tension and continue to knit. Alternatively knit the hem on to the last row of knitting. (See diagram.)

Elastic, continental hem. Using the 1/1 needle pusher bring forward the required number of needles to knitting position – that is every alternate needle. The other needles must remain in non-working position. Move carriage across to line up the needles. Cast on with waste yarn using the nylon cord or cast on comb. Re-thread with main yarn and lower the tension by two points. Knit approximately 40 or 50 rows. Bring forward empty needles to knitting position, making sure all latches are open. Using single transfer tool start at the opposite end to the carriage, pick up each stitch from the first main row and put them onto the empty needles. Return the tension dial to main tension and knit several rows and the waste wool can be removed. Variations on this hem are the 2/1 3/1. The procedure is the same as for 1/1 but the needle selection is different.

Picot hem. Set the machine as for a plain hem and knit half the hem with the tension dial two numbers lower than required for that yarn. Then either by using the lace carriage, which will transfer every second stitch over to its adjacent needle, or by using the single transfer tool and manually transferring every other stitch to its adjacent needle, leave the empty needles in knitting position. Set tension dial to normal and knit the second half of the hem and raise the first row of stitches as in the plain hem. Transferring as above makes a row of small holes on the fold line.

HEMS

Picked up hem, used for waistbands and for hems. Run a contrast thread through the last row of knitting

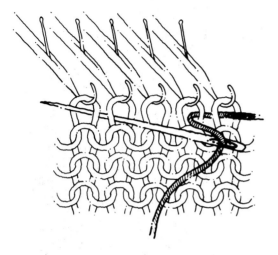

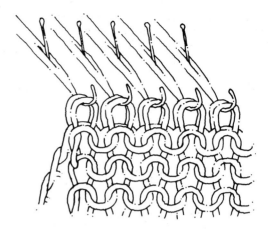

Set tension two numbers higher and knit one row

Knit the hem

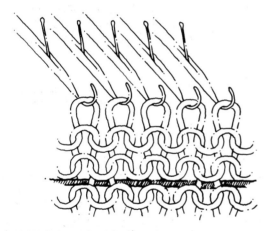

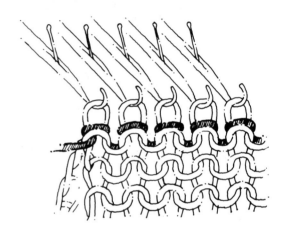

Finish off with back stitch

Pick up the stitches above marked yarn onto the needle hooks

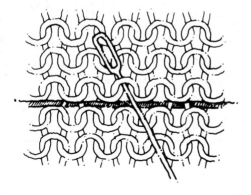

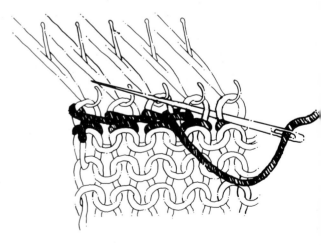

Knitting in a hem on a side edge. Use for hems and edges. With wrong side facing, pick up the side edge stitches leaving out the odd stitch to achieve an even tension

Knit the hem on main tension for the outside section, and on one number lower for the inside hem

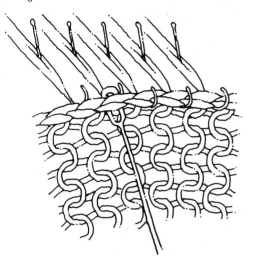

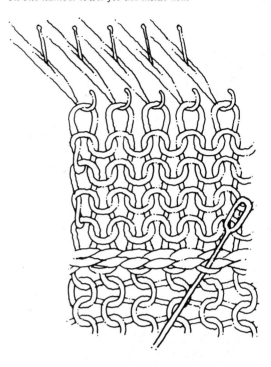

Set tension dial one number lower and knit one row

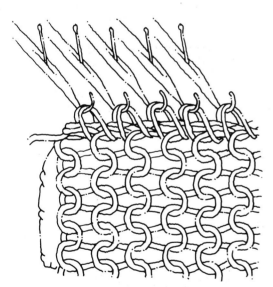

Pick up the loops from the first row. Knit one row with the tension at least two numbers higher. Used back stitch to finish the edge

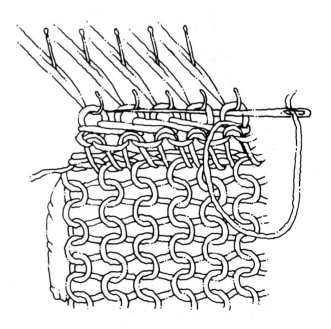

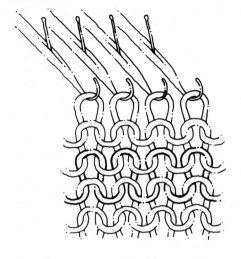

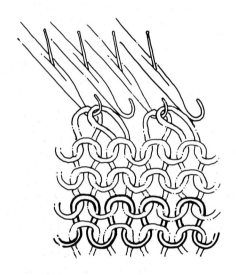

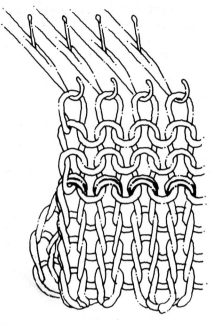

Picot edge

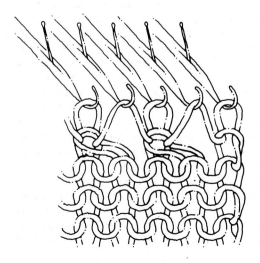

HEM SHAPING. Straight knitting will be the same length at the sides of a garment and the centre. With hems on skirts and dresses, where a garment is flared, and jackets, the outer edges will be longer than the centre length. It is important therefore to shape hems so that they appear straight when worn. On plain knitting the shaping is worked above the hem. An even, large amount of needles at the edges of the knitting are put into hold and as each row is knitted a group of needles on the opposite side to the carriage are put into working position. This shaping on average is worked over about ten rows. On the Passap the lock is set to BX and pushers are in working position. On the opposite side to the lock the large amount of pushers are taken to non-working position over 2 rows. Needles are then returned to working position gradually in groups as described previously.

HEMMING STITCH (see also *Making Up*). This stitch is used for turning double bands, sewing hems and for waistbands. Having steamed the edge and unravelled all but the final row of the waste knitting, turn and pin the hem. Starting on right unravel just 2 or 3 stitches of the waste yarn. Pass the needle down into the first stitch of the main yarn and under the loop of the opposite stitch of the main knitting. Be careful not to pull tight. Continue this method a few stitches at a time.

HISTORY OF MACHINE KNITTING (see also *Aran Knitting, history of, Fair Isle Knitting, history of, Guernsey Knitting, history of, Shetland Knitting, history of*). It is thought that knitting started from the primitive weaving principle, but not the method of knitting with a single strand of yarn used today. The word knitting comes from an old English word meaning a knot. Knitting has survived for over 3,000 years. Nomadic tribesmen of Arabia knitted on circular wire frames, while the women spun wool from their animals. They produced the sandal socks which were knitted on a round frame. The frame had a ring of pins round it with a loop of yarn on each pin. A length or yarn was wound round the outside of the pins and the loops were then drawn over this yarn. When repeated to the length required, this gave a circular piece of knitted fabric. This was two or three centuries before Christ. In the north of Scandinavia, in a Viking tomb, a small piece of fabric was found closely resembling knitting. It consisted of inter-locked stitches based on the weaving principle. It had been worked on a rectangular frame with vertical threads, making a warp. A needle and thread was worked in an open chain stitch up the first thread, starting at the bottom and working to the top until the whole warp was covered. The top and bottom threads of the warp were secured and then the warp threads were removed. This resulted in a fabric that looked like stocking stitch, but the interlocking was through the side of the loops and not through the top of the loop as in modern knitting. Variations were found on this type of knitting and it was called sprang. No date can be put to this fabric.

The next evidence is Peruvian needle knitting. In excavations in Peru some fringes were found which had been worked with a needle to form a series of loops on a single thread; from these loops another row of loops had been made, and a length of fabric was produced. They used cotton and wool, being the only two fibres available. Peruvian knitting was the most like today's knitting. There is now a long gap in the history until the seventh century A.D. A piece of fabric knitting was dis-covered at Fostat, a city which stood on the site of what is now the capital of Egypt, Cairo. It is Arab knitting worked with one strand of yarn. The two-needle method has been used on this very fine knitting. It produced 36 stitches to 2.5 cm (1 in). The thick wools used today give us between 3 and 4 stitches to 2.5 cm (1 in). These early knitters had the necessary patience to produce such fine work. The pattern was a geometric one, in a dark red on a gold background, while the colour not in use was floated at the back of the knitting. (This method is still used today when knitting Fair Isle patterns.) It was worked in a cross stocking stitch. It suggests that knitting may well have been practised from about 1000 B.C. Between the seventh and nineth centuries the Coptic Christians were making caps in colourful designs and this was a craft they could only have learnt from the Arabs. The exact date of these cannot be fixed because of the raiding of tombs, but Coptic art developed from Hellenistic art away from the large cities. The Copts in their weaving took the weft above and below the warp like the ancient Egyptians did. Knitting must have followed closely on from this, being worked on a small board. The Copts had an artistic style which made a great impact at that time, they preferred to design figures and sym-metrical animal patterns; their floral motifs also followed a geometric pattern, showing the influence of Persian and oriental designs. Knitting then reached Spain, brought by traders from ancient Egypt or by the Moors who had conquered the Peninsula in A.D. 711-712. Intricate geometric and floral patterned pillows, knitted in silk in stocking stitch, were found in the thirteenth-century tombs of the Kings of Castille at Burgos. Knitting then moved across Europe through Italy and France, with the making of silk knitted hose. Early in the thirteenth century one of the main industries in France was hand knitting. A guild was set up called The Knitters' Guild of Paris. This guild maintained a high standard of work: a young man had to serve an apprenticeship of three years. During this time he learnt all the techniques of knitting. He was then sent abroad for three years to learn new ideas. At the end of this time he was examined by the craft master of his own guild. The practical work was full of detail and colour, taking up to three months to complete. He then had to knit a carpet of exquisite design, a beret, a pair of socks and a type of woollen shirt. All knitters at this time were men, but later the guild was prepared to admit that women were skilful too, and if a master knitter died the guild would accept his widow in his place, provided she could match the men. The fine knitting seen in museums shows the superb, intricate craftsmanship of such guilds, knitting worn only by people of the highest position. The peasants, however, were producing their tough knitted caps. During the reign of Edward IV hosiery was exported from France to Britain. The hose was knitted in a single coloured yarn to produce a fine, lacy stitch pattern, this fabric was envied by the courts of Europe. Italy at this time was producing coloured brocaded knitting

Manual stocking frame c. *1770.* (With kind permission of
the Public Relations Department, Corah Ltd, Leicester)

and lovely Florentine waistcoats and jackets worked with fine wool. Heavily embossed gold and silver threads and coloured silks were added to these. Gloves were worn by the ministers of the Catholic Church; many examples have been found in ecclesiastical tombs. At the Cathedral Church of Ross, where there is a tomb of a fourteenth-century Bishop, the earliest known pieces of knitting in Britain were found – plain red silk stockings and gloves.

Guilds were set up in other parts of Europe. The guild in Florence helped to perfect colour knitting. Germany and Austria knitted heavy knotted and cable fabrics. During the reign of Elizabeth I knitting made an impact in England, and the ladies of the court knitted as a pastime. When the Spanish Armada was shipwrecked it may have been possible that the patterned fabrics produced in Spain and Italy were taken to the west of Ireland and to the Shetlands. The only surving evidence is that Donegal knitting today still uses the simple geometric pattern designs that the Spaniards learnt from the Arabs. This knitting links up with the first piece of Arab fabric found at Fostat, dating back to the seventh century. The making of felt was being carried out in the Basque country for berets. A piece of knitting several times larger than needed was worked on four needles. The knitting was then soaked in water, beaten and rubbed with stones until it shrank and the fabric became thick and felted. It was then mounted on a large flat stone and left to dry. In

England Tudor-style hats were made from felt and worn in the fifthteenth century by the apprentices in guilds. These hats could undergo as many as fifteen stages before completion. In 1527 Holbein drew Sir Thomas More's son John wearing one such flat cap. After the reign of Elizabeth I knitting became less popular in France and more so in Britain. Hosiery was established as a craft in the Yorkshire Dales and the first knitting school was founded in York. Earlier, in 1589, a minister, Reverend William Lee, had invented a frame knitting machine and this established a frame knitting hosiery trade in Nottingham and Leicester and later in all parts of the world. This machine used the beard needle. Lee died, however, before he knew the impact his machine would have, for Queen Elizabeth refused to grant him a patent. She said she had 'too much love for may poor people who obtain their bread by the employment of knitting'.

The photograph in this book of the manual stocking frame is similar to the original frame invented by William Lee and the detailed drawing explains the action of the frame. Full exploitation of the machine was slow owing to strong opposition by hand knitters. Working models of the hand frame and other old knitting machines can be seen at: Leicester Museum of Technology, The Science Museum, London, Ruddington Framework

Detailed diagram explaining the action of the stocking frame. (Crown copyright, Science Museum London)

THE HAND STOCKING FRAME

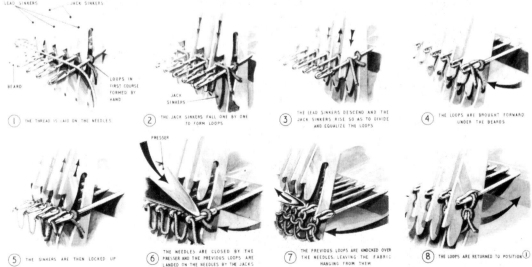

LEAD SINKERS   JACK SINKERS

BEARD

LOOPS IN FIRST COURSE FORMED BY HAND

JACK SINKERS

① THE THREAD IS LAID ON THE NEEDLES

② THE JACK SINKERS FALL ONE BY ONE TO FORM LOOPS

③ THE LEAD SINKERS DESCEND AND THE JACK SINKERS RISE SO AS TO DIVIDE AND EQUALIZE THE LOOPS

④ THE LOOPS ARE BROUGHT FORWARD UNDER THE BEARDS

PRESSER

⑤ THE SINKERS ARE THEN LOCKED UP

⑥ THE NEEDLES ARE CLOSED BY THE PRESSER AND THE PREVIOUS LOOPS ARE LANDED ON THE NEEDLES BY THE JACKS

⑦ THE PREVIOUS LOOPS ARE KNOCKED OVER THE NEEDLES, LEAVING THE FABRIC HANGING FROM THEM

⑧ THE LOOPS ARE RETURNED TO POSITION ①

1957 195

(THE THREAD IS CONTINUOUS BUT TWO COLOURS ARE USED FOR CLARITY)

Museum (five miles to the south of Nottingham), and probably the best collection is in the Musée de Bonneterre, Ville de Troyes, Départment de l'Aube, France.

None of these frames is earlier than the late seventeenth century. They are very solid, made from metal and wood, and built to last. Hand knitted hose was very expensive, and in around 1620 a pair of woollen stockings from Doncaster, Jersey or Scotland cost about 3 shillings, silk stockings cost 33 shillings and a pair of fine worsted hose 39 shillings. The highest paid household servant at this time was getting an annual wage of £5 plus board! Knitting spread from Holland to Denmark; the King of Denmark was presented with a pair of very fine Dutch hose, and he was so delighted that he invited a group of Dutch knitters to settle in his country to teach and establish the craft. Only the King and members of the court were allowed to wear the fine hose. The peasants rebelled at this and were later allowed to wear very coarse wool hose. It was therefore possible to tell to which class a person belonged. At the same time Austria continued to produce simple lace fabrics in thick wool with woollen embroidery worked over the fabric in gay colours. Germany was knitting cables in natural coloured thick wool and France cobweb lace patterns. Several knitted narrow lace samplers have survived from the late eighteenth century. A knitted lace dress from the Great Exhibition of 1851 can be seen at the Victoria and Albert Museum, London, together with many other examples of early knitting. This dress was knitted by Sarah Ann Cuncliffe of Saffron Walden with 6000 yards of No. 100 sewing cotton. It has 1,464,859 stitches and took five months to complete. It won a bronze medal. The Industrial Revolution and the Victorian age slowly killed off the hand knitting industry. During the Industrial Revolution the framework knitters were grouped together; this marked a social change, taking people out of the home or cottage and into the factory. The home knitting industry therefore disappeared and it became a hobby for middle class women in Britain. Beaded knitting was developed at this time. The tucking bar for the knitting frame was invented in 1730, supposedly in either Dublin or France! Two-colour tuck ribs were put onto stocking tops and were very fashionable. The Derby rib frame was patented in 1759 by Jedediah Strutt, a wealthy farmer and a very clever technician. It was not invented by him but by a knitter called Bowman and a framesmith called Roper — who asked him for his patronage. Strutt made a piece of equip-

ment to turn the single bed into a double bed frame, by using a ribbing attachment. He also applied external selection and this led to Jacquard's punchards. He thanked Roper for his success by giving him a cocked hat with gold trims, and free ale for life at his local alehouse. Until the end of the century Nottingham, Derby and Leicester areas bred technical inventions. An Englishman, Matthew Townsend, first used the latch needle (which originates from France) in 1849, to improve upon the hand frame of William Lee, and owing to its semi-automatic function this needle permitted the construction of much simpler knitting machines than those used before. The basic formation of the stitch has remained unchanged since then.

The Shetland and east coast fishermen still continued to hand knit because it was a necessity; the thick knitted Guernsey sweaters were a part of their equipment. Later their wives continued this tradition. By the end of the eighteenth century the machine age was fully established. At the end of the nineteenth century machine spun knitting wool first appeared, from a manufacturer in Scotland. The Crimean War bought a revival of knitting and the balaclava helmet appeared. Warm underwear was the popular thing to make and wear. Machines improved quickly, becoming more efficient and enabling the knitting of circular stockings. The first machine was patented by William Cotton of Loughborough. These machines could produce up to 10,000 loops per minute. Modern stocking machines produce over two million loops per minute, while automatic increase and decrease of stitches provide the fashioning.

In his book *The History of the Machine Wrought Hosiery and Lace Manufacturers*, 1867, Felkin wrote: 'a small domestic knitting frame was contributed by a mechanician named Backenheim to the Cologne exhibition a few years ago. It was highly spoken of. It had 84 needles and the machine was said to weigh not more than 14-15 lbs and might be adapted to any table for ladies work. It is said to produce from 10,000 to 35,000 loops per hour and be worked with great facility. Whether it is a mere modification of the old stocking frame, or of the circular knitting machine, or an entirely new arrangement, was not stated.'

In America in 1870 a Crane Knitter was invented. This machine could knit a full-sized pair of woollen socks in 25 minutes. Various types of sock machines, circular and flat bed machines, began to appear in Victorian homes. These were supposed to be used by the ladies but the idea did not catch on. Victorian ladies were not expected

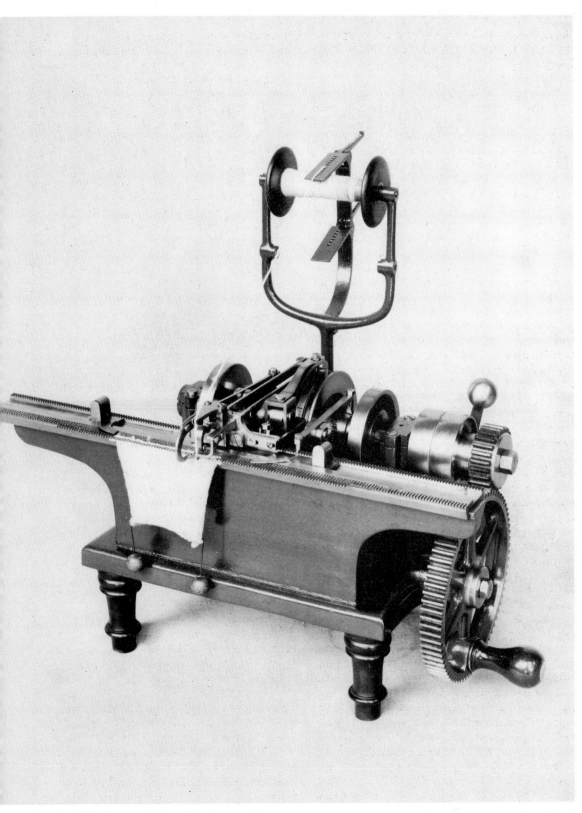

Straight knitting machine, 1846. (Crown copyright,
Science Museum, London)

Circular knitting machine, late nineteenth century.
(Crown copyright, Science Museum, London)

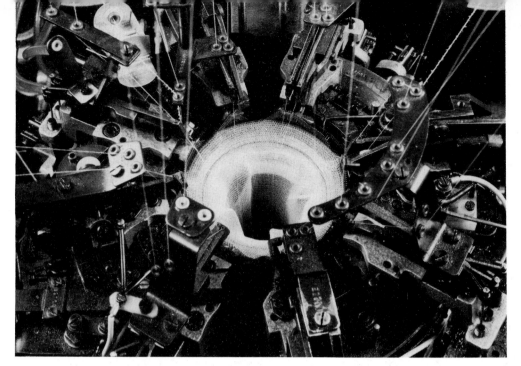

The photo shows the manufacture of panty-hose and
stockings. The knitting head of an 8-feed machine has the
sinker cap raised so that the positioning of the 8-feed
stations can be seen. The yarn is Celon crimped 20 denier
5 filament. (Photographed in 1971). (Courtaulds Ltd)

Production of double jersey knitted fabric. The fibres are
yarn dyed polyester and the fabric is for menswear
suiting. (Photograph taken in 1975). (Courtaulds Ltd)

to be involved with mechanical contraptions. The Harrison Patent Knitting Company manufactured machines around the early 1900s. The New Harrison, a plain and purl machine which could be used with jacquards if required on the single or double bed, was more similar to today's machines than those invented in the intervening period.

Japan became involved in Western industrialisation in 1871 when a group of businessmen came over and returned with a wide range of knitting machines.

Redundant hand frames were sent to museums in Japan and the U.S.A. during the 1920s. In Switzerland Passap patented their fast knitting machine in 1939. This had an open needle system with 120 needles like hooks that pulled, and 18 straight needles.

Knitting patterns first appeared in magazines in the nineteenth century. Spinners followed by providing patterns of knitted garments. These were very simple patterns. In 1899 John Paton and Son first published *The Universal Book of Knitting*, priced at a penny. This was a great step forward in the art of knitting and knitting pattern design. It was so popular that a second edition appeared including, for the first time, some advertising.

Knitmaster started in England in 1952. In the 1950s several European firms joined with Passap to produce single and double bed domestic machines. These were still very heavy manual selecting machines and eventually, in the 1960s, disappeared. In 1958 came the amalgamation of Girotex with Knitmaster. Passap produced ribbing attachments and the French firm Superba manufactured their double bed machine. The Passap Duomatic came onto the market in 1961 with its weightless knitting and the selective pusher system — a new breakthrough in double bed knitting. In 1971 Knitmaster produced the first fully-automatic punchcard machine in this country and it had a 24 stitch pattern repeat. Then other manufacturers followed from here: Jones +

Three-bar Mayer knitting machines producing polyester menswear fabric. Each completed roll is 24 m (about 26 yd) long and there are 26 machines in this one alley. (Photograph taken in 1975). (Courtaulds Ltd)

Brother, Toyota and Singer (U.K.). Each machine, however, varied in its individual features. Modern knitting was published by *Knitmaster Monthly* during the 1950s and ceased in August 1978. Passap Pattern books were available prior to this. *Stitch in Time*, published monthly by Jones + Brother, started later on in the 1960s. In 1970 Jones English Sewing Co. amalgamated with the Japanese firm Brother. This firm and Silver Seiko, who produce the Knitmaster Empisal machines, sell the largest amount of knitting machines on the Japanese home market. In September 1978 *World-wide Machine Knitting Magazine* was launched. They are independent of any one manufacturer. In the 1970s individual people published books. Teaching is now extending through the knitting clubs, on the dealer and tutor basis, in Adult Education Centres and through schools and courses. Today patterns have become very sophisticated, including couture designs for adaption into home knitting. The trend is to use thicker yarn than has been used in the past, as knitting today must be quick and easy to do. Coned and spooled yarns are now available and a great variety of exciting fine and thicker yarns are more commonplace. However, the great satisfaction of creating a garment to wear still exists.

HIRE OF MACHINES. It is not usually possible to hire a knitting machine.

HIRE PURCHASE. Mail order catalogues offer hire purchase arrangements for buying a knitting machine. Some dealers are now also able to offer this facility. A knitting machine can be bought by credit card.

HOLDING CAM. Varies in position on each machine. It is the lever on the carriage which keeps selected needles in holding position. This is where the needles are brought forward from the normal knitting position. When the carriage is passed across these needles they will not knit. This makes it possible to knit one part of the knitting while holding the other, for example, when shaping necklines or circular skirts, etc.

HOLDING POSITION (see also *Hem Shaping, Needle Position, Partial Knitting, Punchcard*). The position when needles are out of action, which can be right at the back of the needlebed, in which case they are placed there by knitting the nylon cord by hand across the knitting, taking the needles singly to the back of the needlebed. Empty needles also sit in this position. To return

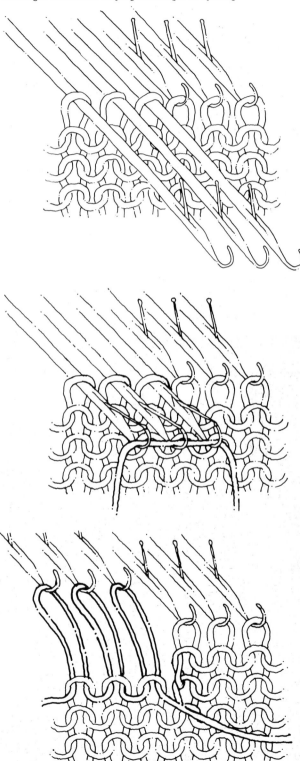

Holding stitches by using the nylon cord and putting each stitch back manually to non-working position. Waste knitting is used when shaping neck edges or opening

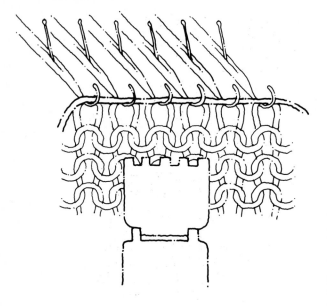

Showing the stitches pulled forward with the nylon cord ready for removing

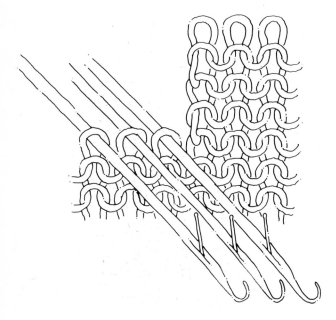

the needles to working position, pull on the nylon cord, so the loops of the last row knitted in the main yarn return on to the needle hooks. The needles are then put into working position again. Alternatively, the second position is the furthest forward position from the needlebed. This is used when one side of the knitting has to be held and the other side is knitted. It is also used for shaping the lower edge of skirts, for darts, socks, or short row designing. This is also known as partial

knitting, hold, etc. Reset the carriage if the needles have been pushed forward; the held needles will knit on the next row. Where forward held stitches are used to avoid a hole remember to take the yarn (when carriage is on the side of the held stitches) under the first inside needle in the held position. When the carriage is taken back across the needles the yarn travels over the top of the held needle, forming a loop. Where other shaping occurs, for example on a V-neckline, the carriage is simply taken back and forth across the needles, having decreased for the neck edge. The second half of the neckline is then knitted when the first part is complete. On the Passap take the pushers to the bottom of the needlebed to hold the needles. The lock must be put to BX, no arrow keys used. Knit one row, lift the yarn and place it over the hook of the needle next to the first inside needle in holding position. Knit one row. Continue doing this until shaping is complete. Back and neck shoulder shapings can sometimes be achieved by using the hold position, rather than casting off. Remember to push needles to holding position on the opposite side of the carriage. Wrap the yarn around the end needle to prevent a hole.

HOOK AND EYE, see *Fastenings*.

HOSIERY. Originally used as a term for knitted socks or stockings but now used to cover all types of knitted garments.

IMITATION FABRIC. Fabrics produced to copy the characteristics of existing textures such as fur fabrics.

INCREASING (see also *Tools*).
1 To increase one single stitch at either edge of the knitting simply bring one needle into working position on the side nearest the carriage. This will be knitted on the next row.
2 To make a fully fashioned increase, use the one, two or three needle transfer tool and move the stitches out by one needle, leaving one empty either one, two or three needles in from the edge. Then pick up from the loops below either on the

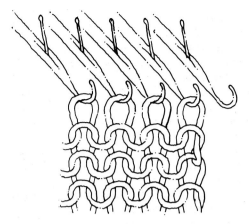

To increase a single stitch

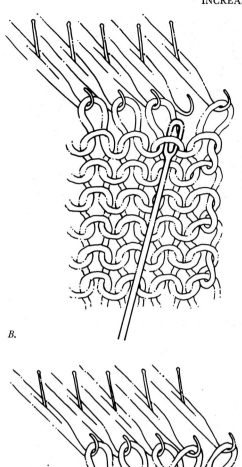

B.

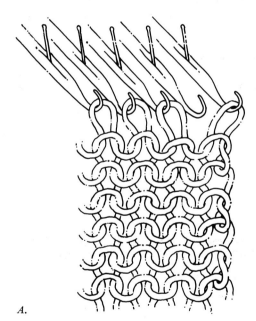

A.

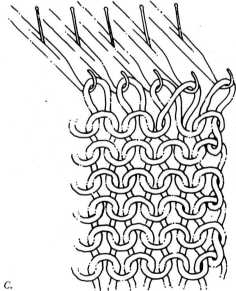

C.

To increase a single stitch fully-fashioned using the single-eyed transfer tool

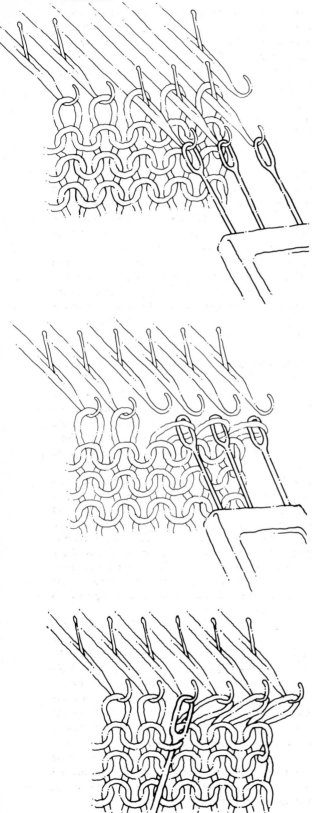

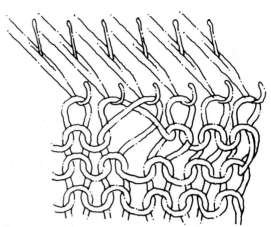

Increasing a single stitch fully fashioned, using the 3/1 transfer tool

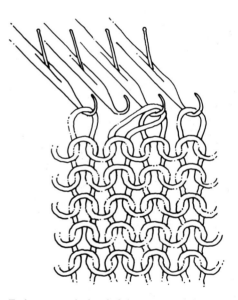

To increase a single stitch in a row, transfer the stitch, then move all the other stitches across so the empty needle has a stitch. At the end of the row the empty needle is pushed back to non-working position. Continue knitting. This method is used for darts

left or right of the gap on to the empty needle. This avoids a hole. A row of holes is quite attractive with a knitted cord threaded in and out. Suitable for lightweight fabrics only. To increase several stitches at either edge wind the yarn around each needle as in a closed edge cast on.

INCREASING DURING LACE KNITTING. To increase one stitch at a time bring an extra needle at the edge of the knitting on the side away from the carriage to knitting position and knit two rows. Then raise another needle to knitting position and transfer the last stitch on to this needle, leaving the second needle empty and returning it to non-working position. Continue transferring this stitch outwards until the desired number of needles are knitting. To increase more than one stitch at a time, select the number of needles required into knitting position so the lace pattern is continued in the needle layout. Wind the yarn as for closed edge cast on around the needle hooks. Lay the nylon cord across the loops (only over the new needles), pull it down firmly and knit.

INCREASING ON RIBBED KNITTING.
Increasing a single stitch on a knit 1 purl 1 rib. 1/1. At same side as carriage, push ribber needle to knitting position and continue to knit. On the same side as the carriage, push the main bed needle for increasing into knitting position, and continue to knit. To increase more than one stitch follow diagrams carefully. *To increase one stitch on a double rib.* Push empty needle to knitting position on main bed at same side as carriage. Pick up the loop from the stitch below and put it on the empty needle. Push the empty needle opposite on the ribber into knitting position. Alternatively, push an empty ribber needle to knitting position on the same side as the carriage and place the loop of the stitch below and put it on to the needle. On the main bed push up a needle to knitting position and continue to knit.

To increase a single stitch on a knit 2 purl 2 rib. 2/2. Push empty ribber needle to knitting position and continue to knit. Push the next needle on the ribber, so making the second of the pair, to knitting position and continue knitting. Or push up needle on main bed as in diagram. *To increase more than one stitch on a 2/2 rib.* Push up the required number of needles on the opposite side to the carriage to knitting position and knit one row. Lay either an edge weight over the stitches or the nylon cord and knit one row, transfer the stitches into the right rib, set the lever to half pitch and continue knitting.

Increasing one stitch during lace knitting

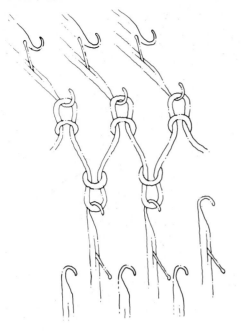

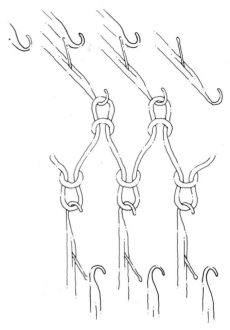

To increase on a 1/1 Rib (Knit 1 Purl 1). On same side as carriage, push up ribber needle

On the same side as the carriage push needle to knitting position on the mainbed

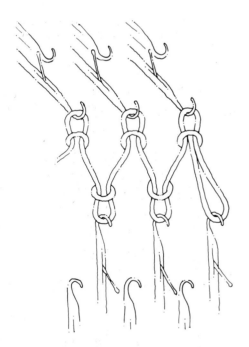

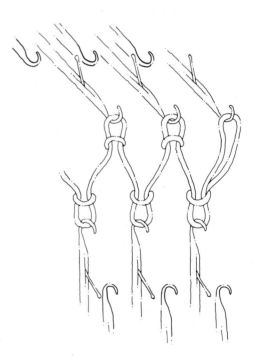

Continue knitting

Continue knitting

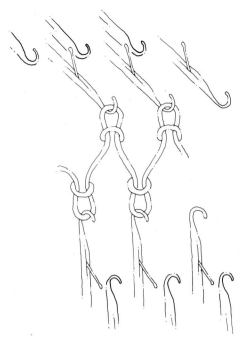

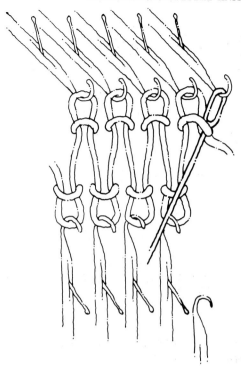

To increase more than one stitch on a 1/1 rib. The needles for increasing are pushed up on the opposite side to the carriage into knitting position, on both the ribber and the mainbed. Knit one row

To increase on a double rib. Push up needle on mainbed and place the loop from the first knitted stitch onto the empty needle

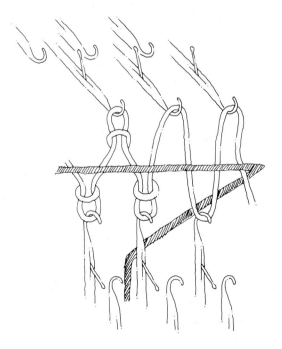

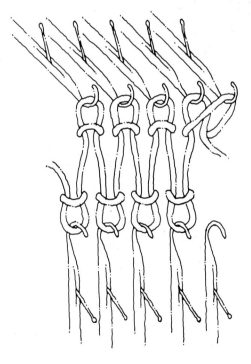

Use the edge weight to hold the stitches down and knit several rows. Then continue knitting

Push up needle on ribber. Continue knitting

INCREASING ON RIBBED KNITTING

To increase one stitch on a 2/2 rib

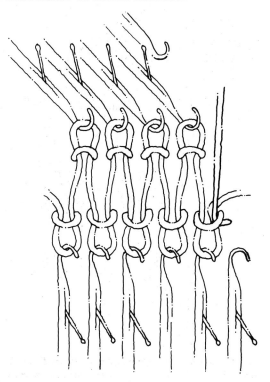

Push up needle on ribber into knitting position. Place the loop from the first knitted stitch onto the empty needle

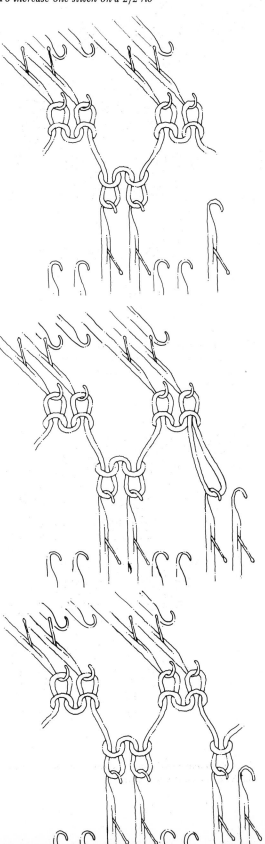

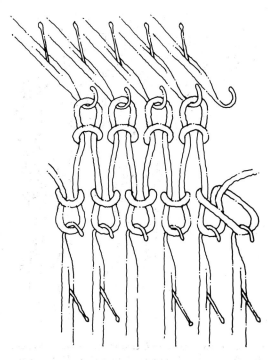

On the mainbed push up needle into knitting position and continue knitting

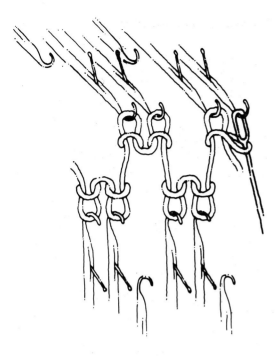

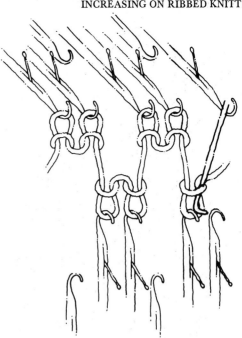

Increasing on a 2/2 rib. Push up needle on same side as the carriage, on the mainbed. Place loop from the adjacent stitch onto the needle. Continue knitting

Place the loop of the stitch onto the empty needle on the ribber. Then push the needle to be increased on the main-bed into working position, and knit one row

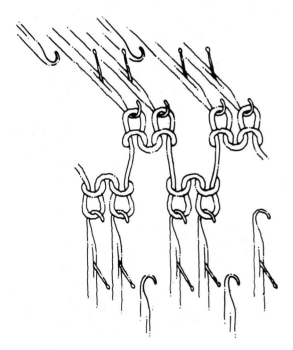

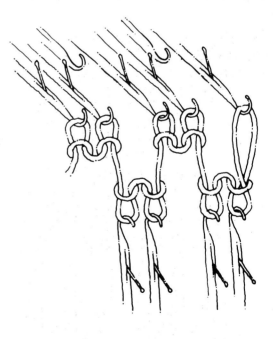

Push the ribber needle to be increased up into working position and continue knitting

On the mainbed the yarn is caught on the end needle and therefore one stitch has been increased on the ribber and the mainbed

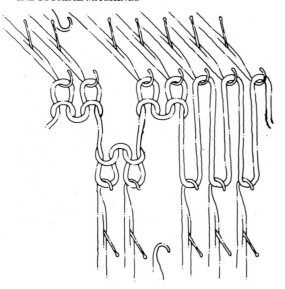

Increasing more than one stitch on a 2/2 rib. Push up the required number of needles on both beds, on opposite side to carriage, and knit one row

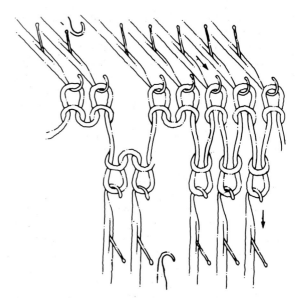

Knit one row and transfer the stitches using the double-eye transfer tool. Continue knitting with half pitch lever set to H. (See Pitch)

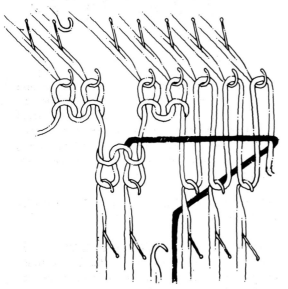

Hang on the edge weight

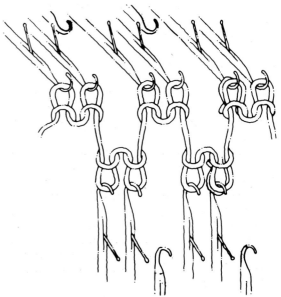

INDUSTRIAL MACHINES (see also *Gauge, History of Knitting*). It is occasionally possible to purchase an industrial hand double bed machine. This is a machine that the designer has used to sample his/her designs prior to placing on the larger powered machines of the correct gauge. These hand machines are normally V beds. However, these are not recommended for domestic use as they are very large and heavy. It is possible to buy a motor for some domestic machines. The majority of power industrial machines have circular needle beds, particularly Jersey machines, so the knitting is continuous. In industry body blanks are used and lengths of fabric, for the cut and sew method, for garments. The industrial machines are also designed to shape several garment pieces across the needlebed at once. Industrial sock machines produce sock after sock and are divided by pulling a single thread. Because domestic machines have a different needle gauge, the designs could not be used on industrial machines unless they were altered considerably. Problems can arise for designers in industry as they are not technicians and vice versa. The industrial machines are very complex, and there are many different gauge machines that have individual limitations.

INDUSTRIAL YARNS (see also *Cheeses, Cones, Count of Yarn, Twist*). Mills in the north of England often run their own shops, or supply yarns by mail order. Town markets and knitting machine shops do too. These are often cheaper and some very interesting yarns can be found. Be careful if you select a weaving yarn for knitting as the yarn sometimes knits with a twist to the left or to the right, making the knitting distorted. This can also apply to some industrial yarns. It is also possible to buy end of line yarns that are excellent for using in striped garments, but beware of weak, knotted, and faded yarns. Yarns may come in hanks or skeins and must be wound into balls before use. Most of these yarns are classified according to their metre per kilo.

INLAY YARN, see *Slip Stitch, Weave.*

INSERTIONS. Although surface decoration can be applied after the knitting has been removed from the machine it is possible to insert items into or on to the knitting while it is still on the machine. If using the double bed, set on tubular, small beads and sequins can be placed in the knitting. The knitting is on normal, then the yarn can be changed to a finer yarn and set to tubular for several rows. The beads will then shine through the finer yarn. Insert beads, threads, sequins, etc. and knit on normal with the main yarn once again. Beads can be threaded onto yarn and hand knitted across the row on the single bed. Many variations are possible using these techniques.

INSTRUCTION BOOK, see *Books, instruction.*

INTARSIA. This is a method of producing colour patterning without the yarns floating at the back of the fabric when not required in the pattern. It can be used on any pattern which is in stockinet. The tension remains the same. The yarn is knitted within its own shape and there is no limit to the number of colours that can be used. This method is excellent for larger areas of colour, and excellent for very original experimentation. Set the machine for normal knitting and place the coloured balls on the floor in front of the machine. If a large selection of colours is being used, small amounts of yarn can be wound on to small cardboard or plastic bobbins. Lay the first colour across the needles selected for this colour, the short end on the side of the carriage, then proceed to the next colour making sure that each colour overlaps by one needle, otherwise holes will appear. Pass the empty carriage across the needlebed and the yarn will be knitted in. Bring the needles back to knitting position, if they have not already returned. Lay the yarn once again across the needles and continue as before. This method can be free, or designs can be worked out on squared paper first.

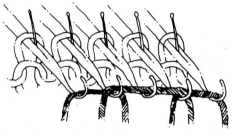

Intarsia

INTERFACING (see also *Vilene*). Vilene and Superdrape are the best known makes. Pockets, hems, collars, necklines, cuffs, etc. benefit from the firmness that an interfacing gives the knitting. Use with the cut and sew method for larger areas, where necessary. Select carefully as there are different weights and types.

INTERLOCK. A double 1 x 1 weft industrially knitted rib construction.

INTERNATIONAL SILK ASSOCIATION (see also *Silk, history of, Silk, production*). The International Silk Association has produced a mark to assist in identifying silk. Silk is the natural product of the silkworm. All silk contains no other textile. Pure silk contains silk with metal weighting only in the dye. Pure dye silk contains only silk and no weighting. Nett silk is a product with continuous cocoon filaments. Spun silk is yarn with silk fibres of 2 to 20 cm (¾ to 8 in) in length, spun together. Schappe silk is spun silk that is degummed by fermentation.

INTERNATIONAL WOOL SECRETARIAT (see also *Shoddy, Wool*). They have produced a Wool-

Silk. The silk mark of the International Silk Association

mark so that every pure new wool garment carries this label. Each garment must have reached certain high standards on fibre content, colour fastness to light, on washing, shrinkage, and resistance to abrasion. This mark also means that the wool does not contain any reprocessed fibres. 'All Wool' labels apply to garments that have a blend of reprocessed and new wool. This, however, is no indication of the standard of the wool.

Pure new wool mark of the International Wool Secretariat

INVISIBLE SEAMING, see *Grafting, Mattress Stitch*.

IRONING BOARD (see also *Ironing Press*). Ironing boards tend to be too small to press the larger pieces of garments without having part of the knitting hanging over the edge. This distorts the knitting and should be avoided. An ironing pad can be made from blankets covered with a clean white cotton cloth. A fast dyed gingham or checked cloth can be used as a blocking aid for measuring. A commercially produced blocking board is available in the U.K.

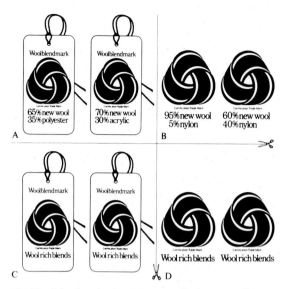

The Woolblendmark. A and B are used when several products all have the same fibre content. The content is quoted. C and D are used when the fibre content is not consistent. The correct fibre content for each product is stated

IRON AND IRONING (see also *Garment After-care, Ironing Board*). Most yarns benefit from steaming when removed from the machine, particularly natural fibres. Steaming draws the bars between the stitches into the stitches themselves. In other words, the knitting contracts. Always set the iron to the correct yarn setting, having checked the fibre content of your yarn. Do not use the steam setting on your iron as it is the incorrect heat for most yarns. Use a test piece first. The heat from the steam is usually sufficient to shrink and set the fabric, and it is not necessary to press the iron on to the fabric. Never try and push the iron, just hold the iron above the fabric, and glide over the surface of the cloth. Press hems first. By steaming hems the stitches are drawn into place and this gives the elasticity necessary in a welt. Use a rib bar which is included in the lid of some machines and looks like a metal ruler. Any smooth length of wood or metal can be used for this purpose. Never iron an acrylic rib. Place the bar through the hem and use the table clamps to pull against. Stretch fabric and lay a very wet cloth on the welt. Hold iron over the stitches and then remove the bar and leave knitting to dry. Pin each piece of knitting to shape on an ironing board or pad. Knitting must fit the board and not hang over the edge. Do not pin welts again. Pins should be inserted so they lie horizontally. (See *blocking*.) Check measurements as you go. Press as before, leave to dry before unpinning.

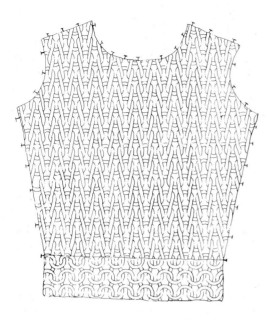

Blocking prior to steaming

Using the steamer bar to press a welt

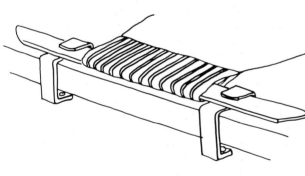

Wool. Press on the wrong side with iron at wool setting over a damp cloth, lightly. For stocking stitch press firmly; for Fair Isle and multi-coloured fabrics press lightly with a wet cloth.

Cotton and Silk. Press on the wrong side lightly at cotton or silk setting over a wet cloth. The pressing cloth should be wetter for these yarns than wool.

Mohair. Press on the wrong side firmly with iron on wool setting over a damp cloth. For rib fabrics press very lightly.

Cashmere. Press on the wrong side very lightly, with iron set on wool, over a damp cloth.

Bouclé gimp, tweed and textured yarns. Pin with the wrong side uppermost. The iron should be set to yarn content heat and a damp cloth used. The steam is sufficient to set the fabric, so do not press, but hold above the damp cloth, and this will avoid crushing the extures.

Angora. Pin with the right side uppermost, iron set to wool. Angora is not pressed but the wet pressing cloth and the heat of the iron above the fabric set the yarn.

Synthetics. Press on the wrong side very lightly with iron at synthetic setting over a dry cloth, unless otherwise directed on the instructions. A slightly damp cloth can be used if wool or cotton has a percentage of synthetic yarn, with a warmer iron. If synthetic yarns are pressed heavily no amount of washing will correct the flat looking fabric. Too much heat will partly melt the yarn and the same flat looking surface will result.

IRONING PRESS. Marvellous for pressing, especially when employing the cut and sew method. A press is also suitable for normal ironing.

Elna ironing press with the vap-o-jet

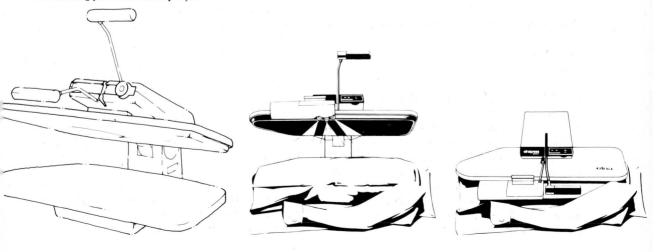

It comes complete with instructions and has a padded ironing board base and a heated lid. A temperature selection knob controls the thermostat. In most cases the electric heater is automatically cut off if the machine remains closed for longer than is allowed on the setting, and an automatic buzzing sound is heard. The Elnapress can be fitted (or bought already fitted) with a vap-o-jet. This is a spray system with three jets. It slips over the left-hand handle of the press and damps the ironing during or before pressing. After spraying, the water is immediately converted into steam when it comes into contact with the heating shoe. The vap-o-jet is filled with ordinary water and will not fur up. Lavender or other oils can be added to the water to perfume the articles.

IRREGULAR PATTERN SETTINGS, see *Pattern Settings, irregular.*

J

JACOB'S SHEEP. Tweed, which is very hard wearing and used in jackets and furnishings, is made from this sheep. It is believed that this sheep originally came from the Spanish Armada which was shipwrecked in the Hebrides in 1588. They had been used for live meat on the boat.

JACQUARD (see also *History of Knitting*). A weaving method invented by Joseph Marie Jacquard in 1798. It is a punch card system, attached to the loom, which selects various individual warp threads, and patterns are therefore woven.

This mechanism has been developed for knitting machines and is now the name also given to the punch card system on domestic knitting machines. For knitting true Jacquard specially-punched cards must be used. On the double bed the order is uneven, even, even, uneven. In other words, on the first row of the punch card the main yarn knits the background. On the second row the design is knitted in the contrast yarn. On the third row the design is knitted in the contrast yarn and on the fourth row the background is knitted in the main yarn. On the single bed the order is uneven, even, uneven, even. The reverse side of the two-colour fabric of true jacquard knitting is the same. Use a

smooth 2-ply yarn as maximum thickness. Variations on this fabric are embossed jacquard and half milano. It is important to sample carefully with a variety of yarns when producing this fabric. The right weight and colour combination is very important so that the floats do not show through on the face side of the fabric.

JAMMING CARRIAGE, see *Carriage Jams.*

JERSEY (see also *Double Jersey, Guernsey Knitting, history of*). Used to describe either a knitted fabric or a knitted garment. The origin of the word comes from the Channel Island of Jersey between Britain and France. Single or double jersey is the name given to a very fine machine-knitted fabric which stretches because of the way it is structured. The British Edwardian actress Lily Langtry was a daughter of the Dean of Jersey and she made fashionable the wearing of a long Jersey garment with a long style of skirt. (She became known as Jersey Lily.)

JOINING KNITTING, see *Grafting, Making Up.*

JOINING YARN (see also *Unravelling*). Never join yarn by knotting as the knot may appear on the face of the knitting. It will show up immediately and cheapen the garment. Always join yarn at the beginning of a row. If the yarn should run out as the carriage is being taken across the needlebed, stop knitting, remove the carriage, unpick the row and knit again with the new ball or cone. Should a spinner's knot appear in the knitting the rows should be unravelled back until the knot disappears.

JONES + BROTHER INTERNATIONAL (see also *Appendix*). Importers of knitting and sewing machines into the United Kingdom.

JUKI KNITTING MACHINES, see *Appendix.*

KEMP. Wool, usually obtained from mountain sheep, containing a coarse fibre called kemp which is used in tweeds. This fibre will not absorb moisture and therefore appears lighter when dyed. This is particularly noticeable in Harris Tweeds.

KNITCOPY (see also *Charting Devices*). The pattern is drawn on to the copy paper which feeds automatically as each row is knitted.

KNIT LEADER (see also *Charting Devices*). Works on the same principle as the knitradar except that it is full scale and drawn on to a special plastic sheet. Working full scale means that dress making patterns can be traced on to the sheets and it involves fewer calculations. The only disadvantage is that the pattern has to be washed off the plastic sheet in order to put another pattern on to it, therefore it is difficult to keep patterns for long.

KNITMASTER, see *Appendix*.

KNITRADAR (see also *Charting Devices*). A system for reading off a pattern as you are knitting. The advantage lies in being able to design original ideas. The Knitradar is a half scale pattern; it consists of a roller inside an open-topped casing. The paper pattern is fed round the roller like a typewriter. The line at the left of the pattern is the centre front or back edge. The four lines at the right are the four different sized sidelines. The inner one is the smallest size and the outer line the largest. The A B C are the hem points and you follow the lines as you knit. On the front of the roller is a gauge which shows the number of stitches needed for the width shown of the drawing. With each row that is knitted the pattern moves down, and so at the end of each row the gauge shows how many stitches need increasing or decreasing. Comes with a set of basic patterns for adults and children.

KNITTING (see also *History of Machine Knitting*). The name given to the method of making a fabric by intermeshing loops either by hand or machine on needles. Methods include: handknitting with needles, warp knitting (which interloops the warp threads), raschel knitting on the machine (which is the same method as warp knitting but produces more complex patterns), weft knitting on a domestic or flat bed machine and weft knitting on circular machines.

KNITTING PATTERNS (see also *Appendix*). It is possible to adapt hand knitting patterns for use on the knitting machine, but now a variety of machine knitting patterns are available and most machine knitting patterns can be adapted for the various machines with practice. It is also possible to add details to a favourite pattern, making a basic pattern work in an original way.

KNITTING FOR PROFIT (see also *Appendix, Labels*). Most important factor is a well-equipped workroom with good lighting, and plenty of shelves. Apart from the knitting machine or machines it is essential to have a good supply of yarns. A sewing machine or overlocker is important to speed up the finishing of the garments. With fine fabrics that are difficult to stitch, sew with a piece of tissue paper underneath which can be removed later. An iron and a pressing table with a thick padded surface are a must. The latter can double as a cutting-out table. Several white cotton pressing cloths should be to hand, and sharp scissors, a tape measure, a good supply of rustless steel pins, a set of needles, a bodkin, various colours of polyester threads, and beside the machine a notebook and pencil to enter details of every sample. Build up a selection of patterns for stretchable knits. (See *Patterns*). Make sample garments in a size 10 as they look neater and more interesting in a smaller size. Larger sizes can then be drawn up from these basic patterns. A filing cabinet is helpful to store the patterns, yarn manufacturers, samples, accounts and records, orders and relevant details. Keep an account book and a separate record of all business payments and receipts. An accountant will give you a list of the items that can be set against tax. Ask for cash on delivery at first; this way it is easier to keep track of incomings and outgoings. Larger stores may not pay immediately and a period of 4-7 weeks can be the normal waiting time. Some shops may only sell the garments on a sale-or-return basis; whilst this is an easier way of getting work into a shop it can be risky. If this method is used then an agreement should be signed that any unsold goods be returned to the owner in as new condition, and agree a limit on the selling time. Never start on an order unless it is in writing, either as a written order or a signature on the order in the duplicate order book. If a delivery date is agreed it must be kept. Decide on the number of garments that are possible to produce in a month, the type of garment and which end of the market to assist. Calculate over the year what your saleable hours are worth, deducting overheads and materials and adding the profit. If the business is to be called anything other than by your own name then it must be registered, and the registered name and address and the owner of the business must appear on the letterheads. Labels should be put in each garment.

(See *Labels*.) If you intend to sell to friends then garment orders will come by showing a garment to one person who will inform and so on. If selling to shops, then a visit to the shop to see the buyer by prior arrangement is best. Keep a photographic record of each garment sold to show future clients. Colour slides are best and they can be mounted in plastic sheets, obtainable from photographic shops, with each slide numbered and details written in a notebook against the reference number. Show a selection of work and offer to produce an exclusive range. Offer a choice of yarns. Bread-and-butter lines are quite important when starting a business; for example, scarves or bags that sell easily and therefore leave a little floating capital. Do not commit yourself to more orders than can easily be coped with. Never let designs and ideas go out of sight and always keep the details of samples in another book with a reference number. If the garments do not sell or the samples, with the fashion ideas, try asking why. Remember that shops are normally working two seasons ahead. Finally, do not be discouraged. Remember, however, that knitting for profit is only for proficient knitters; reputations cannot grow on badly produced garments.

KNITTING SCHOOLS (see also *Appendix*, *Machine Knitting Courses*). Some knitting machine importers operate schools at their head offices.

KNIT TRACER (see also *Charting Devices*). The charting device for Toyota knitting machines.

KNOP. Fancy man-made yarn with small tufted loops.

KNOTTING YARN (see also *Joining Yarn*). A knot detector is now available on the market.

LABELS (see also *Appendix*). If knitted garments are being produced to sell then it is important to advertise the maker by putting a label at the back neck or attached to the seam. They are normally satin ribbon with the details printed on in black or brown. The choice of wording and sizes can be seen in sample books at the printers. The *Draper's Record* and the *Drapers Weekly* magazine in the United Kingdom lists addresses of manufacturers who produce bags and carriers for packaging the knitted garments.

LACE (see also *Cables, decorative, Decreasing for Lace Knitting, Double Bed, Drive Lace, Increasing During Lace Knitting, Shadow Lace, Tuck Lace*). An openwork structure using a fine thread. When made by hand it is produced on hard cushions with threads being wound around pins. The first machine for producing lace was not invented until early in the nineteenth century. Lacy fabrics are produced on Raschel knitting machines. Bought lace can be used as an edging on knitted garments. A lace stitch on the machine is achieved by stitch transfer. A stitch is taken off a needle and put on the next needle and the knitting then continues. The empty needle continues to knit but leaves a hole where the stitch has been transfered. If the empty needle is put into non-working position then the hole will become a ladder until such time that the needle is put in working position once again. On the punchcard the holes make the lace and the blanks knit plain.

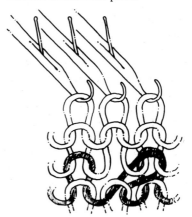

Lace stitch formation

LACE CARRIAGE. An extra carriage supplied with some machines, which enables lace to be knitted over a large area. The carriage is passed across the needles, which preselect for the lace area. This is known as automatic transfer lace. Extension rails are fitted to the machine so that the entire width of the bed can be used, therefore they need not be fitted for sampling. Other machines produce mock lace known as punch lace, where the lace holes are knitted in a finer yarn. This gives the fabric the see-through quality. A fine cotton sewing thread is most suitable, or a fine metallic yarn. The manufacturers recommend a transparent filament yarn (an invisible nylon thread) but this tends to make the fabric very harsh to the touch. True lace can be produced by manual selection but it takes a long time and should be confined to smaller areas only. The punchcard indicates when the lace carriage should be taken across the bed and in which direction. This is according to the type of pattern. However, when the knit carriage is being used the lace carriage is always on the left side of the machine. The instruction manual gives specific instructions for the use of the lace carriage and for mock lace. Remember for all single bed machines that if an end needle is selected when patterning it should be pushed to knitting position to avoid the stitches dropping off the edge needle. The Passap uses the U70 transfer carriage to form the lace stitch. The Superba uses a lace transfer carriage. Both these devices transfer the stitches from one carriage to the other to form the lace.

LADDER (see also *Decoration, surface, Dropped Stitches, Flute, Mock Rib*). Produced by leaving a single needle in non-working position; the yarn floats over the stitch and on to the next needle. Should the ladder be an error, then use the latch tool from behind the knitting and knit up the knitting and back onto the needle. If the ladder is too long or a complicated patterned fabric is being knitted, then insert a piece of yarn through the dropped stitch using the latchet hook. Make sure the latch of the needle is open before starting to knit again and form a stitch on the needle from the bar below. Repair the fabric when it has been removed from the machine. A ladder can also be used to form a mock rib. Ladders can be used as patterns or to thread knitted cords or ribbon through. A contrast yarn can be used for picking up the ladder to form a pattern.

LAMBSWOOL, see *Wool*.

LAPELS, see *Collars*.

LARGE SCALE DESIGNS (see also *Cable, Lace, Intarsia, Picture Knitting*). Most machines can be set to elongate the design. For those machines that have a 24 stitch repeat, a larger design can be knitted partly with the punchcard and the remainder of the needles are hand selected to complete the design. Stitch transfer lace can be used for partial patterning and is a method to produce a variation on a cable over a large area.

LATCH (see also *Needle Replacement*). The moveable part of the latch needle that opens and closes to accept the knitted loops. When the latch is damaged or broken, the needle should be replaced.

LATCH HOOK (see also *Needle, Tools*). Also known as latchet hook and tappet tool. For picking up dropped stitches or binding an edge. It is also used for casting off by the chain method. It looks identical to a needle on the machine bed, except that it has no butt, but has a plastic handle to make it easier to hold.

LATCH NEEDLE, see *Needle*.

LATCH TOOL, see *Latch Hook*.

LATTICE STITCH. Use double transfer tool. Select 12 needles and knit several rows. Put the first two stitches where the second two are and the second to the first. Put three where four is and four where three is. Make sure both times that the right hand needles are transferred first. Swop five with six and then knit several rows. Put pair two where three is and vice versa, leaving pair one. But this time put the left-hand needles first. Change four and five from the left first, then repeat from the beginning again.

LAYING IN (see also *Weaving*). Secondary yarn for patterning is laid across the needles by hand at the beginning of each row or, as in weaving, is fed in front of the sinker plate. It is called the laying-in or secondary yarn.

LEATHER (see also *Blanket Stitch, Eyelet Holes, Renovation*). Can be used in areas to trim knitting. Can be thinned by removing a layer with a sharp knife from the back of the skin; this makes it much easier to handle and the patch can be sewn on by hand using blanket stitch or on the sewing machine. Leather thonging can be used to fasten jackets. Leather patches can be bought with pre-punched holes for easy sewing. Use at elbow or knee of trousers.

LEE, REVEREND WILLIAM (see also *History of Knitting*). Inventor of a knitting machine to produce machine-made stockings. Born in Nottinghamshire between 1559 and 1564. He died in France sometime after 1611 before he knew the profound influence that his machine would have on history.

LIGHTING. When knitting it is very important to sit in a good light. If artificial light is being used be careful not to sit in your own shadow. A bendy lamp or the Superba striplight lamp is the most suitable to position at the rear of the needlebed.

LINEN (see also *Fibres, identification*). Vegetable fibre coming from the inner layers of the stalk of the flax plant. Not very easy to knit with due to its lack of elasticity.

LININGS. A partial lining to restrict the over-stretching of knitting in certain areas is vital. To line a skirt back, cut out the back pattern piece in the lining fabric. Make it the length of the skirt or cut off the just below the buttocks so it will take the sitting strain. Transfer the appropriate markings and tack lining to the fabric wrong sides together, along the seamlines and darts. Then treat these two layers as one and complete the skirt. Trousers at the knees are lined in a similar way, approximately 25 cm (10 in) long and the width of the knee area of the front trouser pattern. Try trousers on and mark the horizontal centre of each knee cap. Remove trousers and place lining sections over the centre of these marks. Stitch the sides of the lining to the front seam edge. Then blind stitch the upper and lower edges to the outer fabric. Lining is not generally used with stretch knits but there are exceptions. Where the garment is of a fine construction a lining will help it retain its shape and can be used as a backing contrast to show off the pattern. A lining will keep the fabric away from the skin, where a yarn may irritate. It is possible to purchase a stretchy lining or, where appropriate, a lightweight bought fabric can be used as a lining. Make sure lining material is of a good quality to avoid shrinkage when washed. It is recommended to wash or dry clean the lining prior to construction. Garments can be lined where the floats are likely to catch on jewellery and where the reverse side of the garment is likely to be seen, for example cross-over skirts, hoods, jackets and coats. For dress, skirt and trousers, cut the lining from the main pattern pieces (if cut and sew method is used); if not lay knitted pieces that have been blocked on to the lining and cut out. Pin the lining to the garment wrong sides together at the neckline and armhole edges or at the waistline before joining the facings, sleeves or waistband. Slip stitch lining to the zipper tape and tack. Attach other garment sections and the lining is then permanently in place. Hem the lining separately to the knitting. For jackets, coats or vests use the main pattern pieces but cut the front along the fold line and add 5 cm (2 in) of extra fabric down the centre back to form an ease pleat. Construct the lining separately. A cross stitch holds the back pleat in place. Where possible the lining is inserted before sleeves, collars or facings are attached.

LINKERS. Machines that are now available on the market and are also used in industry to join pieces of knitting together with a row of knitting. The open stitches are fed onto a rigid bar of metal spikes, one for each stitch. A linker comes as an accessory which automatically casts off by linking one stitch through another. It is used to join side seams, edge to edge, and for decorative fabrics. It is also useful in the knitting of neck bands and buttonhole bands. In industry it is generally used for attaching bands, collars and sleeve heads and they are joined by a straight line of elastic chain stitches. Knitted pieces that have been taken off the knitting machine with waste knitting can also be joined on the linker. It is important when using the linker that every needle has a stitch. When thicker yarns are being used over every other needle, all needles should be put into knitting position and one row is knitted from left to right. Use a thinner yarn and a loose tension and knit one row to the left. Link off as per the instructions. When using any textured yarn knit the last row on a loose tension in a smooth yarn to avoid the knitting being caught up. This also applies for weave, punch lace, tuck or slip patterns. Fair Isle can, however, be knitted in the pattern in the last row. When knitting on the main bed and ribber, the stitches are transferred to the main bed; the close knit bar, if used, is removed and one loose row is knitted before using the linker. Some knitting machines have an automatic linker which is a small carriage that fits onto the needle bed and forms a chain stitch castoff. The last row of knitting is worked as a very loose row. This linker can also be used for joining any two pieces of knitting, providing they are not too textured. The last row, however, on textured knitting, should be knitted in a very loose smooth yarn.

LLAMA (see also *Fibres, identification, Yarn Combinations*). Comes from the camel family of South America. The fibre is 20 to 30 cm (8 to 12 in) long and is very soft, shiny and fine. Normally found in natural colours ranging from white through brown to black.

LOCKING PLATE, CARRIAGE (see also *Tools*). Is used to hold the carriage on the needlebed and prevent it from moving when being packed away.

LOOP YARNS. Formed by two binder yarns that are twisted tightly, one at a faster speed that forms the loops. Mohair is used for this yarn a great deal as the fibres are long.

LUREX (see also *Yarn Combinations*). Trade name for a shiny metallic yarn made from thin strips of aluminium covered in a plastic film. Can be bought supported or unsupported; this means either twisted around a central core or in a smooth strip. The finer lurex is better run with another yarn for strength, is more subtle and feels less harsh than the thicker lurex. Helps when fine to take it twice round the disc spring. Some lurex will take dye, particularly the pearlised type, which dyes into very pretty pale colours.

M

MACHINES, KNITTING, TYPES OF (see also *Gauge, Industrial Machines*). There are two basic types of machine, one with a single set of needles which produces a stocking stitch fabric, the other with two sets of needles that are set opposite to each other and produce a double knit or a rib fabric. The first is called a single bed machine and the second a double bed machine. Most domestic knitting machines are single bed and, with the addition of a ribbing attachment, can be made into a double bed machine.

MACHINE KNITTING CLUBS (see also *Adult Education, Clubs, knitting*). Most towns have a knitting club that caters for all levels of machine knitters. Local dealers normally know of a club, and the clubs advertise in the local paper or local library.

MACHINE KNITTING COURSES (see also *Adult Education, Appendix*). Courses are advertised in *Worldwide Machine Knitting*, a monthly magazine, and *Crafts* magazine, which appears every two months. Postal courses are run by Jones + Brother International, in the United Kingdom, for their machines. Passap run various knitting courses: Beginners, Passap Deco Part 1 and Part 2, and General Knitting Techniques.

MACHINES, SEWING, see *Sewing Machines*.

MACRAMÉ (see also *Fringes*). It is based on two knots; a blanket stitch, which is a half-hitch, and the flat knot, which needs a minimum of four threads to make it. It can be used to make fringes and edges, belts, cords, etc.

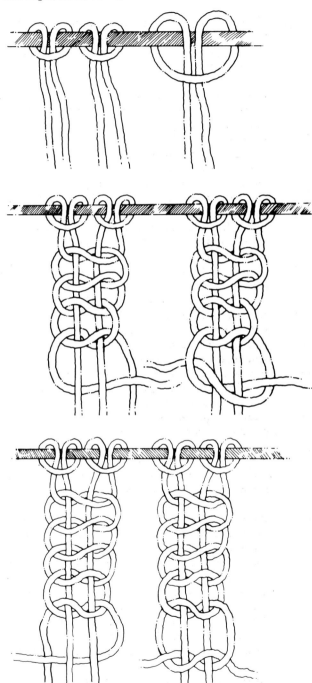

Macramé: making flat knots

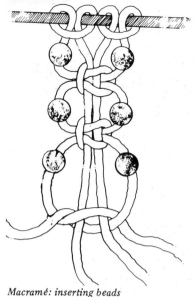

Macramé: inserting beads

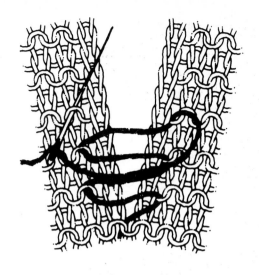

Seam joining of garter stitches

MAGAZINES, see *Appendix*.

MAIL ORDER MACHINES (see also *Hire Purchase*). Machines can be bought by mail order. Some places offer better discount than others, but are often far away. Provided that tuition is not needed and the machine is familiar to the buyer then a considerable amount can sometimes be saved by shopping around on the telephone for the best buy. If a machine is purchased by mail order and a knitting problem should arise, bear in mind that the local knitting machine dealer may be reluctant to help you, having purchased elsewhere.

MAIL ORDER YARNS, see *Yarn Suppliers*.

MAKING UP (see also *Bands, Grafting, Iron and Ironing, Mattress Stitch*). The construction of a garment must have as much care as the knitting. Most yarns benefit from steaming when removed from the machine. A perfectly pinned garment will be easy to make up. The type of edges to be joined will dictate the stitch that should be used. If the knitting tends to curl on the edges and it is being constructed on a sewing machine, then it is helpful to buy a roller foot attachment, used mainly for pile fabrics, which will help the knitting flow and lie flatter.

    Seam joining. Tuck and weave garments need to be sewn with a tiny stitch, working from bottom to top. Remember to darn in all loose ends. Follow this order for construction where possible. Join shoulder seams for cardigans, join one seam for tops. Make sure the join is in a straight line,

Joining edge to edge for an invisible seam

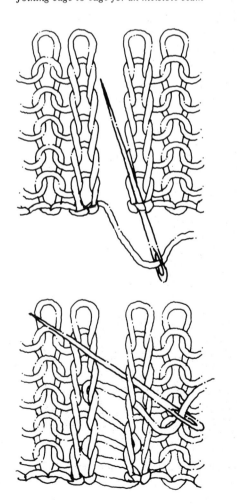

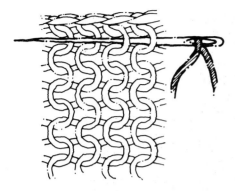

Seam joining with back stitch, two side edges. With right sides facing each other

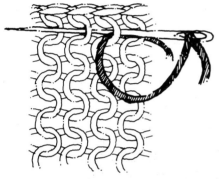

Put needle through the last loop worked and pick up two more loops side by side. Continue until joining is complete

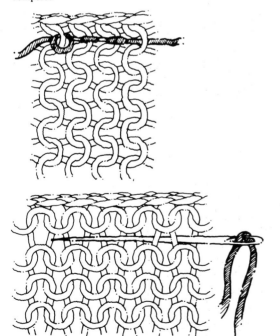

Seam joining with back stitch, two closed edges. With right sides together

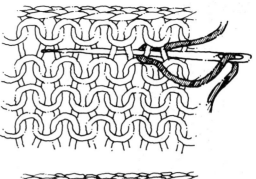

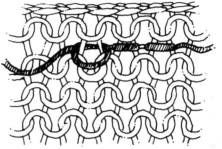

Use this stitch for shoulders on patterned fabrics. On side seams and on sleeves

and where there is a possibility of shoulder dropping include a narrow tape across the shoulder, sewn in carefully. Stitch on the right side of the neckband, collar, etc. and turn. Seam the second shoulder with the neckband. Set in the sleeves. The arm and side seams can be joined in one. Stitch down the right side of the front bands and turn. If a zip is to be inserted, put into place as soon as possible. The crotch seam of trousers should be stitched last. Having constructed the garment give one final press.

Grafting, using the tapestry needle, is mainly for sewing knit stitch to knit stitch, but can be used for purl stitch to purl stitch and on garter stitch. Use on shoulders and for plain fabric on socks. (See also *Grafting*).

Mattress stitch. (See also *Mattress Stitch*.) Used where an invisible seam or blind stitch is required. On patterned fabric at shoulders, stitch raglan sleeve with mattress stitch and F/F side seams, sleeve seams, neckband ends.

To join a 1/1 rib. With right sides facing pick up the bars between the last two stitches from the edge, firstly from one side and then the other for every row. Pull gently and evenly. Continue to the top of the seam. This also applies to a purl stitch to knit stitch, and for a 2/2 rib. For purl stitches: purl side facing, pick up the bars of the second stitch from the edge of the first fabric, on the

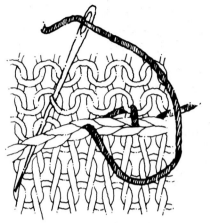

Sewing on a hem or waistband (slip stitch edge)

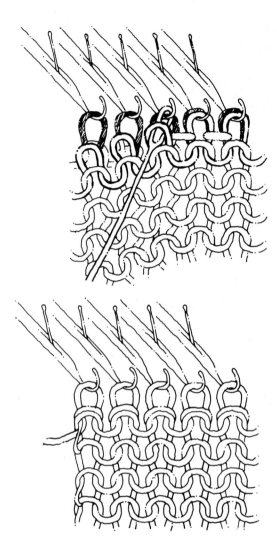

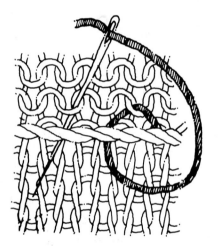

Sewing on a hem or waistband (back stitch edge)

Joining knitting stitch to stitch. Both fabrics face each other when picked up onto the needles. Knit side facing on the first and purl side on the second. Use at shoulder join

Break off the yarn with a long end and thread up the tapestry needle

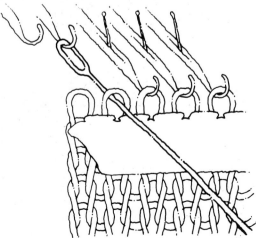

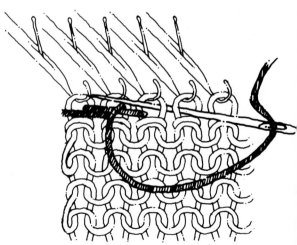

Cast off using back stitch

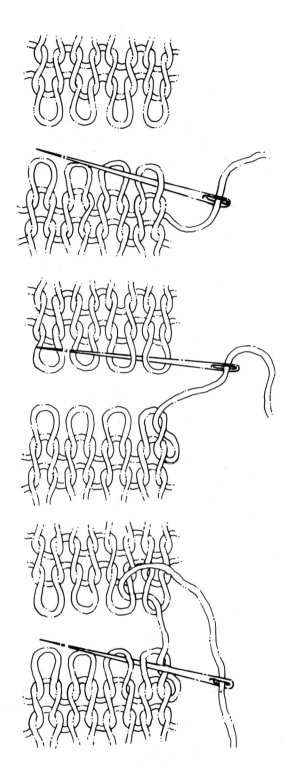

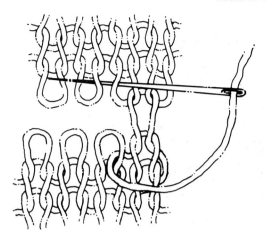

Grafting

Finishing off a 1/1 rib. Insert the needle into the first stitch from the back. Then follow diagrams

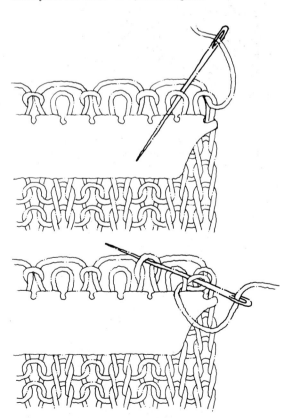

Finishing off a 2/2 rib

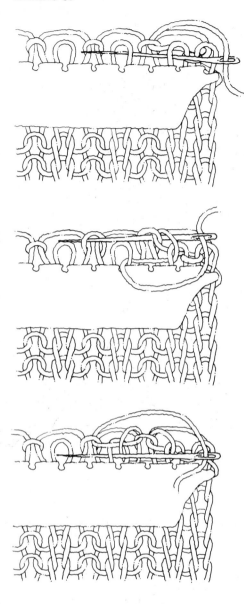

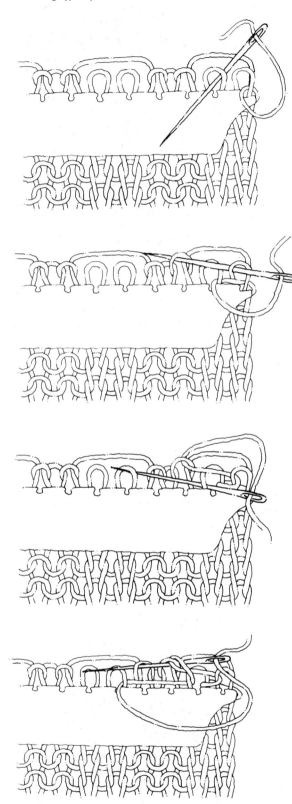

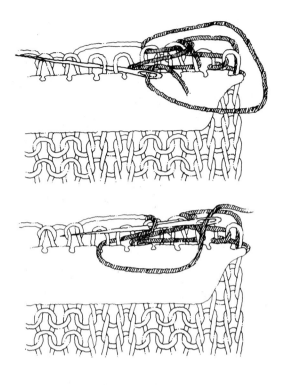

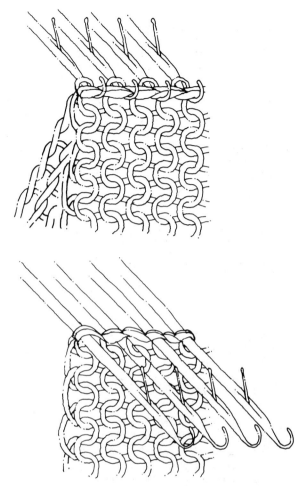

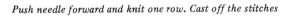

Joining knitting — ribbed knitting to side of knitted fabric. It is used for cardigan bands. The side edge of the fabric is placed onto the same needles as the main knitting, leaving some spaces so that it is evenly placed

Push needle forward and knit one row. Cast off the stitches

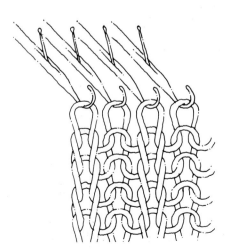

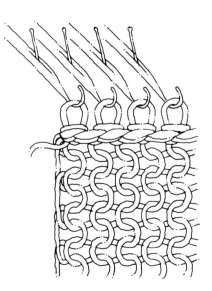

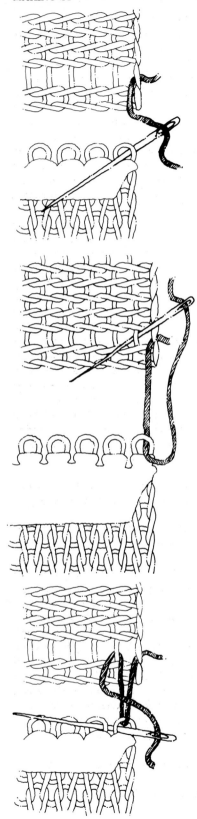

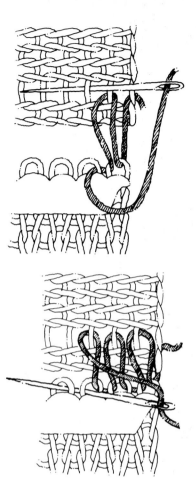

For joining a side edge stitch to a stitch with waste yarn, by hand, using a tapestry needle. Useful for borders

second fabric pick up the bars between the last two stitches; repeat this alternately until the seam is complete.

To cast off by hand a 1/1 and 2/2 rib, follow diagrams carefully.

Joining a side edge stitch to an open stitch. Used for joining a band to a cardigan. Follow diagrams carefully.

Slip stitch using the crochet hook. Put fabrics with right sides together. Using the crochet hook insert into the edge stitches and catch the yarn. Pull back the hook and insert into the next stitch, catch the yarn. Pull back the hook and insert into the next stitch, catch the yarn and pull the hook back again. Repeat until complete. Use for turning in hems and waistbands to the wrong side. Also for pockets. Some seams can be *picked* up and joined on the knitting machine, as seen in the diagrams. The edges are picked up on to the machine, one

Finishing open stitches with the crochet hook — waste knitting is then removed. This method is used if the carriage finished on the left side of the knitting

row is knitted, then closed edge cast off. Seams can be *crocheted* together. By using a double crochet a firm neat finish can be obtained. Follow diagrams carefully.

Seaming using the latch tool. Use on fully-fashioned plain knitting. Knit garment pieces up to the casting off stage. The first stitch which is normally cast off is left to ladder down the knitting. Cast off all the other stitches except the last one, drop this also and then remove the work from the machine. When the two pieces of knitting are to be joined, pull the dropped stitches so that a ladder is at each edge to be joined. Insert the latch tool through the first two loops on one piece of knitting, push through so that the loops are behind the latch. Insert it through the first two loops on the other piece of knitting, keeping these on the hook and pull through with the latch. The first two loops drop off the tool. Insert the latch tool in the next two loops on the first edge as before and pull through the two already on the tool. This is a method of crocheting the two seams with the latch tool. Always use two loops from each edge for every stitch. Can be used for skirt sections, reglans or anywhere where a fancy seam will look attractive. If the yarn is thicker, three loops can be picked up instead of two for a bolder effect.

Blanket stitch (see also *Blanket Stitch, Cut and Sew, Edgings, Fastenings, Zips*). The sewing machine can be used for seaming a garment but is best not used on rib-based stitches.

MAKING UP ON SEWING MACHINE, see *Bands, Buttonholes on Sewing Machine, Cut and Sew.*

MAN-MADE FIBRES, HISTORY OF, see *Acetate, Acrylic, Nylon, Polyester, Rayon, Viscose.*

MAN-MADE FIBRES, PRODUCTION OF (see also *Metallic Yarns, Roving*). New fibres are being developed all the time all over the world. Man-made fibres fall into two basic categories: regenerated cellulose, which is rayon and acetate, and synthetic polymer, which is acrylic, nylon, polyester, polyethylene, polyurethane, polypropylene, and polyvinylchloride (PVC). They are made by squeezing plastic liquid through a nozzle, which becomes solid and forms filaments of thread. A single filament is called a monofilament. These are then spun with other fibres into yarns.

MANUALS, see *Books, instruction.*

MANUFACTURERS, KNITTING MACHINE, see *Appendix.*

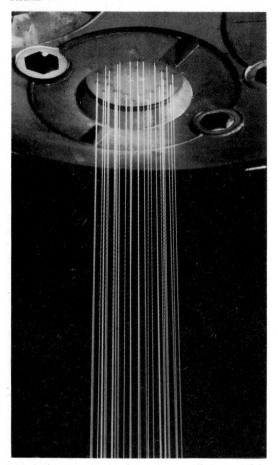

Spinning 100 denier 28 filament Celon yarn

bars, one stitch only, in from the edge of the knitting at the top. Then under the bars opposite one stitch in from the edge on the lower piece of the knitting. Pass the needle back into the same hole where the yarn came out in the top piece of knitting and under one or two bars. Continue this for several stitches, then gently pull the threads to draw the edges together, but stretch the seam out afterwards, so that it remains as elastic as the main knitting. Where double ribs or hems have to be sewn, start on the reverse side, work down the hem and up the outside.

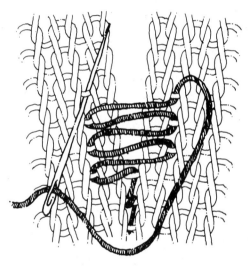

Seam joining with mattress stitch

MARL. A fancy yarn produced by one yarn being twisted around another one to keep it from wearing. One yarn is usually smooth and strong, and the other is a more fancy, hairy yarn.

MARKING FOR CONSTRUCTION, see *Tailor's Tacks.*

MATTING (see also *Felting, Pilling*). The tangling of knitted fabric which shrinks the cloth and makes it hard to the touch. Usually caused by incorrect washing.

MATTRESS STITCH. Is used where an invisible seam is needed, and where there is very little bulk. Hold the two pieces of knitting edge to edge, having been pressed, with right sides face up. Working from the right to the left, pass the needle threaded with the main yarn under one or two

MEASUREMENTS (see also *Charting Devices, Children's Sizes, Diagram Patterns, Pattern Adjustments*). Basic measurements are required when knitting a cardigan or a pullover. Length at centre back, underarm length, width of shoulder measuring from centre back, width at the top of the sleeve, armhole and the width of the sleeve at the wrist; bust measurement, neckband, width of neck at the back from shoulder to shoulder seams. Allow an extra 5 cm (2 in) on the measured length of the garment to allow for natural riding up. If using a charting device check measurements against the patterns and alter where necessary.

The pattern can be drawn onto squared paper. To calculate the number of stitches to cast on, measure width at the bottom of the shape.

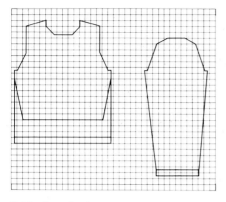

Set-in sleeve jumper

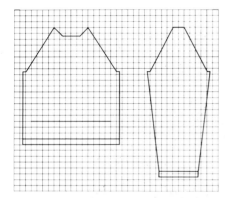

Raglan sleeve jumper

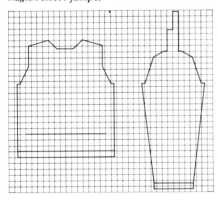

Saddle sleeve jumper

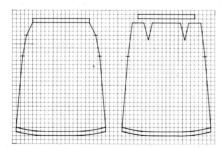

Basic skirt

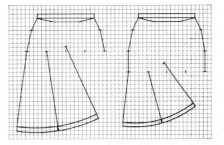

Panelled skirt. (Diagrams © Stanley Paul and Company Ltd, 1978)

Multiply the number of centimetres by the number of stitches per 10 cm on the tension swatch (see *Tension Squares*) and divide the answer by 10. If it happens to be an odd number take the next number up. To calculate the rows to be knitted, for a straight-sided garment, measure the length of the shape and multiply the number of rows per 10 cm in the tension swatch and divide by 10. Multiply the number of rows per 10 cm; this is the total number of rows. Measure the difference between the width at the top and bottom of a piece of knitting and multiply this by the number of stitches per 10 cm from the tension swatch and divide by 10. This gives the number of stitches to be increased. Divide the total number of rows by this number, and this will give the rows when to increase. The following diagrams are drawn over 2.5 cm (1 in) squares. These are the basic garment shapes and from these can be drawn and adapted the required shape. The tension square must be measured accurately and the rows and stitches calculated to every 2.5 cm (1 in). These figures are then applied to the diagrams as already explained and knitting can start.

Standard sizing for men (centimetres)

Chest	91.5	96.5	101.5	106.5	112.0
Finished measurement	96.5	101.5	106.5	112.0	117.0
Length from the back neck					
Sweater	63.5	65.0	66.0	67.0	68.5
Cardigan	65.0	66.0	67.0	68.5	70.0
Pullover as sweater					
Waistcoat	57.0	58.5	60.0	61.0	62.0
Shirt as waistcoat					
Jacket	67.0	68.5	70.0	71.0	72.0
Long sleeve	46.0	47.0	48.5	50.0	51.0
Depth of armhole	20.5	22.0	23.0	24.0	25.5
Upper arm	37.0	38.0	39.0	40.5	42.0
Wrist	23.0	23.5	24.0	24.5	25.5
Back neck	14.5	15.0	15.5	16.0	16.5
Width across back neck after armhole shaping for sleeves	37.0	38.0	39.0	40.5	42.0
Neck depth without band	7.5				

MEDULLA

Standard sizing for women

Bust	81.5	86.5	91.5	96.5	101.5	106.5
Finished measurement	86.5	91.5	96.5	101.5	106.5	112.0
Hips *as above*						
Hips finished		91.5	96.5	101.5	106.5	112.0	117.0

Length from the back neck

Sweater	53.5	55.0	56.0	57.0	58.5	60.0
Cardigan	55.0	56.0	57.0	58.5	60.0	61.0
Long sleeve	42.0	43.0	44.0	46.0	47.0	48.5
Armhole depth	16.0	18.0	19.0	20.5	22.0	23.0
Upper arm	30.5	32.0	33.0	34.0	35.5	37.0
Wrist	20.5	21.0	22.0	22.5	23.0	23.5
Back neck	13.0	14.0	14.5	15.0	15.5	16.0
Width across back after shaping armhole with sleeves	33.0	34.0	35.5	37.0	38.0	39.0
Shoulder slope	2.5					
Neck depth without band		7.5				

MEDULLA. Found in coarser wools, it is the central coloured core. Not found in the fine wools but there is a very small one in the medium range wools.

MERCERISED (see also *Cotton*). A process which gives a lustre to cotton.

MERINO (see also *Botany Wool, Wool, Wool Production*). A breed of sheep.

METALLIC YARN (see also *Appendix, Lurex*). These are made from 100 per cent metal, metal-coated plastics, plastic-coated metal, or metal wound round a core yarn. Metals used are aluminium, copper, gold, silver and stainless steel.

METRICATION (see also *Hand Knitting, Measurements*). Buy a tape measure with both inches and centimetres, which will help in the gradual change-over process. The basic unit for weight is the kilogram. One gram is very small; it equals 0.03527 oz. With balled yarns 50g = 1¾oz., 25g is slightly less than 1 oz., 20g is just under ¾oz., 1k = $2^1/_5$lb (2.205 lb), 1lb = 454g. 1 centimetre is exactly 0.39 inch, and 1 metre is exactly 39.37 inches. There are 1000 millilitres in a litre, 1000 grams in a kilogram and 100 centimetres in a metre. In general, 20g balls and 40g balls are man-made yarns, and 25g and 50g balls are natural wools. Man-made yarns are lighter than natural yarns and they give the same length of yarn and area of knitting if sold in these quantities. It is far easier to buy and measure in metric than to convert back into inches. The basic unit for length is the metre and for small lengths the millimetre. For everyday measurements the centimetre is used. The kilometre is used to measure distances. 1 in = 25.4 mm, 1 ft = 0.3048 m, 1 yard = 0.9144 m. For an area the square metre is used, and for larger areas the hectare. 10 sq cm = 1½ sq inches, 1 sq m = $1^1/_5$ sq yd (slightly more than 10 sq ft). Body measurements are taken in centimetres. For example, 20 in = 51 cm, 25 in = 64 cm, 30 in = 76 cm, 35 in = 89 cm, 40 in = 102 cm, 45 in = 114 cm. Height, too, is measured in metres, to two decimal places, and for small children in centimetres. For example, 2 ft = 61 cm, 3 ft = 91 cm, 4 ft = 1.22 m, 5 ft = 1.52 m, 6 ft = 1.83 m. When buying textiles 36 in becomes 90 cm, 54 in becomes 140 cm, 60 in becomes 150 cm. Eventually textiles will be supplied in widths of steps of 50 cm, 50, 100, 150 and so on. Paper patterns and sewing machine needles are also in metric units. The following is an example of the most widely used British system — the Singer system.

British	Metric
11	70
12	80
14	90
16	100

Crochet hooks are sold under the International Standard range; the diameter of the hook is in millimetres. Zip fasteners are now in metric measurement, for example, 4 in = 10 cm, 8 in = 20 cm, 12 in = 30 cm, and so on.

MILANESE. A type of warp-knitted silk fabric originally made on machines in Milan, Italy. It is a very lightweight cloth but a very strong one, and is used for gloves and lingerie.

MILL SHOPS. It is possible to visit some yarn mills and see the range in their shop. These are quantities of yarn that are excess to requirements at the mill. Mill shops are more common in Scotland and Yorkshire.

MISTAKES (see also *Carriage Jams, Cones, Dropped Stitches, Iron and Ironing, Punchcard, Racking, Unpicking*). *When knitting a pattern.* If a mistake occurs, unravel the necessary rows. Turn the row counter back for each row that is unpicked, as well as the pattern card. Lock the pattern card and take the carriage across the knitting set for non-knitting; the correct row has now been set on the punchcard. Re-thread yarn and continue knitting. When dividing for a neck and for patterning, make sure to note the number of the pattern panel row.

If a yarn is difficult to cast on with, cast on with waste yarn and then put the needles forward to holding position and cast on with the difficult yarn by hand. *If thick textured yarn catches in the yarn brake* then slacken off the yarn brake, and as the carriage crosses over the needles pull the yarn upwards slightly from the feeder with the free hand. This is slow but it works well with fancy yarn. Ease the yarn through the carriage and help it knit.

If the knitting is rising off the needle hooks then is is not weighted sufficiently. *If the balls of yarn are small,* and they have to be changed frequently, knot them with long ends showing; when the knot appears simply pull the yarn through the yarn brake at the beginning of a row. It wastes a little yarn but it speeds up the knitting considerably.

If sleeves or garment body have been knitted too short cut the edge stitch of the row above the hem and pull the thread to unravel the row. Pick the stitches up onto the machine unravelling a row if necessary to make the stitches even, and then knit the required number of rows. Knit the rib or welt and cast off.

If the garment or sleeves are too long cut the knitting as before, unravel the rows and then knit the hem. *If a pattern does not knit at all* check setting of all levers. If the stitches knit instead of tuck, the weights may be too heavy. *If the punch-card is catching* check it is overlapped the right way, or it could be that the holes were punched off centre. If this is the case put sticky tape over the holes and repunch them.

When using the cast on comb be careful before it reaches the floor that the knitting is turned up. Weight the comb evenly. Make sure to position cones correctly. *If using several cones* or balls of yarn be careful that they do not touch.

If the yarn breaks or splits it is possible that it is of poor quality, that there are knots in the yarn or that the tension is too tight. *If the knitting is uneven* then the yarn is not feeding correctly into the machine, the sinker plate is loose or the yarn itself is uneven. *If stitches hook on the gate pegs* the latch of the needle is not working correctly.

There should never be any *slack between the yarn brake* and the carriage. If you knit with slack yarn it will result in big loops or dropped stitches at the sides of the knitting. If the *tension is too tight* it will be hard to knit and more yarn than necessary will be used. If the *tension is too loose* the garment will be shapeless. A bad tension can also jam the carriage, create faulty patterns and harsh knitting. Dropped stitches or loose loops will occur at the side of the knitting if the carriage is taken across the needlebed too far. Listen for the click at the end of each row and then return. *If too much yarn is pulled down from the yarn brake* between the carriage and the knitting, pull any slack down at the back of the yarn brake. *Over-oiling* can stop this clicking and result in oil marks on the knitting.

Knots in the yarn can cause dropped stitches if a ball is wound too tightly. Dropped stitches must be caught either with a piece of thread for patterned knitting, or caught up again on to the needle with the latch hook. Each row takes at least two-and-a-half times its own length in yarn to knit. Do not force the carriage back once it has started a row of knitting.

If the garment is too long but the width is correct the fault is that the stitches per centimetre are correct but there are too few rows per centimetre. *If the garment is too wide but the length is correct* the rows per centimetre are correct but there are too few stitches per centimetre. *If the garment is too short but it is the right width* the stitches per centimetre are correct but there are too many rows per centimetre. *If the garment is too narrow but the right length* the rows per centimetre are correct but there are too many stitches per centimetre.

Loose edgings, cuffs, hems and neckbands are caused by incorrect tension for the yarn and pattern used, or this can be caused by pressing, and with synthetics it cannot be rectified. Redamping and ironing can often correct wool. With a neckline, for example, if the nylon cord is threaded through the band and pulled into shape and then steamed, it is possible that it may go into shape. *If a hem is too deep* several rows of sewing machine stitching with shirring elastic in the bobbin will bring it into shape. If this method cannot be used then the hem should be re-knitted. Cut the hem and pull a thread through the stitches to avoid running, several rows down. Replace knitting on to the machine. With wrong side facing, unpick a row until all needles have an even stitch. Knit 1 row on the main tension and then transfer for a 2 x 1 or 1 x 1 rib if a mock rib is required, or transfer on to the ribber if it is to be used. Knit the number of rows for the hem, weighting the work well and then cast off loosely. Cast off behind the bar gate to avoid knitting pulling. On a single bed hem, slip stitch the edge to the inside, sandwiching the picked up edge. For a ribber hem the work is completed on the cast off row. Make sure, however, that the picked up point is neat. To lengthen or shorten a garment this is the method to use.

With Fair Isle knitting, if an occasional stitch

has been knitted in the wrong colour, it can be corrected by embroidery, called swiss darning. If a punchcard causes this error, check the card carefully to make sure the hole is central or not distorted. If it looks faulty cover the hole on the back and front with sticky tape and re-punch. To see which row the machine is programmed for, put the card lock to hold; the teeth come forward and the needle selection for that row can be seen clearly. (See *Punchcards*).

Dropped stitches are repaired by using the latch tool and an oddment of yarn to secure it at the back of the knitting. Smocking can correct a rather loose top as it pulls the garment in, or a ribbon could be threaded through the neckline and tied. For small tops the sides can be replaced on to the machine and the required number of rows knitted. If it is likely to show where the rows have been added, use a contrast yarn and make a feature of it. Should the garment sides be too long for the machine, knit the pieces separately and sew them on to the main garment pieces. If a line of knitting is too tight or has a fault, a fancy edging can be added to cover the error.

MOCK ARAN (see also *Bobbles, Cables, Cords, knitted*). On the knitting machine it is possible to produce an Aran effect. Bobbles and cord knitting are applied to a simple stocking stitch pattern either on the plain or purl side of the knitting. More elaborate effects are achieved by using a tuck stitch pattern and applying the bobbles and cord on to their surface. For the cord instructions see under the separate heading. This cording can be made of various widths, usually with four-ply wool. To estimate the required length, measure the length of your pattern panel and multiply by three for each strip needed for the pattern. The bobbles are made by casting on approximately six stitches and knitting approximately six rows, according to the yarn used.

Knit a row manually of a contrast yarn. Leave a length of wool hanging as this will be used for sewing up the bobble. Repeat this procedure for the number of bobbles required. Press knitting with a damp cloth to prevent unravelling. Pull out waste yarn knitted in at every sixth row, so the work is separated into small sections. Thread the long end of yarn into a darning needle and thread through each loop at the top, then thread through the side and through each stitch at the bottom and up the other side. Draw up the thread and tie to the other loose end. The bobble is formed and can be attached to the main knitting by the loose ends. A wooden bead can be inserted prior to drawing

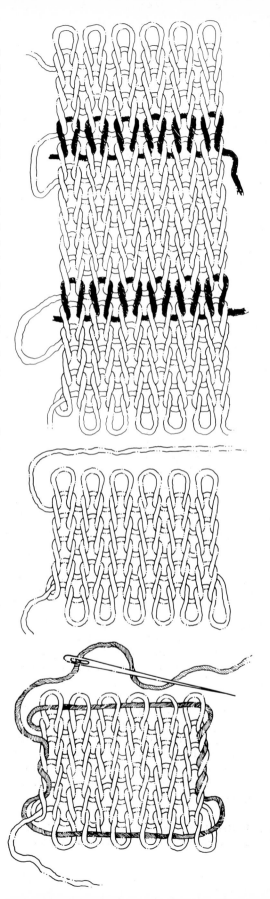

How to make a bobble

Mock Aran, showing cable and diamond patterns with bobbles. (©Stanley Paul and Company Ltd, 1978)

single bed are referred to as mock ribs. Because they are a double band bent in half, and the needles are left out of working position, the rib effect is achieved by the yarn floating over the needle space on to the next needle. Another rib effect can be achieved by laddering a stitch and using the latch tool to catch up the stitch the opposite way, creating a rib. Excellent for dresses at the waist, to retain shape.

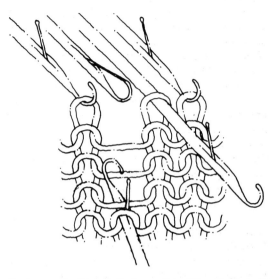

To form a rib stitch. Push the needles of the stitches to be re-formed forward into non-working position, across the needlebed. Insert the latchet hook into the first held stitch where the ribbing is to start and ladder the stitch to this point. Reform the stitches from the front, back onto the empty needle in working position

up the threads. The cord is laid on the garment in a pattern and pinned, then stitched carefully on to the knitting by hand. The bobbles are then sewn into place. This mock Aran can also incorporate cables. It is also possible to knit Aran panels on the machine and sew together, a clever way of producing Aran as every panel can be varied. Plan out carefully on a diagram pattern first.

MOCK FAIR ISLE (see also *Fair Isle*). The background colour for a true Fair Isle pattern can be natural, brown, grey or white; a narrow pattern follows a broad pattern and two colours only are used on any one row. Mock Fair Isle simply means using a space-dyed yarn to give the effect of changing colour.

MOCK RIB (see also *Casting On, Flute*). 1/1 2/1 3/1 and variations on these welts knitted on the

MOHAIR AND MOHAIR LOOP (see also *Brushed Yarns, Iron and Ironing, Wool, Yarn Combinations*). Fibre from the angora goat from Turkey, South Africa and the United States. The goat hair is removed twice a year. The fibre is smooth and silky and these long fibres are teased out to make the surface hairy. The loop is formed by two tightly-twisted binder yarns and a thicker yarn that is fed far more quickly, causing it to loop.

MOTIF, SINGLE, see *Single Motif*.

MOTIF, SINGLE AND ELONGATED, see *Single Motif*.

MOTOR. Some knitting machines can have a motor attached so that the carriage is powered. Of course, it can only do more straightforward knitting. It is advisable never to leave a knitting machine while the motor is in operation.

NAP. The surface pile that lies in one direction only. Dressmaking patterns when appropriate, have a 'with nap' layout.

NARROW FABRICS (see also *Edgings, Embroidery, Plaiting, Swiss Darning*). The general name given to various braids. They are produced by the following methods: twisting or plaiting, embroidering, knitting, lace, macramé and weaving.

NATURAL DYES, see *Dyes, natural, Dyes, natural, history of, Yarn Dyeing.*

NECKBANDS, see *Bands.*

NECKLINES, see *Collars.*

NEEDLE (see also *Stocking Stitch*). The latch needle used on domestic machines consists of the hook, the latch, the stem, the butt and the shank.

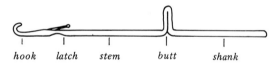

| hook | latch | stem | butt | shank |

The latch needle. (©Stanley Paul and Company Ltd, 1978)

NEEDLE CHANGING, see *Needle Replacement.*

NEEDLEBED (see also *Gauge*). Holds the needles in place. The needles are set into slits or grooves on the needlebed.

NEEDLEBED COVER, see *Accessories, machine.*

NEEDLEBED MARKINGS. Each punched line on the punchcard controls one group of needles; the width depends on the machine. The numbers either side of the centre 0 normally increase by ten and refer to the number of needles. There are also marks for every fifth needle. The other marks refer to the centre and the edge of each pattern repeat, and this depends on the number of stitches in each pattern repeat and on which machine. If a pattern is being followed always work from the centre 0 so that the number of stitches corresponds with the pattern.

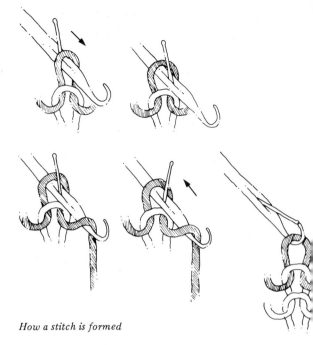

How a stitch is formed

NEEDLEBUTT (see also *Cams, Needle*). The needle is made up of two parts, the latch hook and the butt. The butts protrude above the needlebed and the needle is moved by pushing the butts back and forth. The raising and lowering movements are obtained by cams which are on the carriage of the machine. In its highest position the raising cam is out of action. It passes above the butts of the needles leaving them unworking. In its lowest position the raising cam is right down and causes the butts to work. Long stitches give a slack fabric and short stitches a tight fabric. The adjustment of the lowering cams is called the stitch length. The cams are adjustable so that the butt is controlled to give plain, tuck or slip stitch.

NEEDLE, MACHINE KNITTING, see *Mistakes, Needle, Needle Positions, Needle Replacement, Stocking Stitch.*

NEEDLE POSITIONS (see also *Needle, Needle Position Conversions for Other Models*). There are three basic positions on which the needles can be placed. The non-working position is when the butts of the needles are as far back as possible on the needlebed. They cannot hold stitches and will not move when the carriage is passed over them. The working position is when the needles are in the centre of the needlebed, and they move forward when the carriage is passed over them to form new stitches. Some machines have two

NEEDLE POSITION CONVERSIONS FOR OTHER MODELS.

CONVERSION TABLE FOR NEEDLE POSITIONS

Machine	Non-working Position	Working Position	Upper Working Position	Patterning Position	Holding Position
Silver	A	B	C stitches behind latches	at B	D
Brother	A	B	D stitches in or behind latches	D	E
Toyota	A	B	D stitches in or behind latches	D	E
Juki	A	B	D stitches in or behind latches	D	F
Double Bed Machines					
Passap Duomatic	Out of Working Position	Working Position	—	at Working Position	use BX with pushers for partial knitting
Superba	0	1	2	at 1 and sometimes 2	3

Ribbers have non-selective patterning mechanism, but the settings are marked the same as the main bed:

Silver	A	B	C	at B	D
Brother	A	B	D	at B	E
Toyota	A	B	D	at B	E
Juki	A	B	D	at B	F

N.B. For all machines please read your instruction book for partial knitting directions.

working positions, therefore refer to manuals. The holding position is when the needles are pushed forward as far as they will go so that twhen the carriage is passed over them the held stitches will not knit. With this position some machines have a knob or lever to press or push to make them hold, and when released they will automatically knit the stitches when the carriage is passed over the needlebed. The needle positions for single bed machines are marked on the edges of the needlebed. The Passap has three positions for the pushers: out of action, working position, non-working position. There are two positions for the needles.

Basic needle positions. (a) Non-working position.
(b) Working position. (c) Upper working position.
(d) Holding position

NEEDLE PUSHER. There is a pusher on the needlebed for every needle and this pusher bed is situated below the needles. The pushers are used for certain stitch patterns. On the simpler machines needles are selected manually by bringing them forward with a needle pusher. These are found in the tool box, and either include some or all of these combinations, depending on the knitting machine model: 1 x 3, 3 x 1, 1 x 2, 1 x 5 and 1 x 1 with a straight edge for every needle. These pushers are used mainly for ribs but can be used for patterns.

NEEDLE REPLACEMENT. Needles that have damaged latches will cause faulty knitting and must be changed. The opening for the bar that holds the needles in place is situated on the left or right of the needlebed. Push with the bar pusher or the end of the latch tool on the left side and withdraw the bar from the needlebed on the right until it has freed the damaged needle. Pull the needle forward as far as possible, push down the hook at the front until the back end of the needle appears above the needlebed. Take hold of this with the other hand and remove it from the machine. Put the new needle into place by opening the latch and push into place. Put the needle to non-working position, push the bar back into the machine, and knitting can resume. If a needle is damaged during knitting, and a replacement is not available, a needle can be removed from the end of the knitting machine bed and put in place of the faulty needle. This only applies if the full width of the needlebed is not in use!

NEEDLE SELECTIONS (see also *Hand Selection, Needle Pusher, Punchcard*). With some machines a series of needles are selected and by pressing a lever this selection is repeated across the needlebed. The machine could alternatively have a set of buttons; the sequence is selected and the lever operates the needles to repeat across the needlebed. For both processes the needles have to be reselected for each pattern row knitted. On most machines now the patterns are produced by using a punchcard.

NEEDLE SETTINGS, DOUBLE BED (see also *Hems, Pitch, Rib*). Set needlebed up from right to left and set the needles with the first and the last needle to knit on the main bed. Put the half pitch lever on to P; this will make the ribber central. Push the needles into working position on both beds. Using needle selector, push back needles for rib starting from right and making sure that on opposite beds the needles are staggered, creating a zigzag set up. When an extra needle has to be left on the end of the main bed this is not included in the number of stitches in the pattern. This applies to 1/1 and full needles rib. It is important to consider the set up for ribs as the seams have to match when sewn together. Where the set up is unequal so that the ribs would be uneven, it is solved by adding a couple of extra stitches to the cast on number and then the edges match and the extra stitches make very little difference to the overall measurements. Where larger ribs are being knitted and it would be impractical to add stitches, the first set of needles can be split to be set at either end of the beds, therefore not adding to the stitches at all.

NEP YARN. This is yarn spun with contrasting spots of another colour caught up in the main yarn, which is smooth and strong. Donegal tweed is produced by this method.

NON-WORKING POSITION, see *Needle Positions*.

NOTEBOOK (see also *Knitting for Profit*). Always keep a record of every sample, plus a piece of the yarn used for future reference. It saves time and is particularly important if you have a further order for a garment that has been sold.

NYLON, see *Synthetic Yarn*.

NYLON, HISTORY OF (see also *Fibres, identification, Iron and Ironing*). The first man-made fibre made from mineral sources: carbon and petroleum or natural gas, oxygen and nitrogen from the air, and hydrogen from water. The very first nylon stockings were produced in Delaware and sold to the employees of the Du Pont Company in 1939. In 1940 nylons were available throughout the U.S.A., but World War II stopped this production as the military needed nylon. Since the war different types of nylon have been made all over the world, and there are now over one hundred types manufactured for textiles. Nylon is very strong and does not absorb moisture.

NYLON CORD (see also *Cast On Comb, Casting On*). Used for an open edge cast on, for hems and sampling. A cast on comb is used for casting on over larger areas. The nylon cord is usually supplied in the tool box, and is laid, after the first row of stitches has been knitted, over the top of them between the sinker gate pins and the needles. The two ends are held in one hand and pulled down firmly while the carriage knits several rows across the needles. The nylon cord is then pulled out of the knitting and an open edge cast on has been made. This type of cast on will unravel if pulled. Do not allow the cord to become knotted. A new nylon cord is obtainable as an accessory. If the nylon cord is unusable, a strong smooth piece of waste yarn can be used.

O

OIL IN YARNS (see also *Oiled Wool, Wool*). Wool yarns often have a lanolin dressing to prevent them from fluffing up during knitting or weaving. This washes out on the first wash and the yarn becomes bulkier. Allow for this when working out the tension; make sure to wash sample well.

OILING MACHINE (see also *Cleaning Machine*). It is important that the knitting machine does not become dry, as this could affect the knitting. Always leave a very light film of oil on all parts between the rails under the carriage, unless otherwise indicated in the instruction manual. Old oil should be removed from the knitting machine before applying new oil.

OILED WOOL. When yarn is supplied direct from the mills on cones (mainly Shetland wool, lambswool and tweed types) the oil is usually left in. As this yarn is spun in oil, the oil gives the yarn a completely different feel; it is hard and stringy. A larger stitch size must be used so that the knitting is loose and open. The garment must then be washed, either before construction or after, to remove the oil. Wash in detergent and squeeze well. The yarn will then thicken out and the knitting will become firmer. Four ply should be knitted on tension 7-8 and 2 ply on stitch size 5-6. This is for plain knitting. When knitting a tension swatch with oiled yarn it must be washed and pressed before measuring. At this point the texture can then be seen to be correct or incorrect. Because the yarn is soft it lacks strength, and it is the oil that strengthens it and stops it breaking during knitting.

OPEN EDGE CAST ON, see *Casting On*.

OPENINGS (see also *Crochet, Edgings*). Can be finished off by a row of crochet to help strengthen and neaten the edges. Stitches can also be picked up along the opening and either a fancy edge or a plain one knitted.

ORIGINS OF KNITTING, see *History of Knitting*.

ORLON (see also *Acrylic*). Trade name for an acrylic man-made yarn also called a polyacrylic.

OUTSIZE. Limitation of the needlebed means only a certain size of fabric can be produced. Outsize garments have to be specially designed using the charting devices and the diagram patterns. Extra panels can be incorporated to give an increased size.

OVERLOCKERS. These trim, overlock and join in one process. They are used to construct garments by the cut and sew method. These types of machine are used in industry and are not necessary in the home unless a great number of garments are to be made by this method. It is occasionally possible to buy ex-factory stock in the *Exchange and Mart*, but the machines take up a lot of space and are very heavy. Domestic overlockers can be bought; the Babylock is sold on the market, but most modern sewing machines are perfectly adequate, especially those that have an actual overlocking stitch. Otherwise, a row of zigzag and a straight row is sufficient to hold knitting, according to its structure. More stable knits are easier to handle and patterned fabrics are best used for cut and sew. Plain fabrics benefit from the look of the fashioning points.

OVERLOCKING STITCH (see also *Overlockers*). The seaming stitch used in industry to cut, oversew and join the edges of garments. Most domestic sewing machines now do an overlocking stitch.

PAPER PATTERNS (see also *Cut and Sew*). It is possible to buy garment patterns that are only for stretch knits. Because these patterns are quite expensive they should be kept so that they can be used again. This also applies to home-made patterns. The paper pattern pieces should be ironed carefully to remove creases. They should then be stapled on to thin card, the card trimmed, the pieces neatly folded and put in a cardboard folder, together with the instructions and the information from the reverse of the packet that held the pattern. The front of this packet should be pasted on to the folder for easy selection. Never use pins through pattern pieces; use weights to keep the pattern in place.

PARTIAL KNITTING. Only part of the fabric is being knitted and the other part is in holding position.

PARTIAL PATTERNING. A method to knit vertical patterns in plain and pattern at the same time, in conjunction with the punchcards (i.e. part area is patterned and part plain). Bring needles for plain knitting to holding position before each row is knitted. Some machines have extra cams for this method.

PART KNITTING, see *Slip Stitch*.

PART ROW KNITTING, see *Short Row Designing.*

PASSAP (see also *Accessories, Appendix, Diagram Patterns, Double Bed*). Swiss manufacturers of double bed knitting machines. The double bed does not have a removeable ribber, but works purely as a double bed machine.

PATCHWORK KNITTING (see also *Intarsia, Quilting*). Knitted patches can be knitted into garments by either joining them together on the machine or by hand. It is far more interesting if the patches are all odd shapes. Edge patches can have shaping so that the garment fits well. This is ideal for using up oddments of yarn or sample squares for children's garments. The patchwork can be random or planned, according to the garment being made. This method also enables another design element. There are two ways of achieving the patchwork effect, either by using separate pieces of knitting and sewing them or by crocheting them together. The second way is to work the patchwork as a single piece of knitting. This is easier to tackle if worked out on graph paper first, to ensure that the co-ordination is correct. Draw the basic outline and then fill in the shapes. If problems arise from the number of colours being used, it is advisable to wind small amounts around bobbins and let them hang over the knitting. Make a groove in the top of the card to stop the yarn unravelling.

Patchwork knitting worked in squares of varying textured yarn and stitch formations

PATTERN ADJUSTMENTS (see also *Diagram Patterns, Measurements, Tension, Tension Squares*). The most important information needed before knitting a garment is the tension. This is the number of rows and stitches to 2.5 cm (1 in). Check body measurements against pattern measurements. *The length of a top* is measured at the back

from the first vertebra. *The back width* is measured across the shoulders, from shoulder point to shoulder point. *The sleeve length* is measured from the shoulder point to the wrist over the elbow. *The hips* are measured over the fullest part. *For trousers and skirt length* measure from the waist line to the required length. Adjust patterns before knitting, bearing in mind the natural elasticity of knitted garments. If the person for whom the garment is intended cannot be measured, then the standard sizing chart can be followed. Adjustments will also affect the amount of yarn to be used. A simple addition of bust darts on a basic cardigan pattern can make a garment fit better, or the changing of a welt can alter the look completely. *To adjust diagram patterns* use the following methods. *For a pullover and a cardigan*: on the back pattern measure required length from the centre back. Lengthen or shorten as required and draw a new starting line. Alter the front pattern by the same amount as the back pattern. The shoulders of the garment are stretched slightly by the sleeves. This is important for a correct fit. If the shoulder line has to be altered, extend it to the correct bust size and draw the curve line for the armhole. Check sleeve length against the pattern by measuring from the sleeve top and lengthen or shorten accordingly; at the same time check the sleeve seam width. *For a raglan pullover*: on the pattern measure the length at centre back. Lengthen or shorten, also drawing a new side line, and then draw in a new horizontal starting line. Adjust the pattern front by the same amount. Measure sleeve and also adjust the length and width accordingly and draw a new line, not forgetting to calculate for the length of the cuff. For a skirt measure the

Pattern adjustments and alterations For narrow shoulders

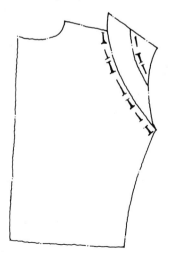

To widen shoulder

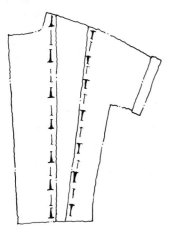

For a hollow back to stop the garment wrinkling

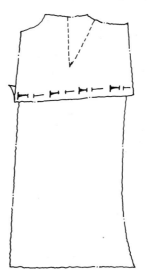

To increase pattern for a large bust

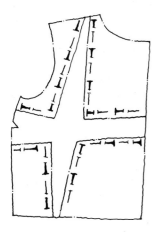

For large hips

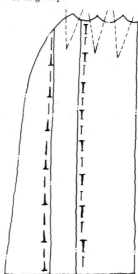

For a hollow chest, trim armhole edge

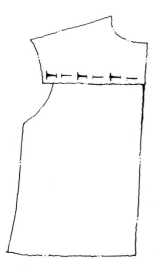

When widening trousers length and width must be added

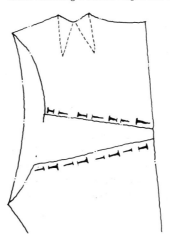

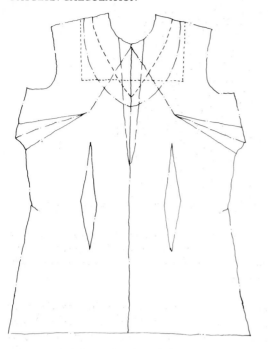

Pattern adjustments and alterations

length from the centre of the waistline, adding 3 cm (1¼ in) for the hem. Draw a new seam line and a new horizontal line. Panel skirts are adjusted in the same way. *A dress pattern* is adjusted in the same way as the pullover and skirt. Check all measurements above and below the waist and draw in the new line. Trouser length is measured from the waistline to the required length, adding 3 cm (1¼ in) for the hem. Check other measurements and redraw a new horizontal and vertical line. To create *a slim-fitting waistline* on a pullover mark on the pattern the required width adding at least 1 cm (³⁄₈ in) for ease, and draw a new line from the underarm to this point and then to the hip. To make *a sleeveless pullover* from a pullover pattern, a new line must be drawn for the armhole, accounting for the width of the armband. Cardigan band patterns can be redrawn to take collars.

PATTERN CALCULATION, see *Designing*.

PATTERNS, CONTINENTAL. Patterns can easily be adapted provided that there is a picture of the garment and a sketch of the outline of each garment piece with numbers next to them. Ignore these figures and take your own measurements. Knit a fabric sample and work out the rows and stitches. Convert all the measurements to rows and stitches and place these figures against the

garment pieces. Work out the increasings and decreasings and proceed to knit.

PATTERN DRIVER, see *Charting Devices*.

PATTERNS, HAND-KNITTING (see also *Mock Rib*). Some hand-knitted designs can be adapted for the machine but many are unsuitable, therefore think carefully before trying to adapt from a hand pattern. It is far safer to adapt the design details from the hand-knitting pattern that appeals to you onto a basic machine-knitted pattern, or to design with these details on to a diagram pattern. It is possible to hand knit ribs and then place them on to the knitting machine to knit the main body pieces. This is very time consuming though, and it is far easier to ladder a welt and catch it up with the latch tool to form a mock rib.

PATTERN MEMORY (CARRIAGE), see *Punchcard*.

PATTERNS, PROBLEMS WITH (see also *Appendix, Designing, Mistakes, Yarn Substituting*). The main problems that arise are caused by incorrect tensions due to lack of tension swatches. When using charting devices make sure that each step is followed correctly. Set row counter, insert sheet correctly, follow the right line and for ease cast off at armhole for both sides on the same row. When deducting or adding rows to garments, they must be gradually and evenly added. This applies to any shaped piece of knitting.

PATTERN SETTINGS, IRREGULAR: DOUBLE BED. When knitting a tension swatch on an irregular setting, e.g. when all needles are knitting on main bed but only several on the ribber, then knit it with this irregular set up and count the stitches as if stocking stitch has been knitted. That is, only count the regular stitches. Where increasing or decreasing occurs the needles on the ribber opposite the cast off stitches are cast off too, but are not counted in the decreasings.

PATTERN SYMBOLS, see *Diagram Patterns*.

PETERSHAM. A heavy corded ribbon used to reinforce belts, hat bands, etc. It can be used at the top of knitted skirts and folded to the wrong side. It is fairly stiff and retains its shape.

PICOT EDGE (see also *Hems*). Creates a fancy edge to a single bed welt by transferring stitches along the fold line. Suitable on hems, cuffs, neck bands, it is also particularly well suited to children's garments.

PICTURE KNITTING (see also *Beads, Cords, knitted, Embroidery, French Knots, Fringes, Intarsia, Pile Knitting, Pipe Cleaners, Single Motif, Swiss Darning*). Pictures can be built up by using part patterning and hand selection, and then adding various surface techniques, having removed the knitting from the machine. References for picture knitting can be obtained from books, by drawing ideas out of doors, or from museums, etc.

PINS. Use good quality pins that will not catch on the knitting. Never use a rusty pin as it will mark the knitting permanently. Ball point pins or silk pins are best. Do not leave pins in knitting for very long.

PILE. The word comes from the Latin *pilus*, which means hair. The pile is the surface of the fabric that stands out from the main construction.

PILE KNITTING (see also *Fringes*). Best used for collars and cuffs, baby jackets. Small piles can be formed in stripes either side of textured yarns for heavier type garments, for example, with jackets, coats and in picture knitting. Sometimes known as carpet stitch.

PILLING (see also *Garment Aftercare*). The removal of hair caused by friction on soft yarns. Avoid using yarns such as angora on a tight fitting garment, or where there is likely to be rubbing, for example under the arm. Perspiration can also cause these yarns to matt and become hard. Shoulder bags can rub knitted garments, particularly on the shoulder and hip. It causes the wool to wear and to become thin and see-through. If pilling occurs remove the loose little balls of fibres by picking them off, by brushing them or by using self-adhesive tape with the sticky side down to pull them away. There is also a little tool available for removing pilling. This can be purchased at local wool shops or haberdashery departments.

PINNING OUT, see *Blocking*.

PIPE CLEANERS. Can be bound with yarn and used to create a three-dimensional surface on knitted garments. They can also be dyed and used in this way. Useful for cleaning the knitting machine, having been dipped into white spirit.

PITCH. A lever is positioned below the needlebed.

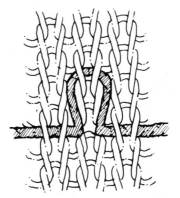

A piece of pipe cleaner inserted through the knitting

Pitch is when plain needles and purl needles are directly opposite each other. Half pitch is when the purl needles are half-way between two plain needles.

PLAIN KNITS. These have a flat front surface composed of the knit stitch, and a back characterised by the short horizontal loops of the purl stitch. Bought knitting, velour, panne, terry knit, and fake fur are pile variations on the plain knit theme.

PLAIN SIDE. Known as the technical face of the fabric.

PLAITING (see also *Cords, Twisted Cord*). Can be used to make a cord for a belt. The ends of a plait can carry beads to tone with the garment, and this will make the plait hang better by giving it extra weight. A plait can be made into any thickness and is made by hand. Plaited cords can be used as a drawstring to pull in cuffs of mittens and jumpers at the waist and cuffs. Seam lines can be covered by top stitching a plait along the join. To make a

Plaiting

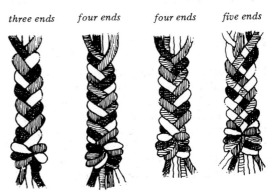

| three ends | four ends | four ends | five ends |

plait the ends are secured together at one end and the strands are passed over one another in turn, working from the outside to the middle.

PLATING. The knitting of two yarns, normally of varying weights. The fabric is made in different colours on the right and wrong sides. The plating yarn occurs on one side of the knitting. It is also possible to make patterns in many colours by turning the feeder. Not all machines have a plating accessory, therefore check with manufacturer's knitting machine accessory list. This technique is useful for using an expensive yarn with a less expensive yarn on the reverse side. An unstable yarn can be made firmer by plating. If a yarn is likely to irritate the skin, then a smooth plating yarn can be used. Plate with no more than a 2 ply yarn, fine rayon or metallic yarn. Tension needs to be at least one whole number higher for plating.

PLEATS. The regular folding of the fabric during or after construction which gives more fullness to the finished garment. They are put into fabric by pressing or steaming, or by special needle construction when knitting. Various types of pleats are called accordion, knife and box knife pleasts, and are formed by using tight and loose rows. The tight row makes a fold in one direction and the loose row makes a fold in the other direction. The pleats have to be pressed well. A knife pleat is three times its own size. Box pleats are formed in the same way but with different proportions of tight and loose rows. Knitting can also be made to pleat by pleating on to the machine before the waistband is knitted. Mock pleats can be knitted by leaving a needle in non-working position (the ladder then gives the appearance of pleats) or by using thick and thin yarn, particularly with the short row method used to produce a circular skirt.

PLEATING ON DOUBLE BED. Set needles for full needle rib. Cast on. Certain needles are then taken out of knitting position and these needles form the fold of the pleat. It is the number of needles left in working position between the empty needle on the main bed and the next empty needle on the ribbing attachment that decides the width of fold, as they are formed in zigzag intervals across the two beds. If the pleats are too big the garment can become unflatteringly bulky. It is advisable for adults to have the pleats start at the hip line and have plain knitting above. Use 2-ply or a fine 3-ply only for pleats.

PLY. The single spun thread of any thickness.

POCKETS (see also *Bands, Pocket Top*). Never use a soft fine yarn or have a loose knitted construction for a pocket. The knitting should be firm so that the pocket can be used. Use a yarn that will take interfacing, if necessary, for strengthening the top of the pocket and helping it to retain its shape. Bust pocket openings are placed 2.5 cm (1 in) above the beginning of the armhole shaping and centrally. On a V-neck a pocket is placed between the armhole and the V-neck shaping. On other garments a pocket is placed between the armhole and an imaginary line down the centre front. If,

Classic open pocket

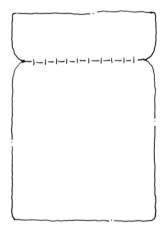

Flap over pocket. A row of garter stitch is worked on the turnover edge of the flap

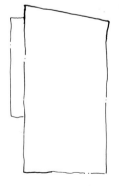

Slit (side opening pocket)

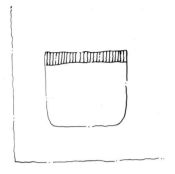

Patch pocket. A row of holes can be worked below the ribbing line and a cord threaded through to make a fancy drawstring pocket

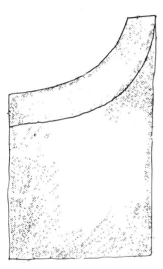

Top curve pocket

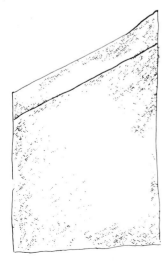

Top slanting pocket

because of the weight of yarn, an inset pocket is likely to bulge, use the following most suitable method. Knit the pocket lining in a finer yarn of a matching colour, or knit the pocket lining singly and then join it to the main garment by grafting to the pocket top and seaming the sides to the main fabric on the inside of the garment.

For an inserted pocket. When the point for the pocket has been reached, push up the number of needles for the pocket width and knit them back by hand with contrast yarn. Knit in knit 1 purl 1 rib the length of the pocket opening, making sure that two knit stitches are knitted on either side. With wrong side facing and the fabric upside down, pick up the stitches of the last row knitted before the waste yarn. Put the stitches of the last row of the pocket knitted in the rib on to the same needles. Some needles will have two stitches at intervals so that the stitches are evenly placed. The two knit stitches are placed together on either end needle. Set tension dial two numbers higher and knit one row and back stitch through the stitches with a needle. With the wrong side facing, pick up the loops of the first row after the contrast yarn has been knitted and place them on to the needles. Knit the inside length of the pocket and cast off using back stitch. Pull out the waste yarn.

For a patch pocket. Looks best if edges are turned in as this type of pocket is knitted separately and sewn onto the knitting. It is easier to use a matching coloured sewing thread. A contrast yarn can be used to top stitch fancier yarns to the garment. (See *Top Stitching.*) They can also be sewn into place on the sewing machine, which saves considerable time. To make a fold line for the pocket leave one needle out of working position; a fold line along the bottom is also recommended. Interface the actual pocket area only to reduce bulkiness. A lining can be used which enables a zip to be inserted if desired. Patch pockets can be any size and set at any angle.

Little pockets can be knitted by selecting the width and position and then putting the needles in

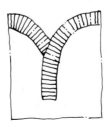

Double curve pocket

holding position on either side of the pocket opening. Knit the rows for the pocket and then bring the needles back into knitting position. The top edge can be crocheted having been removed from the machine and pressed. Sew the inside of the pocket.

Tubular pockets can be knitted on the double bed. If knitted slightly longer than needed, the top can be turned over to form a cuff. Decide on the size of the pocket and cast on for turbular/circular knitting and knit the length of the pocket. Cast off using waste yarn. Interface if necessary and then neaten the open edge of the pocket.

Pockets can be framed with bought fabric and the garment can be edged with this fabric too.

POLYESTER (see also *Fibres, identification, Terylene*). All the different types of polyester fibres that are used in textiles are made from petroleum chemicals. The first polyester was sold in America in 1953 and in British shops in 1955. It was discovered in Britain and originally sold under the trade name 'Terylene', manufactured by Imperial Chemical Industries Ltd (I.C.I.). Du Pont in America used the name Dacron. Polyester is now produced all over the world. It is very resilient and is often blended with other fibres. It resists moth and damp but can feel clammy in warmer weather; it also tends to pill.

POLO NECK/COLLAR. Normally knitted in rib so that it can be pulled over the head and still retain its shape to fit well around the neck. It is simply an extension of a neckband. The collar is knitted separately. The inside half that fits to the neck is knitted on the original number; for the outside of the collar, the first part should be 2 points of the stitch dial lower, the second part 4 points lower and the third 2 full numbers higher. Finish the knitting with waste yarn and join the collar to the neck edge of the garment on the machine. Join the first half nearest the garment on the right side and join the second half on the wrong side, down the side seam of the polo neck. The normal length of a polo neck is 18 cm (7 in) and the width depends on the size of the neck line. A detachable polo or cowl collar can be knitted to fit over a garment with a round neck. It is made slightly larger than the attached collar so that it sits well over the neck opening.

POMPON. Cut two circles of card to the size required. Cut out a hole in the centre of both and place the two circles together. Thread a tapestry needle with the yarn; wind the yarn round the

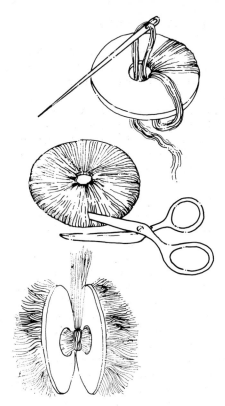

Making a pompon. Use two circles of card

card and through the centre hole until it is full. Cut the threads around the outside edge of the circle between the two pieces of card and then separate them slightly. Take a thread and wind it tightly round the centre of the pompon and knot securely, leaving a long end to attach to the garment, cord, etc. Pull the card away, fluff up the pompon and trim. A pompon can be used at the ends of scarves, having gathered in the bottom edges, or at the end of twisted cords, to tie-close cardigans — particularly on infants' clothes. Short lengths of cord can be used in place of buttons, or in place of bobbles scattered over a garment. For fun small pompons can be used on the turnover edge, in a row, on socks.

PRESS FOR IRONING (ELNA), see *Iron and Ironing*.

PRESS STUDS (see also *Fastenings*). Can be used on garments where there is to be little strain. They can also be used as a false closure with a knitted band and buttons on top. Attach them to the garment with overhand stitches through each hole as for buttonhole stitch, picking up a small amount of the knitted fabric with each stitch.

PRINTED KNITTING, see *Printing*.

PRINTING (see also *Appendix, Batik*). The following techniques can be applied to knitting before construction, having been removed from the knitting machine.

Fabric crayons. Finart Fabricrayons and Pentel pastels. The Finart crayons can only be used on synthetic fibres or fabric. If used on a striped fabric with natural and synthetic yarns it will only take on the synthetic yarns, and therefore some interesting effects can be achieved. The design is drawn onto white paper. The excess crayon specks are brushed off; to make a clean edge the design can be cut out. The knitting is placed on the ironing board and the paper design is placed face down on to the fabric. Use the cotton setting on the iron. Put a clean sheet of paper over the paper design to stop the colour coming through onto the iron. Exert a steady pressure over the entire design until the image can be seen through the back of the paper. Be careful that the knitting does not scorch and be careful not to move the iron too much otherwise the design may blurr. Remove the paper. If the pattern is to be used again, colour must first of all be reapplied. The colour is permanent.

Pentel pastels are used to draw directly onto the knitting. They work particularly well on cotton. Cover with clean paper and press.

Dyes can be painted on to knitting, and this is especially successful on wool. The dye is dissolved with salt and a little acetic acid or vinegar if being applied to wool. It is then drawn on to the knitting with a paint brush or sprayed on using an infuser, and a stencil if required. To make the colour permanent it has to be steamed; make sure the design does not touch other parts of the knitting. It can be steamed by being suspended above a saucepan of water. If shapes are being filled in with dye do not paint the dye right up to the edge, as steaming makes the dye creep and it will spread a little over the knitting. For sampling, the dye can be fixed when wet by covering with paper and pressing with a hot iron.

Silkscreen. By using a simple wooden frame and stretching organdie or terylene (according to the dyes) over the frame, stencils can be screened over the knitted surface. Uni-Dye sell small pots of dye and give the instructions for making dye into a paste; it needs to be made, thick enough to squeegee across the knitting without bleeding under the stencil or design. A squeegee is a wooden wedge with a rubber edge that fits the width of the silkscreen.

Discharge printing is the reverse of the normal printing. The colour is removed from a previously dyed dark fabric, using the design and a bleaching agent for removing the dye. Then the design is reprinted with the new colour where it was previously removed. It is therefore a process for putting light coloured prints onto a dark background.

Stretching fabric over a silk screen and securing with staples

Centralising the paper for a test print

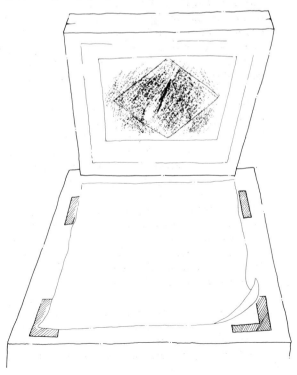

PRINTING

The screen is ready to take the ink

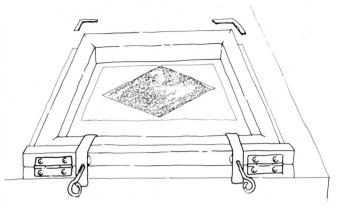

The squeegee is pulled across the print by hand

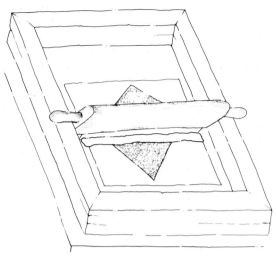

Pouring the ink across the top of the screen

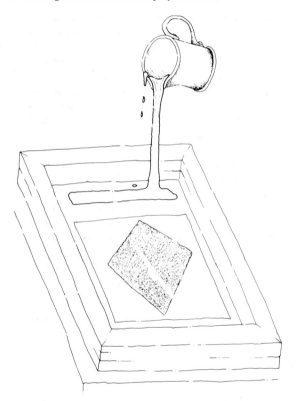

The excess ink is banged off the squeegee and onto the gummed paper on the edge of the screen

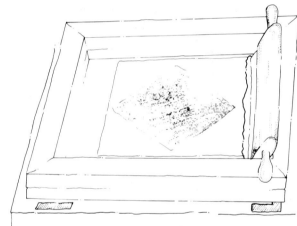

The squeegee is lifted carefully away from the print, taking care not to lift the screen. The silk screen is then lifted off the paper, and the print is complete. For a more complex print, a screen has to be prepared for each new colour that appears on the design

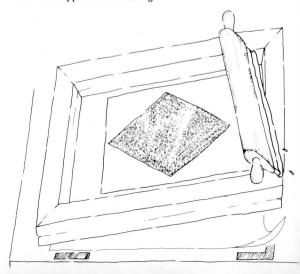

Dryad produce fabric inks and a binder, and Dylon make inks that can be drawn directly on to the fabric. They come with full instructions. Masking tape can be pressed onto the underside of a silk screen in strips to form diamond shapes, for example. The dye will only take where the screen is not covered. An effective diamond pattern is therefore achieved, and if different colours of inks are dripped across the top edge of the screen and then pulled across with the squeegee a mottled or marbled effect is achieved. This fabric has to be steamed as with spray dye in order to set it into the fabric and remove the hard feeling of the surface.

Wax resist can be used to make designs. (See *Batik*).

Tie and dye can be applied to knitting, but is best used on fine fabrics such as rayon or cotton. The knitting is bound securely with string or a colourless yarn, at varying intervals. Where the yarn covers the knitting it resists the dye. The dye colour has to be darker than the original knitting and if more than one colour is to be

used on to the knitting then the dye must get darker after each dyeing. The dye is mixed in the dye bath with plenty of salt and the dyed knitting is put either right into the dye pot or held so that the edge of the fabric does not dye. If more colour is to be applied then the knitting is tied in more places and put into the second colour dye pot. Where the knitting was first tied, the colour of the main knitting is retained and on the second dyeing the colour from the first dye bath is retained. Having removed the string, the knitting has three colours. This is a very effective way of making fancy pockets.

Tritik is a version of tie and dye except that it is produced by running a long and strong thread along a line on the fabric, and then pulling the thread tight when the line is complete. The fabric is dyed and the dye resists where the thread has been run. Use a running stitch and oversew several times at the beginning of the row, to take the strain of the pulling. Transfer printing is acheived by using colour transfer paints (obtainable from Lowe and Carre Ltd). The paints are drawn onto paper and then pressed with an iron onto the fabric, so that quite fine detail can be achieved. (See *Appendix*).

Dylon fabric paints. These can be bought from most large stores and can be used to paint directly onto knitting. The paint must be left to dry and then fixed into the knitting by ironing lightly or putting the garment into the tumble dryer. It can then be washed to remove any stiffness. The dyes can be mixed together to create other colours. Apply with a wet artist's paint brush and dilute the dyes slightly with a little water before applying. Do not use them on textured yarns.

Tie and dye. Fabric ready for dyeing

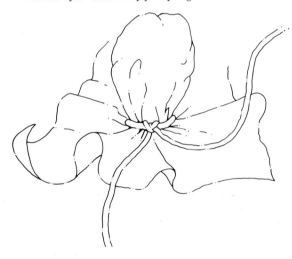

Fabric bound ready for marbling

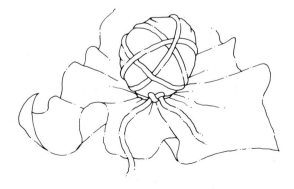

Tie and dye. Fabric is folded and bound with string ready for dyeing

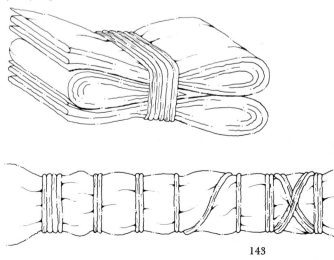

PRESSING, see *Iron and Ironing, Steaming*.

PUBLICATIONS, see *Appendix*.

PUFF SLEEVE (see also *Sleeves*). To alter a diagram pattern to take a puff sleeve, draw a line out from the main sleeve centre for the extra width required and take this line vertically down the diagram. Measure around the arm and draw a pattern for the cuff, the sleeve is then gathered to fit the garment and eased onto the cuff.

PUNCHCARDS (see also *Mistakes, Punchcard Clamps, Single Motif*). These are plastic cards with holes punched in them that produce patterned fabric on the knitting machine. A set of pre-punched cards are normally supplied with each machine and a set of cards for the single motif, which is an isolated single pattern. Sets of cards are also available as an accessory. The holes and the blanks on the cards relate to various stitches. *Tuck:* the blanks tuck and the holes knit plain. *Slip:* the blanks slip and the holes knit plain. *Lace:* the holes knit lace and the blanks knit plain. *Weave:* the holes float and the blanks weave in. Each row of holes and blanks on the card controls which stitches will be patterning across the entire width of the needlebed in working position. Some punchcards have a maximum repeat of 24 stitches and others have a 40 repeat. The selected card is fed into a slot on the machine and the ends held together with little plastic clamps. Put the starting line parallel with the panel where it was inserted. Make sure that the letter markings on the card are used for reference, as this would affect an uneven pattern. The card must be the correct way up. Different machines have varied starting points for the card; check instruction manuals. The way each machine picks up the information on the card also varies, as the pattern has to be set into the memory. The Passap has an 0 to start on, and this is seven rows down from the first row of the pattern. The carriage is set to the appropriate settings for the pattern selected. The carriage is then taken over the selected needles in working position and the needles are selected automatically for that pattern. The card then moves on to the next row and the carriage is taken across once again. Passap only supply pre-punched cards called Deco cards; on their machines the cards move upwards, but on the Japanese machines they move downwards. Blank cards, for designing original ideas with the use of the hand punch or ratchet punch, can be bought separately. If the design is being punched by hand and it is longer than one card, continue onto another card, clamping the two together, having trimmed the card down to the size required.

The electronic machines vary, but usually have a wider repeat of 60 or more. Instead of punching a card, squares are blocked in on a sheet with a special pen; the machine is programmed where the pattern is to appear. Many varied designs can be drawn or a part pattern repeated on this sheet. Motifs can be mirrored widthwise or lengthwise, and the length doubled both ways. The colours can be reversed or two different motifs knitted at at the same time. *Knitting designs that are more than 24 stitches wide*. This can be done either by *(i)* knitting garments sideways or *(ii)* using small areas that are blank on a card. With *(i)* the width, therefore, becomes the length. If knitting letters or numbers which were punched for vertical knitting they have to be lengthened to account for the difference between the proportion of the stitches and rows. With *(ii)*, if an abstract, more random design is being knitted, several extra stitches can be added by punching part of the design on a blank area. When the pattern is knitted the extra punched part will link up with the main part of the design.

Holding position for patterned knitting. Do not use the normal holding position when knitting patterned fabric, the only exception being on bust darts, on a curve of a hem or where it had to be used. For holding stitches for neck shaping, knit back the stitches manually using the nylon cord into non-working position at the back of the needlebed. Place the nylon cord over each needle hook, having pushed the needle forward so that the stitch goes behind the latch, then push the needle backwards. A new long knitted loop will form on the needle. This method is also excellent when using light coloured yarns either on a patterned or plain fabric, as it avoids the dirty line and fluffing often caused by the movement across the knitting of the brushes under the sinker plate. This can be avoided to a certain extent by using the other method of holding and placing a strip of self adhesive tape over the top of the held knitting. When using the Deco card on the Passap the stitches can be put on to Decker Combs. The hold on BX can be used for Fair Isle. The needles are placed in hold; the pushers will probably have to be returned to the blocking rail, so make a note of their position before moving them. When using only the singlebed, stitches can be transferred to the back bed to hold them. If the normal hold position is used, then each stitch must be replaced onto its needle hook by using a single transfer tool.

Remember when dividing knitting for holding position to write down the row on the punch card. When one side of the knitting is complete the card has to be reset for the second half. Therefore the carriage must cross the knitting once without knitting the stitches to set the row into the patterning mechanism.

To reset the pattern after a mistake. Unravel the rows of knitting by pulling gently on the yarn so that the next row of stitches slip on to the needle hook. Turn the punchcard back for the number of unravelled rows. Lock punchcard and set carriage so that it crosses over the needle without knitting to preset the pattern row. Reset machine and continue knitting. On the Passap the punchcard moves one row every two or four rows of the lock (carriage), so the knitting must be unravelled until the row of stitches are on the last row of either the two or four rows. The card is then turned back one row. The selector is put to 0 to disconnect the lock. It is then moved to the left past the trip cam. This cancels the pattern. The pushers are then put into line at the bottom of the needlebed. The card is turned back to the correct row. The selector is taken across and connected to the lock. Bring pushers to working position in a straight line. Make sure to reset row counter — this applies to all machines. Turn selector dial to 2 or 4 for pattern and continue knitting.

PUNCHCARD CLAMPS (see also *Punchcards*). These clamps are also known as snaps; they simply hold the punchcard together. They are inserted through the connecting holes at the top and bottom sides of the card, keeping it circular so that the pattern continually repeats itself automatically. It is important that the lower half of the card overlaps the top of the card and not vice versa, otherwise the card could jam as it passes through the machine.

PUNCHCARD GUIDE PIN (OR HOLDER PIN). A metal rod inserted in the hole behind the slit where the punchcard is fed. Keeps the punchcard upright.

PUNCH, HAND (see also *Punchcard*). A hand punch for punching holes into blank cards.

PUNCH LACE, see *Lace Carriage*.

PUNCH, RATCHET (see also *Punchcard*). This is a heavy version of the handy punch. It sits on the table and a knob is turned to move the card for punching.

Punchcard guide pin

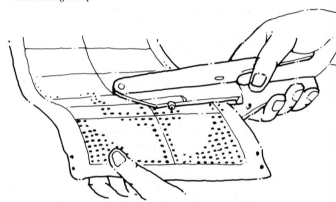

Hand punch for punching blank cards

PURL KNITS. These have pronounced ridges that travel across in a horizontal direction from edge to edge. Entire rows are formed alternately of knit and purl stitches. This fabric has considerable lengthwise and crosswise stretch and excellent recovery. It is usually reversible as the back is identical to the face of the knitting.

PURL SIDE. The technical reverse of the knitting which faces the knitter on the machine.

PUSHERS, PASSAP (see also *Needle Positions, Needle Position Conversions for Other Models*). There is one pusher for every needle, and they are positioned in the pusher bed below the needles. The pusher is only used for special stitch patterns and for making shaping easier.

Q

QUILTING. Areas of knitting can be quilted by sandwiching padding between knitting and top stitching, either with the sewing machine or with hand stitching. Alternatively, bought quilting or quilting made with woven fabrics can be used to contrast with the machine knitted fabrics, to make a complete outfit. Quilting is also very warm and is therefore excellent for making knitted jackets. The machine stitching can become part of the pattern on the knitting.

Quilting, showing wadding tacked between the knitted fabrics

R

RACKING (see also *Pitch*). A means for moving the ribber from side to side. It is achieved by the racking lever or swing lever, and can only be used on the double bed. Racking can make a plain fabric more interesting. Where instructions refer to 'pitch', turn the lever one needle setting or half pitch enabling the bed to be moved half a needle position to the left or right. The swing indicator shows the direction of the lever. Main bed is set to tuck; cast on with lever at central position. Ribber is set for normal knitting. Knit two rows, then set the lever one whole position to the right; this pulls the knitting diagonally. Knit two rows, and the pulled stitches are now part of the pattern. If the lever is then put back to the starting position, which is in the opposite direction, the knitting is once again pulled the other way and two rows are knitted. If the end needle on the main bed that is tucking causes loops when racking, then bring up another needle on the ribber opposite this needle. However, loops may be rectified just by using weights.

RAGLAN SHAPING (see also *Designing, Fully Fashioning, Measurements, Sleeves*). A sleeve head must fit the armhole shaping accurately for a well-finished garment.

RANDOM DYED YARNS, see *Space Dyed Yarns.*

RASCHEL KNIT. Industrial knitting, ranging from fragile tulles to coarse fur clothes but usually recognised by their lacy construction. A fine yarn restrains and stabilizes a heavier textured yarn, often resulting in limited stretch.

RAYON, VISCOSE (see also *Cones, Fibres, identification, Iron and Ironing, Yarn Combinations*). This man-made fibre was patented in 1884 by Count de Chardonnet. In 1892 viscose rayon was developed in Britain and patented by C.F. Cross & Partners. In 1904 Samuel Courtauld & Company became interested, bought up the patents and produced the yarn. It is known as artificial silk. The first viscose filaments were used in electric lamps. It is made by the addition of caustic soda and other chemicals to wood pulp. Rayon is made either as a soft or very hard fibre. It home-dyes very well and drapes easily. Industrially-dyed rayon, however, tends to vary between dye lots and, therefore, if buying in quantity be careful that the colour is uniform.

RECYCLING YARN, see *Shoddy.*

REMOVING WORK FROM MACHINE. Remove work either by closed edge cast off, casting off with big loops, straight thread cast off (see *Casting Off*), or by knitting six rows of waste yarn when a garment is being knitted, taking the yarn out of the sinker plate and taking the empty carriage across the needles – the knitting then automatically drops off the needles. (See *Waste Knitting*).

RENOVATION (see also *Darning, Leather*). Knitted garments cannot last indefinitely and they also become out of date. With careful application garments can be rectified and altered. A snag should be pulled through to the reverse of the garment and caught down by sewing with a needle and thread, otherwise the snag can cause the stitch to gape. Hems and sleeves can be extended and a worn knee or elbow section can be covered with suede or fabric which can be appliquéd on to the garment in an interesting contrast colour. A pocket can be added to disguise a hole. Garments can be unpicked, tied in hanks and steamed to remove the crimp of the knitting, and then the yarn can be re-knitted. A garment that has been cut and sewn cannot be unpicked but new parts can be added. Patches can be the same colour as the buttons, which could match the garment worn under or on top, or below. New contrast button-bands can be placed on cardigans. A patched elbow can match a patched yoke. Dresses and skirts can be lengthened by adding a frill or frills or by cutting off a section of the knitting approx-imately 15 cm (6 in) from the hem line, adding a bought piece of fabric and then replacing the knitting. Alternatively, the dress can be cut short and made into a top.

REPAIR, see *Darning, Renovation.*

REPEAT. Where a pattern occurs repeatedly across the knitting it is called a straight repeat. The uniformity of this can be broken when punching onto blank cards to vary the repeat. Examples are half drop, mirror, diamond, etc.

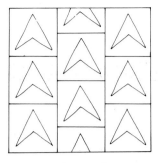

Half-drop repeat

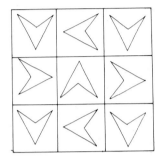

Quarter-turn repeat

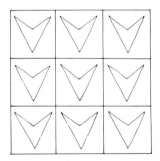

Repeats. Straight repeat

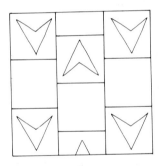

Half-drop turn over, on alternate repeats

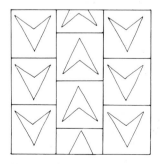

Half-drop turn over repeat

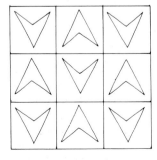

Straight repeat printed half turned

RETURNING WORK TO MACHINE (see also *Bands, Edgings*). Work is returned to the machine for bands, for joining two pieces of knitting together or purely because the knitting is too heavy to leave overnight on the machine. If it is not being placed onto the machine according to a pattern, then it is placed with the technical reverse showing, but pick up from the face side on to the machine. Open latches and place each loop of the knitting on a separate needle. When picking up sideways do not stretch the knitting; pick up two rows in and catch several on to the needles across the knitting to take the weight and then carefully and evenly pick up stitches on to the remaining needles.

RE-USING YARN, see *Unravelling*.

REVERS, see *Collars*.

REVERSIBLE FABRIC. Where either side of the cloth can be used as the right side. It is extremely useful when knitting a cardigan or a jacket, so that the cuff can be folded back on to the reverse side, and can be complemented by the reversing of the collar or neckband.

REVERSIBLE GARMENT. A garment that is made in such a way that it can be worn with the inside to the outside and vice versa.

REVERSE SIDE (see also *Technical Face*). The side of the knitting that faces the knitter on the machine. It is the back of the knitting, but with some patterns this becomes the front of the fabric. Fancy yarns nearly always show up better on the reverse side of the knitting.

RIBBER ADJUSTMENTS. Use a sturdy screwdriver. Slacken the clamps of the ribber, not the main bed. Slacken off the large ribber screws at each end, without removing. The ribber will move slightly. Gently push the ribber on the edge inwards towards the main bed. A part of the screwhole is showing at the front and the two ribber stops are close to the main bed. Tighten the two large screws at the same time so that the front part of the holes can still be seen. Tighten the clamps by hand only. If the knitting is piling up on the needles and not knitting correctly the height of the ribber might be at fault. The space between the needle base and the sinker pins is most important and should accommodate the thickness of a postcard with slight pressure being felt. If this is not the case then the ribber needs raising. Rack the ribber to the far right. On far left a large nut must be loosened – it is right at the end of the machine in line with the needle hooks in non-working position. Behind this nut is a round disc with two little slots on it. Put a screwdriver into one of these and turn slowly. The ribber moves slightly. Bring out main bed needles and slide the postcard through the gap in the beds to see if the resistance is felt. When the width is right tighten the nut. Rack the ribber to the left and make the same adjustments on the right side. Take the carriage across the bed and check that it moves freely.

RIB (see also *Casting Off, Casting On, Hems, Making Up, Mock Rib, Pitch*). On the double bed full fisherman's rib is tucking on both beds, but using one bed one way and the second bed the other way. The half fisherman's rib is single row tucking on the ribber bed only, and is also called English rib. (See *Bands, Rib*.)

2 x 2 rib. Both needlebeds are set with 2 needles in working position and 2 needles in non-working position. This rib is not quite as firm as a 2/1 but is simple to knit for decreasing. The number of stitches cast on should always be uneven so that the ribbed lines match on construction. Cast on with two extra stitches, one on one bed and one on the other. Having cast on plus 2 rows of circular and 1 row of rib, the 2 extra stitches can be put on one bed. This then remains the same for the knitting of the garment. With carriage at right knit the initial zigzag row and insert the comb. Both carriages are set for circular and three rows are knitted. The machine is then set for ribbing and the knitting can continue. (See *Hems*).

2 x 2 rib for double bed. Put the swing lever to 5 and the half pitch on P. On main bed put the required total number of needles into working position. From the right take every pair of needles down alternately into the non-working position. On the ribber put 2 needles into working position opposite the empty needles. Then swing lever to 4 and the half pitch lever to H. Cast on and knit two circular rows, then move the swing lever to 5 and the half pitch to P and continue knitting.

RIBBONS (see also *Dropped Stitch, Embroidery*). Can be threaded through holes created by transferring one stitch as for a picot hem. This can be used on a cuff or hem to make a feature and to pull the width into shape. Ribbons can be used to make a pretty feature, on either side of the neckline, and top stitched on the machine, with long ends left to hang free down the back and over the bustline, either in stripes or checks. Beads can be added to the ribbon to give it weight. Ribbons can also be threaded through a laddered fabric, or used to trim cut and sewn garments. Bought ribbons with loops down the edges can be hooked onto the needles and used for a fancy edging. If included on the centre of the knitting, the ribbon can be caught down on either edge so that it remains flat against the knitting. However, it is important to steam both ribbon and knitting on a sample to calculate the number of rows to be knitted between the ribbon width.

RIBBING ATTACHMENT (see also *Double Bed*). This is an extra needlebed which is attached to the main bed and converts the machine into a double bed machine. It is then possible to produce tubular garments, ribbing and fabrics based on rib stitches. The ribbing attachment can be put out of action once the ribbing has been knitted, and work can be done on the single bed.

RIBBING ATTACHMENT, see *Ribber Adjustments*.

RIB EFFECT. Can be achieved by using tuck patterns that have a vertical bias effect, but with short single tuck; for example, card on hold, knitting stripes of tuck and plain. A ridged effect can be achieved by sideways knitting. With two ends of fine yarn knit for several rows and then introduce an additional one or two strands and put the tension tighter; knit for several rows. Return to original yarn and tension and this results in a ridged fabric.

RIB KNIT. Has pronounced vertical ridges. Made by alternating sets of knit and purl stitches in the same row. The purl stitch recedes while the knit stitch advances, creating a wavy appearance and giving considerable crosswise stretch that automatically gives a closer fit.

RIPPLE FABRIC. A ripple effect is achieved by knitting pin tucks.

ROLAG (see also *Spinning*). A roll of wool formed ready for spinning after the fleece has been teased and carded.

ROLL COLLAR, see *Collars*.

ROLL NECK, see *Polo Neck*.

ROUND NECK (see also *Measurements*). Knit left and right of the neckline separately. Set carriage to hold — refer to manuals. Bring forward all needles

at opposite edge to carriage from centre 0, plus 3 extra from the centre stitches. These will not knit. Decreasing at the neck edge is done with the transfer tool. (See *Decreasing*.)

Decrease according to pattern until required number of stitches remain for the shoulder width. Bind off the stitches or knit waste yarn and remove from machine. Leaving centre stitches, return remaining needles to working position by using the transfer tool and placing the stitches back onto the needle hooks. Knit this side of the shoulder as before and cast off. Bring neckline needles to knitting position and cast off. Knit the back in the same way.

If pattern knitting, mark on the punchcard the line where the decreasing began when the knitting is divided so that both sides can be knitted the same. Having knitted side one put the punchcard back to the marked row and lock in place. Set the machine so that the carriage crosses the needlebed without any yarn. This selects the needle setting. Release card lock, thread yarn into feeder and complete as before.

ROVING (see also *Wool*). Staple fibre must be spun to make a yarn, and it is drawn and twisted until it is the right size. When it is at the bulky but untwisted stage it is called roving. It has less strength the less it is twisted; if it is twisted tightly it will become hard and strong. It may be twisted either way and is known as S twist or Z twist. Roving is excellent for weaving in.

ROW. Knitting from left to right or right to left over selected needles.

ROW COUNTER (see also *Tools*). Can be positioned either side of the rear cover plate at the back of the carriage. This is important if only one half of the needlebed is being used to shape a garment. The row counter is very important when following a pattern, for every time the carriage passes across the needles the number of rows that have been knitted are indicated.

RUGS (see also *Floats, Fringes, Pile Knitting, Space Dyed Yarns*). Can be knitted on the machine by using a stable construction and strong yarns. A pile effect can be made or a woven fabric can be used with cut floats. These can be varied in length to give a more varied texture. Rugs can be backed according to their construction to give them more stability and a longer life.

RUNGS, see *Flute*.

SADDLE SHAPING (see also *Designing*). Sometimes called an epaulette sleeve, it is used on pullovers and cardigans. The top of the sleeve head is extended and the shoulder line is shortened.

SADDLE SHOULDERS, see *Saddle Shaping*.

SAMPLING (see also *Yarn Combinations*). It is essential to have a good knowledge of the yarns available and to understand how they can be used — their construction, durability and suitability for certain garments. It is impossible to overstress the importance of sampling, for time well spent sampling will result in far better garments. Sample over approximately sixty needles and see the effect of the various fibres: wool, cotton, chenille, angora, mohair, and mohair loop, gimps, slubs and the man-made fibres. It is the only way to discover how they work, if they work and how well they work together. Keep a record of each sample and pin the record to the sample as you go along. It is not a waste of yarn because it is far better and more exciting to learn from mistakes and discover ideas on a small area rather than buy enough yarn for a garment that may not work out right. The samples can be made into a patchwork later on. Try knitting the same pattern with different yarns. The various tensions and textures can completely change the design. Remember that the feel of the fabric is so important, and a well-constructed fabric is generally a correctly-tensioned one.

SCARVES. Can be knitted on the single or double bed. If using the single bed, knit double the required width, leaving a needle in non-working position in the centre of the knitting for the fold line. The knitting can be joined on the inside with a small gap left in the centre to turn the knitting the right way, and this is sewn invisibly. Alternatively, the scarf can have two fold lines which are on the outside of the scarf when folded and the seam can be joined down the centre back. The scarf can be seamed from the outside matching yarn. Tassels, pompons, fringes, plaited or knotted fringes and macramé can be applied. Ribbed scarves are best made on the double bed. Scarves are an ideal way of experimenting with yarns, patterns and textures for using oddments of yarns

that can match garments. This can complete an outfit. If using a patterned Fair Isle border that has a definite right way up, be sure to reverse the punch card when completing the far end of the scarf.

SCISSORS. Use very sharp scissors to cut knitting, and keep them just for cutting fabric. Cut with steady, even slashes and never lift fabric from the table. When buying scissors make sure they fit the hand well and feel comfortable, and that they are the correct weight for the task they have to do. It is possible to purchase left-handed scissors.

SCOURING. Prior to spinning, the wool is washed in soapy water to remove the dirt, grease and perspiration; this is called scouring.

SEALSKIN (see also *Imitation Fabric*). Sealskin is a knitted or woven pile fabric made to look like real seal fur.

SEAM JOINING, see *Making Up*.

SEAMS, see *Making Up*.

SECOND-HAND MACHINES. These are advertised in local newspapers, in *Exchange and Mart* in the United Kingdom and in machine knitting magazines. Dealers as well as private individuals also advertise. Machines may also be purchased from dealers, direct. Do remember to check the age of the machine and the name of the model, and to check with the manufacturer whether parts and tuition are still available for that model. Check that all tools that are listed in the instruction manual are in the box and that the knitting manual itself is complete. If buying from a dealer check to see if the machine has been serviced, ready for re-sale. Try the movement of the carriage to see if it runs well. Ask to see the type of patterned fabric that can be produced on the machine and ask for a list of accessories that are available for adding to the machine, if required at a later date.

SELLING KNITWEAR, see *Knitting for Profit*.

SEQUINS (see also *Beads*). Varying sizes of fine, shiny metal or plastic discs with a hole to attach to garments. Sequins look stunning when actually knitted in on a double bed during the construction of the fabric. The fabric is set to knit tubular in sections and the sequins are placed in the pockets. Tiny sequins with a bead on top look attractive on a yoke and cuffs, combined with embroidery, and this is applied when the knitting has been removed from the machine. Too many sequins can spoil a garment – they should be used sparingly. To knit them in during construction, thread onto yarn and knit across the needles by hand.

SERVICING. Manufacturers vary with their repair service. Any machine that is taken good care of and cleaned regularly is unlikely to need servicing.

SET-IN SHAPING (see also *Designing*). The basic set-in sleeve for a top or cardigan, where the armhole shaping follows the line of the shoulder.

SEWING IN ENDS (see also *Darning*). Thread yarn end through a tapestry needle and insert it into the seam of the garment. If the yarn end is too short insert needles first and then thread the yarn. The yarn is oversewn or run down the seam edge. Alternatively, sew the yarn end in along the stitches using the tapestry needle if it is likely that the seam will become too bulky.

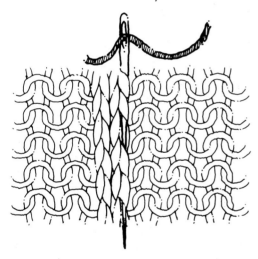

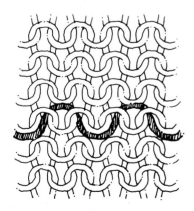

Two methods of sewing in ends of yarn

SEWING MACHINES (see also *Cut and Sew*). Can be used to construct knitted garments and to add small embroidered areas, and can be used with the cut-and-sew method to overlock or zigzag the edges.

SEWING MACHINE, CONSTRUCTION WITH, see *Cut and Sew*.

SEWING MACHINE STITCHES. The two stitches mainly used on the sewing machine to construct knitted fabrics are plain and zigzag. Some machines have an overlocking stitch and this is excellent for the cut-and-sew method. (See *Cut and Sew*.) Some fancy stitches can be applied to very stable knitting to embroider a small area. Shearing can also be used at shoulders or on children's garments. Shearing elastic is very fine and is put onto the spool, while the cotton is retained on the top. Shoulders that need taping can be stitched on the machine, and a piece of heavy cotton yarn is caught into place at the same time to stop the knitting dropping.

SHADE CARD (see also *Appendix*). Small strips of coloured yarn supplied by manufacturers on a card to show the variety of yarns, their prices and which are available at that time. Because of the ever-rising cost in producing these shade cards some manufacturers now make a charge for these.

SHADOW LACE. Patterns made in double rib. While the ribber knits rib stitches, the main bed knits slip stitches according to the punch card. Stitches are transferred from the knitter to the ribber at an interval of several rows as required. The stitches are transferred by using the shadow lace transfer tool which is available from knitting machine stockists, with full instructions.

Shadow lace transfer tool

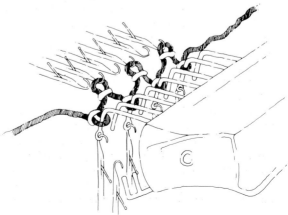

SHAPING (see also *Cut and Sew, Decreasing, Fully Fashioned, Increasing*). Achieved by two methods. The first is by transferring needles using 2- or 3-transfer tool to achieve fully-fashioned shaping for plain fabrics, or by transferring using the single transfer tool or pushing up single needles to increase for basic shaping. The second methods is to use cut and sew. This is when a long piece of fabric or a body blank is knitted and the garment constructed after cutting by using dressmaking techniques.

SHEEP, WOOL-PRODUCING, see *Wool.*

SHETLAND KNITTING, HISTORY OF (see also *Aran Knitting, history of, Fair Isle Knitting, history of, History of Knitting*). These original hand-knitted patterns from an island in the Shetlands are worked with one background colour, worked as an overall pattern or in bands of patterns on a plain background. Natural colours are used in undyed shades of off-white, natural, brown and grey, and a blackish-brown that helps the patterns to stand out. Sometimes a bright colour is introduced in very small areas of the pattern. These patterns originally came from Scandinavia and go back as far as the early Norwegian settlers. The same patterns can be found today in Iceland. The Shetland Knitters are also known for their lace knitting. In Unst, where the lace knitting started, several knitters remain to continue the tradition of lace fabric. It is so fine that a 'wedding ring' shawl can be pulled through a wedding ring. The origin of this fine lace is unknown except that the knitters on the island copied lace and adapted it for hand-knitting from a collection belonging to a Mrs Jessie Scanlon, early in the nineteenth century. She collected Brussels, Madeira and Valencia laces. The adapted lace was gradually evolved into the type of lace made today. Only approximately ten original stitches exist, although many more are used today. They have been given names to represent the beauty of the Island: Ears o' Grain, Print o' the Wave, etc. Because of the fineness of the lace it is knitted on 'wires', which are finer than the finest needle. Soft fine wool is used that generally comes from the area of the sheep's neck. To dress such fine knitting, it is stretched after washing between wooden frames so that it dries naturally and retains its shape.

SHETLAND YARN (see also *Oiled Wool, Wool*). This wool is coarse and soft fibres mixed together, and is probably the warmest of all sheep's wool.

Use this yarn double when stitching the seams as it is a fairly weak yarn.

SHIRRING ELASTIC (see also *Elastic*). Very narrow elastic bought in various colours on reels. It can be used in the spool of the sewing machine with ordinarily cotton on the top for smocking. It can be put into very lightweight cuffs to gather them into the wrist, or into the top of socks for extra support.

SHODDY (see also *International Wool Secretariat, Wool*). The name given to old woollen rags and garments that are shredded, so that the fibres can be reused. It is blended with new wool and made into garments carrying the 'All Wool' label.

SHORT ROW DESIGNING (see also *Intarsia, Partial Knitting*). It is used to make multi-coloured or textured fabric worked diagonally and horizontally. Can be worked by bringing one needle to holding position on the opposite side to the carriage. Knit one row and take the yarn under the held needle and knit back again. Bring the next needle forward and knit one row, taking the yarn under this needle and over the second. This must be continued every row otherwise holes will appear. (These can sometimes look attractive on a light-weight fabric.) Keep bringing a needle forward until one is left in knitting position. Remove the yarn from the carriage, put the last needle into non-working position, take the carriage across to the other side and thread up with the second colour. Put the first needle back in to working position on the opposite side of the carriage, using the transfer tool, and knit two rows. Continue this until all but one needle is in working position. Continue as before. Weight fabric well. More than one needle may be brought out at a time to create

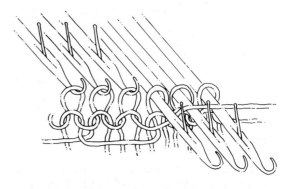

Short row designing — taking the yarn around the first needle in holding position to avoid a hole

a steeper shape. This method is excellent for using a variety of textured yarns, but don't forget to adjust the tension accordingly. Use for skirts, darts, yokes and flared jackets, pockets, circular mats, socks, baby garments, and on parts of other garments. If groups of stitches are brought out, when all the required needles are in hold, set machine for knitting in and start the process again. Skirts are better if a number of rows are worked across the knitting after all the needles have been returned to working position. Alternatively, if a contrast colour is used, when the needles are all in hold return them gradually in their groups; a square is then knitted with a diamond stripe.

SHORT ROW KNITTING, see *Partial Knitting, Partial Patterning, Short Row Designing*.

SHOULDER PADS. Can be inserted into stable knitted garments to help maintain the shape of the shoulder line. Do not make the pad too thick as this may distort the garment. Position pad while garment is being worn.

SHOULDER SHAPING (see also *Making Up, Sleeves*.) The shaping must correspond with the sleeve head shaping. There are several ways to shape a shoulder and it is worth practising to find the correct finish for a particular garment.

1 Over 30 stitches. Carriage at left, cast off five stitches at the left and knit 2 rows. Repeat the casting off and row knitting for four more times. Cast off the remaining 5 stitches.

2 Carriage at right. On left push 5 needles furthest forward and set them for non-knitting. Knit to the left and place yarn under the first pushed up needle at right. Knit to the right. Repeat this four more times. Carriage is now at the right. Reset carriage to knit in needles in holding position and then set the tension three numbers looser and knit one row. Cast off all the stitches with the latchet tool, starting at the right.

3 Is worked the same as No. 2 until the 30 needles are in non-knitting position. Set the carriage to knit in and leave the tension the same and knit two rows. Using waste yarn knit several rows and remove the knitting from the machine.

4 Best used for patterned fabric. Carriage at right; using nylon cord from the left return the first five needles individually to resting position. Knit two rows and using the nylon cord return a further

five needles to the back of the needlebed. Repeat the knitting of the two rows and the pushing back of five needles until 25 needles are in non-working position, and knit two rows. Raise needles to working position and pull out the nylon cord so that the stitches drop on to the needle hooks. Using a high tension knit one row, but not a patterned row, then cast off with the latchet tool all the stitches starting from the right.

5 Also for patterned fabrics. Work as for No. 4 until all needles are in the back position. Raise the needles to knitting position and pull out the nylon cord carefully. Using waste yarn, knit several rows without patterning and remove knitting from the machine.

SHRINKAGE. The reducing in length of a piece of cloth by steaming, washing or dry cleaning. It is essential to steam knitted lengths (depending on fibre content) prior to construction. Cotton and wool shrink more than man-made fibres.

SIDEWAYS KNITTING (see also *Partial Knitting*). When the horizontal knitting is used in construction vertically.

SILK (see also *Fibres, identification, Silk, production, Tusser Silk, Yarn Combinations*). A very strong yet soft, shiny filament yarn. Excellent shape-retaining qualities and resistance to creasing. The fibre is produced by the larva of the silkworm moth, and is formed by the hardening of a liquid emitted from the spinning glands. *Artificial silk* is made by forcing a viscous solution of modified cellulose through small holes. It should be knitted in the same way as rayon.

SILK, HISTORY OF. The cultivation of silkworms (sericulture) dates from around 2640 B.C. The Chinese reeled silk from the cocoon in secret until approximately A.D. 300 but eventually this process reached Japan, Korea and India early in the fourth century. According to tradition the secret first got out when a Chinese princess left China, concealing the silkworm eggs in her headdress. Silk was introduced to Europe in the sixth century by the Emperor Justinian, who persuaded two Persian monks to bring out a supply of silkworms hidden in a hollow cane. In about A.D. 1147 sericulture came to the western countries of Europe, to Sicily and Northern Italy. However, it took over four hundred years before it was established in France. Japan today is the main supplier of raw silk, with China second and Italy third. In the seventeenth century French Protestants escaped to England, among them being a number of silk weavers who were equipped with the knowledge of weaving velvets, satins and brocades, and the first English silk mills opened in 1740 at Sherborne.

SILK, PRODUCTION (see also *International Silk Association*). There are several different species of silk moth, but the most important is the *Bombyx mori*; the caterpillar of this moth feeds on mulberry leaves (and the Latin for mulberry is *morus*). The leaves of plants change within the caterpillars' bodies to protein, and silk is a continuous filament of protein. Some silkworms produce tusser silk (also known as Tusseh, Tussah, Tasar, etc.) or wild silk, the better known being the *Antheraea* and related species. *Antheraea mylitta* is also known as the Tussore Silkmoth. *Antheraea pernyi* is also known as the Assam silkmoth. These feed on the leaves of oak, ilex, beech, apple, willow and other trees.

The silkworm has a pair of glands running through its body. It has two holes in its head where the solution comes out and becomes solid under tension. The worm moves its head from side to side and gradually builds up the cocoon from inside. This continues even when the worm can no longer be seen. After about ten days the chrysalis has formed and the silk can be unwound from the cocoon. Some cocoons are put to one side and these hatch into moths that will produce eggs for the next season's silk production. It is estimated that one cocoon can produce a filament of silk two or three miles long. The cocoons are boiled and this de-gums the silk, making it easier to be fed through nozzles, eight ends at a time. This produces a standard 20/22 denier thickness. The last stage in the production of quality silk is called throwing, when it is doubled into thicker yarn for weaving, knitting and embroidery. The silk is put through processes of soaking, drying and winding and this puts a twist into the yarn. Some silk, however, is not thrown but spun and this is usually done to second grade silk, the waste silk. Slub effects in silk can be introduced into the spun silk yarn or by the silkworms being brought close. They often combine and make communal cocoons; when reeled, these cocoons produce a thread with slubs at intervals, which is known as Douppion. Fabrics made from this yarn are also known as Douppion fabrics. Silk work rearing and reeling can be seen at: Lullingstone Silk Farm, Compton House, Sherborne, Dorset, DT9 4QN).

SILK SCREEN, see *Printing*.

SILVER KNITTING MACHINES (see also Appendix). A Japanese knitting machine manufacturer.

SIMULKNIT. The colour changer for the double bed Toyota knitting machine which gives smooth plain knitting on the reverse side.

SINGER KNITTING MACHINES, see *Appendix*.

SINGLE BED MACHINE. A single set of (normally) 200 needles all facing in the same direction producing stocking stitch fabrics. The gauge — which is the number of needles per 2.5 cm (1 in) — is 6 gauge, giving a knitting width of 89 cm (35 in). Some manufacturers produce varying gauge machines, but most domestic machines are the 6 gauge. Stitch sizes are set according to yarn and type of stitch selected, therefore the tension varies the width of the knitting when it is removed from the machine from a maximum of 92 cm (36 in) to 60 cm (23½ in).

SINGLE MOTIF (see also *Intarsia, Punchcards, Swiss Darning*). When only one pattern appears on the knitting. It is knitted by the same method as Fair Isle pattern but single motif punchcards are used, and can be knitted on most punchcard machines. See instruction manual for information. Some have settings especially for single motif knitting. The punchard is inserted, the machine set and then knitted as normal. Other punchcard machines have stops on the main bed and the carriage is set to Fair Isle. The stops allow the pattern to knit or not to knit, when the carriage is taken across the knitting. It is also possible to mirror the design image on some machines using the stops. On the electronic machines the single motif position is set according to the manual and the pattern automatically knits.

For older punchcard machines that can knit Fair Isle, a single motif can be selected. Needles on either side of where the single motif is to be knitted are returned to working position. Knit 1 row. Repeat the selection of needles for each row.

For machines that do not bring needles forward a single motif is punched out in reverse on the card. In other words, the background is punched out and the second colour patterning is left blank. The motif is knitted between the same markings found on the needlebed. The contrast colour is put into the main feeder where the background yarn is normally put. The main yarn is put where the secondary colour is normally put. Push out the stitches to non-working position either side of

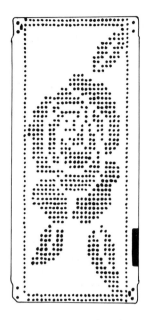

Single motif punchcard

where the motif is going to be. The carriage is set to Fair Isle and you knit across the bed. This procedure is repeated until the motif is complete. Then continue as for normal knitting, remembering to change over the yarn in the feeders so that the main yarn is in the main feeder.

For single bed basic non-punchcard machines where two yarns cannot knit in the same feeder, knit the needle using the contrast yarn for the motif by hand, then push the needles to holding position. Set the carriage so that they will not knit, and knit one row of the main yarn. Return the held needles to working position and work the next set of needles for the contrast yarn by hand and pushing them once again into holding position. Repeat the process until the single motif is complete. The yarn laid across can be more than one colour and worked according to the design for the whole or part of the single motif. It is important to remember to take the yarn round the first needle in holding position before knitting across the row. This keeps the motif section and the plain part joined together. Any size of motif can be knitted in this way.

To produce a single motif wider than 24 stitches. This is achieved by using squared paper and drawing the design on to the paper. The centre part is punched and the unpunched part is hand-selected on either side of the motif. The two edge needles of the punchcard motif must be marked on the needlebed. This makes it easier to select by hand on either side of the centre motif. The needles that

are selected by hand should sit with the stitches on the open latch and never behind it. Motifs can be added to in picture knitting by this method. The pattern width can be increased by punching the card sideways. On the electronic machine the single motif can be made much wider.

Alternatively, for a larger motif, set needlebed to neutral so that the needles will not select. Set carriage for laying in patterns and select the needles for the single motif by hand on each new row. If more than one contrast colour is being used then it is easier to follow a chart. Fair Isle patterns are produced on the passap by re-arranging the pushers and the single motif is knitted in a similar way. For double bed Fair Isle on a full needle rib, set the back bed carriage to N or to BX ◄───► according to model and how you want the pattern to look. Front carriage is set to BX ◄───. Pushers are needed under all working needles on the front bed, and if the BX setting is used on the back bed pushers are needed under these working needles too, in a 1 up 1 down position, and they need no re-setting throughout the pattern. Knit a two-colour pattern in alternate stripes of two rows. Starting with the main colour, the pushers of the contrast colour should be in upper working position and the pusher of the needles for the main colour should be in lower working position. Knit 2 rows in the main colour, then 2 rows of the contrast colour. Re-arrange front bed pushers for the next patterning row. For contrast, pushers should be up and main colour pushers down. Repeat the four-row order until the motif is complete. There is no limitation on the width as each pusher is independent.

To avoid a ragged edge with holes around the outside of a single motif it is important to wrap the motif yarn around the hook of the first needle in the background colour in the shape of an 'e'. This is done on every row on the edge that is nearest to the carriage. This method should also be used on Passap machines with the Deco attachment and on single motifs on the Superba.

SINGLES. One strand of yarn, not plied.

SINKER BRUSHES. Situated under the sinker plate assembly which is attached to the carriage and holds the knitting against the sinker pins when the needles move. Be careful that yarn is not trapped around one of the brushes otherwise the flow of the carriage is impaired.

SINKER GATE. Positioned on the front of the knit carriage. When the carriage crosses the bed each needle protrudes from the needlebed through the centre of two gate pegs. It holds the cast on comb, and casting off can be done going behind the pegs instead of in front. By using this method the knitting is tensioned and the knitting sits on the gate pegs until casting off is complete. Work is simply lifted off and away from the gate pegs. Should a gate peg become damaged or slightly bent the carriage will not operate properly.

SINKER PIN, see *Sinker Gate*.

SINKER PLATE. Screws hold this to the carriage. In the centre is the yarn feed where the yarn sits during knitting. This assembly also holds the weaving brushes and the weaving yarn guide.

SINKER WHEEL. This is underneath the sinker plate and works in the same way as the sinker brushes.

SKEIN HOLDER, see *Skein Winder*.

SKEIN WINDER, (see also *Yarn Dyeing*). Used for holding hanks that have to be wound into balls, for winding old garments into hanks for washing before re-use and for winding hanks for dyeing. Metal skein winders can be bought from machine knitting suppliers and wooden ones can be bought from weaving supply shops. The skein can also be

Skein winder holding a hank of yarn being taken to the wool winder. (Below) Yarn is run from the centre of the ball and should flow evenly

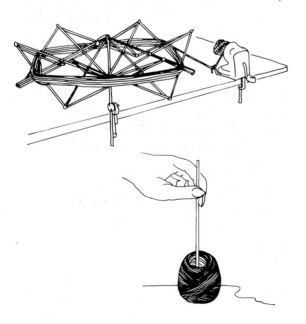

stretched over the back of two chairs. The winder, however, is fully adjustable to the size of the skein or skein-to-be, and has a handle for winding quickly. Be careful if winding from hank to ball that the ball is not wound too tightly. The skein should be held very firmly on the winder other wise it may become tangled. The ties are cut and the outside end is run to the ball winder. The ball is wound smoothly and evenly and is used from the centre of the ball so that it flows steadily without the ball moving at all.

SKIRTS (see also *Garment Distortion, Hems, Intarsia, Pleats, Ribs*). Can be knitted by the short row method, so that a circular skirt is knitted by holding needles. A skirt can be pleated or panelled from the waist or hips. Types of skirts are: A-line skirt, long skirt, tight skirt, gathered skirt, and culottes. Holding position is used on the loose edge of skirts, always making sure the yarn is taken around the first needle in holding position, to prevent a hole forming. The method for straight skirts, using three ends of yarn and the needle set up of 3 working 1 out selection, is to knit straight to hipline and then remove one end of yarn leaving two ends, and reduce tension. To lengthen or shorten on a diagram pattern measure the required length from the waistline and draw in a new horizontal starting line. To make a short pattern into a long pattern for a skirt, the required length is measured and the side line taken from the hips to the bottom width required. This also applies for narrowing a skirt; the new line is drawn from the hip line, provided that the hip width is correct. To extend a basic skirt diagram to make a gathered skirt, draw a new line out horizontally from the line below the waist band; take this line straight down the centre front to the hem line.

SLASH NECK. Straight-across neckline, which can be made deeper in the front, when it is called a boat neck.

SLEEVE (see also *Designing, Dolman, Dropped Shoulder, Measurements, Raglan, Saddle Shaping, Set-In Shaping, Shoulder Shaping*). Dolman, dropped shoulder, raglan, saddle and set in are the basic sleeves. Variations of these are short set-in fitted sleeve, three-quarter length fitted sleeve, long puff sleeve, short puff sleeve and flare sleeves.
Sleeve lengths. There are seven basic lengths of sleeve and all shaped sleeves and sleeve heads are variations of these. *Cap* is a very short sleeve, normally a sleeve extension of the shoulder and does not continue under the arm. *Short sleeve* lies

with its edge across the upper arm. *Above elbow* means that the sleeve reaches to the elbow point. *Three-quarters* ends halfway between the elbow and the wrist bone. *Seven-eighths sleeve* ends about 5 cm (2 in) above the wrist bone. *Wrist length sleeve* sits on the wrist bone. *Full length* covers the wrist bone by approximately 2.5 cm (1 in).

Whichever sleeve is being knitted, it needs to be shaped from the lower edge (other than fuller sleeves) to the underarm, to fit well. For example, with a long fitted sleeve the measurements needed are the length of the underarm seam, the width at the wrist and the width at the upper arm. From the underarm seam measurement always deduct 2.5 cm (1 in) for an exact fit. The sleeve head needs to be about two-thirds the depth of the armhole. The number of stitches to be decreased should be broken up into three steps. The shaping should start as the shaping for the armhole, which is quite fast. Next the shaping slows and a gentle curve is knitted, the shaping is fast again for the round top and the remaining stitches are then cast off for a straight line.

SLEEVE LENGTHS, see *Sleeves*.

SLIP KNOT. Is used to secure the yarn to the first needle when making a closed edge cast on.

SLIP STITCH. The machine is set to slip, the selected needles remain inactive and the carriage crosses over them. The yarn crosses over the selected needles so forming a raised pattern, and the reverse side/purl side of the fabric becomes the front. This type of pattern on the double bed produces a very firm fabric. By knitting thicker yarns on every alternate needle and combining this with slip stitch, interesting chunky effects can be achieved. Refer to instruction manuals for settings.

Slip stitch

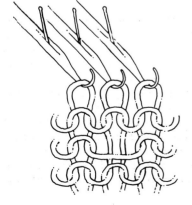

SLIT NECK, see *Slash Neck*.

SLUB YARN (see also *Yarn Combinations*). Textured yarn is made at the spinning stage. The fibres are spun unevenly, some sections tightly and some sections with very little twist. The coarser of the slubs should only be used for laying in. Any slub is better knitted with another yarn to keep the overall tension of the garment even. It shows mainly on the reverse side of the fabric.

SMOCKING. Gathering, usually on yoke and cuffs, with embroidery. There are many varied smocking patterns: the three most common are honeycomb, diamond and cabled smocking. It is the combination of such simple stitches that results in the attractive designs. (The diagram shows a trellis stitch.) Smocking is normally worked by hand, although it can be produced on the sewing machine and is given more stretch by using shirring elastic in the spool of the machine. Most machines give instructions for smocking. It is best suited to fine fabrics, including rayons and fine wools. Smocking tends to take up three times the final width, and is worked before the garment is made up. The gathers should be even, and a dot transfer helps. These are available from most department stores or appropriate suppliers. A thick embroidery thread is used to work the smocking. The needle is brought up in the centre of each dot and down into the next one. Return on the row underneath and secure the two ends together, having worked the number of rows required and gathered the pleats into the correct width. When the smocking is complete press very lightly and remove the gathering threads. (See also *Further Reading*.)

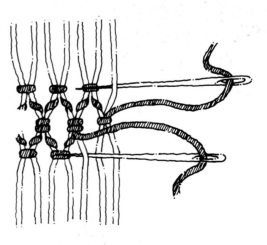

Smocking

SMOCKING, MOCK. Attractive used at the shoulders and in small areas, and on little girls' dress tops. A mock rib is made on the single bed by casting on and knitting a plain piece of knitting, then laddering down every third stitch for eight needles. Catch these stitches up from the front, so that there are knit stitches in rows on the reverse side of the fabric, or leave odd needles in non-working position and then catch up the bars in the same way. (Tighter smocking is achieved by using a double bed 1 x 1 tuck rib and is best worked on knitting of two rows tuck and two rows of stocking stitch on the back bed. The ribber is set as normal. On the Japanese machines use Empisal card 3.) Take a yarn of the same weight but a contrast colour and thread a blunt-ended needle. Bringing the needle from the back to the front of the knitting on the left of the first knit stitch, take the yarn across this stitch and the next 3 purl stitches and the next knit stitch. Take the yarn to the back of the knitting on the right hand side of this knit stitch. Carry the yarn at the back of the knitting for the next 3 stitches and bring out again on the left of the knit stitch. Carry work over 2 knit stitches as before. Continue this over the 8 knit stitches. Start the next row approximately 6 rows down. This time float over the

A smocking effect is achieved by a hand sewn back stitch pulling the stitches together at equal intervals

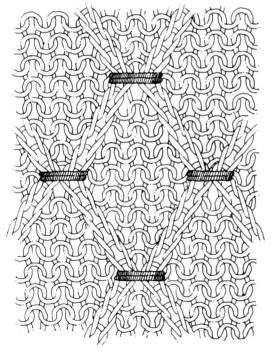

same knit stitches but float over the purl stitches that were not smocked on the previous row. On the third row smock as the first row and so on until the desired length of smocking is achieved. A smocking effect can also be achieved by applied back stitch embroidery. (See diagram.)

SNAGGING. Should a fibre end be pulled by accident during wear never cut it, but pull it through to the reverse of the knitting with a latch hook. Pull it gently so that the stitch becomes the right size at the front and then knot the excess yarn at the back.

SNARL. A fancy yarn with strong central core. The yarn is twisted faster than the core yarn so that it twists back on itself, resulting in a little twisted end of yarn protruding from the central core.

SOCKS (see also *Turning a Heel*). Knitted flat on the single bed. Most types of patterns can be used but the heel, toe and sole are normally knitted plain. The ribbing at the top can be mock rib or ribbed on the double bed and transferred to the main bed, for patterning. On a longer sock the leg has to be shaped but short socks are knitted straight. The leg part is knitted and the stitches for the heel are put on waste yarn, which is an even number either side of the needles to be left in working position. On these working needles the instep is knitted, the patterning stops at the toe shaping and the rest of the sock is in plain. Socks can also be knitted by the holding method. An ankle sock, for example, can be knitted in a square; the ribbing is knitted plus a length of plain knitting, and then a small pocket is formed on the right hand side of the knitting by gradually pushing needles into holding position as for short row designing. The yarn is caught around the end needle, so a hole does not form. The centre of the sock is knitted straight, another pocket is formed on the left-hand side of the sock, several rows of waste yarn are knitted and the sock is then removed from the machine. The sock is pressed, folded in half and the two ends are mattress stitched together, which then forms the ball of the foot. For the heel and toe sections the tension can be tightened by one point or a polyester sewing thread can be run with the main yarn. This will strengthen the areas that have the most wear. Any sock pattern can be adjusted to make long socks by adding the extra length and then decreasing until the original number of stitches on the pattern at the heel have been reached.

Circular socks. The ribbing is worked and then

the knitting is replaced on the machine to form the circle for tubular knitting. The machine is set for circular knitting. For extra leg length for every row needed the carriage must be worked twice. When the leg part has been knitted the ribber is lowered with the stitches still remaining on the needles and the heel is knitted only on the main bed. The ribber is then brought back to working position to knit circular for the foot. When a sock has part pattern and part stocking stitch a tension square must be knitted for both and the rows adjusted. Fair Isle takes less rows. For half sizes add six rows to the number of rows for the instep and the sole on a three-ply yarn. As a general rule be careful regarding the choice and thickness of yarn used, to avoid the socks becoming too bulky. Shearing elastic can be knitted in with the main yarn at the top of the sock or on a small welt; elastic can be threaded through prior to finishing.

SPACE DYED YARNS (see also *Sampling, Yarn Dyeing*). Can be bought commercially dyed or can be dyed at home. The hank is dyed in sections in different colours. The commercially-dyed yarns are more evenly spaced, home-dyed yarns more random and uneven. The dye pots are prepared, for example, red, blue and yellow, the three primary colours. The dye is dissolved, salt added and acid where necessary. It is best to use white or cream yarn, but pale coloured yarns can be dyed or a lighter yarn spun with a dark yarn. The dye will only take on the light coloured yarn. The hank is hung from a glass rod or ruler and a section

Space-dyeing a hank of yarn

is dipped into the red pot. Leave it to dye until sufficient dye has been absorbed by the yarn. Squeeze a piece of the yarn between the thumb and forefinger to see the shade of dye, remembering that yarn is a shade darker when wet. Remove the hank and rinse this dyed section well. Then turn the hank a little way and dip it into the blue dye pot overlapping the red colour slightly. Where the colours overlap a third colour is made – purple. Dye the blue in the same way as the red, rinse well and then put another section of the hank into the yellow dye pot, overlapping a little of the blue. Yellow and blue make green. Also overlap the yellow on to the red to make orange. Either space dye the whole hank, or part of the hank, or space dye the hank without overlapping the colours, leaving an amount of the base colour showing. If several space-dyed hanks are used to make a garment, the width of each dyed section does not have to be the same. When the yarn is rewound into balls the dyed sections are so fine that the random widths do not seem to vary a great deal from ball to ball. The space-dyed yarn can be as delicate and pale or as bold and rich as required. It is also interesting to dye different fibres in the same dye pots, some plain colours and some space dyed. The dye reacts differently to each fibre. When dyeing quantities of yarn keep laying them together on the floor to see if the combinations are successful. By laying them in different orders they will react differently to the colour that they lay against. Gradually build up the range of colours to be used. This applies mainly to the synthetic dyes as natural dyes blend well together. Commercially bought dyed yarn can be re-dyed but its colour will obviously be affected by the original colour. For example, a yellow bought yarn that is put into a red dye bath will give an orange yarn! Remember always to keep notes of colour combinations together with a sample of the fibre before and after dyeing. To re-dye skeins of yarns that have streaked, or to bring two skeins dyed with the same dye at different times to the same colour, simmer the yarn in a clean dye bath with 1 cup of Glauber salts to each gallon of water used.

SPARES, see *Servicing*.

SPINNING (see also *Carding, Rolag, Roving, Scouring, Twists*). Fibres are twisted or spun to form a yarn. Newly spun yarn is a single ply. When these yarns are twisted together the familar 2, 3, or 4 ply results. In industry it is referred to as 2, 3, or 4 fold yarn. Knitters and weavers often like to create interesting and unusual yarns by spinning wool (being the easiest fibre to spin) for themselves from the raw fleece. Before the sixteenth century, when the spinning wheel was invented, spinners only used a drop spindle. Raw wool can be bought undyed, already sorted and in small quantities. These are called matchings and are graded according to their quality. Natural colours vary a great deal from almost white through to black. The wool has to be teased out by taking small amounts, pulling the fibres out until they are really fine and removing any dirt. The wool then has to be carded so that the fibres are broken up and then mixed together well, and eventually the fluffy fibres all lay in the same direction. Before commencing spinning with only a spindle, about 45 cm (18 in) of woollen thread has to be prepared from a rolag. Take a rolag (q.v.) in the left hand and with the right hand pull a few fibres, twisting them clockwise to form a thin thread. Tie or secure this thread to a hook or something firm, and then continue pulling and twisting the thread so that it grows longer. If the thread breaks, overlay the last 2.5 cm (1 in) with fibres from the rolag and hold the weak point between left finger and thumb and continue to twist in the clockwise direction. When this thread is 45 cm (18 in) long tie the end to the spindle just above the wooden disc. Take the yarn over the edge of the disc and around the dowel rod. Bring yarn up over the disc to the notch at the top of the rod and secure it around the notch with a knot. The spindle is now prepared. Put the rolag over the back of the right hand, pinching the thread between first finger and thumb. Twist the spindle clockwise firmly, move the left hand up from the base, pinch the thread below the right hand, pulling a few more of the fibres, and release the right hand. In other words, turn the spindle with the left hand and pinch the fibres with the left hand. Pull out more fibres with the right hand. Pinch the fibres with the right hand. Using the left hand spin the spindle. A rhythm should develop. when the spun yarn reaches the floor, wind the yarn around the rod, crossing it so the spindle is evenly balanced. The wool must then be washed before use in warm water with pure soap or soap flakes. Squeeze gently, rinse well. Let the wool dry naturally, having rewound it onto a winder or back of a chair.

SPINNING WHEEL. The advantage of the spinning wheel over the spindle is that it is possible to spin and wind at the same time, making the process much quicker. The wheel has a treadle so that both hands can be used to draw out the fibres.

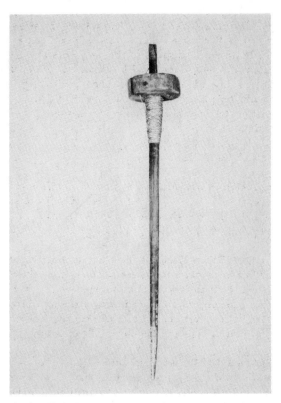

Ancient Egyptian spindle 1375-1360 B.C. (Science Museum, London)

This makes finer yarns more possible. Spinning wheels vary in size and form depending on the country they are made in. They do, however, all have in common a wheel with foot control, a bobbin and a spindle flyer. To spin on a wheel several rolags should be ready before starting. The wheel should turn slowly and regularly. Secure a piece of bought yarn to the bobbin and one of the hooks on the flyer arm. Using a bent-ended hairpin thread the yarn through the hole in the spindle. Turn the wheel, holding the thread tightly in the left hand. Stop the yarn from winding onto the bobbin. The wheel will twist the yarn in the same way the spindle does. Hold a rolag beside the yarn and the spinning process will start in the same way as the drop spindle. The hooks on the flyer arm are for placing the spun yarn evenly on to the bobbin. Build up one area of yarn and then move along to the next hook so that this area also is built up.

SPOOLS (see also *Appendix, Cheeses*). Some yarn is bought on spools and this can be run directly from the spool to the knitting machine. The tubes or spools need to be held upright by being placed on a home-made stand on, for example, a vertical piece of dowel rod or nail. The smaller the spool the more likely it is that the yarn will catch under the bottom of the spool. If the yarn does tend to catch it should re rewound into a ball. If the yarn is very fine an attachment (called an 'Ooslum') should be placed on the ball winder to assist in winding the ball. The yarn is removed on the spool and run from the outside.

SPRAY DYE, see *Printing*.

SQUARE NECKLINE. Worked by knitting one side, the centre, and then the other side. The back and sleeves are worked the same as a basic pullover; only the front neckline is altered.

STABILITY. Weaving or inlay fabrics are created by the secondary yarn passing across the fabric. Stocking stitch is knitted as normal but the inlay yarn is caught under every alternate stocking stitch. The fabric is very stable because the inlay yarn has not formed loops and therefore will not stretch.

STABLE KNITS (see also *Cut and Sew*). Knitted fabric with very little stretch. Ideal for more tailored garments. Weave or slip knitting is most suited to stable knit construction.

STAIN REMOVAL, see *Garment Aftercare*.

STAPLE FIBRES (see also *Fibres*). Short natural or man-made fibres. The length varies according to the fibre.

STEAMING (see also *Cut and Sew, Iron and Ironing, Renovation, Shrinkage*). Water is heated to damp the knitting by using a wet cloth and an iron. Irons are also made with a steam setting.

STENCILLING, see *Printing*.

STITCH DIAL, see *Stitch Size*.

STITCH FORMATIONS, see *Fair Isle, Lace, Slip, Stocking Stitch, Tuck, Weave*.

STITCH PATTERNS. The different types of stitch patterns are plain or stocking stitch, weaving, slip and tuck, which give greater texture on the reverse side of the knitting. Lace and Fair Isle are used on the face side of the knitting. Combinations of these patterns can be used together, provided the face side is the same.

STITCH PATTERNS, MISTAKES, see *Mistakes*.

STITCH SIZE (see also *Tension, Tension Squares*). The tension dial is set at the centre of the carriage, according to yarn being used and the required number of stitches and rows if following a pattern. Fair Isle should be set one whole stitch size higher than stocking stitch. A four row tuck needs a size increase too.

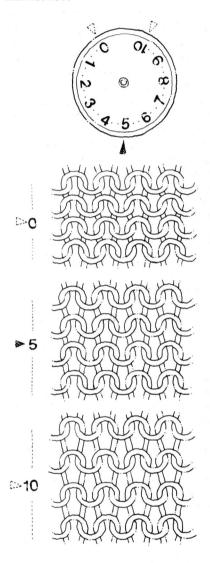

The stitch dial regulates the size of the stitch. The smallest stitch is 0 and 10 is the largest. The diagram shows variation in stitch size 0, 5 and 10 on the stitch dial

STITCH TRANSFER, see *Lace*.

STOCKINETTE (see also *Stocking Stitch*). A knitted fabric, its name deriving from stocking stitch.

STOCKING STITCH. In hand-knitting it is formed by one row knit and one row purl. The right side appears as a series of chain stitches. It was given its name as its original use was for stockings, as it stretches lengthways. It is also the basic fabric produced on single bed machines. It is a single knit fabric and the technical reverse faces the front when being knitted on the machines. The stitch sits on the hinged latch hook and as the needle slides forward the stitch goes behind the latch. The new yarn travelling across with the carriage is placed onto the hook of the needle and the needle slides back; the latch closes and the first loop slips over the closed needle forming a new stitch and sits under the loop being held on the needle hook.

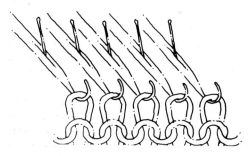

Stocking stitch

STORING OF WOOL (see also *Yarns, storage*). To avoid attacks by moths never enclose wool in cupboards or non-ventilated bags, but hang it in linen bags or lay it on a wire mesh shelf.

STRIPES (see also *Sampling, Space Dyed Yarns*). Knitting stripes is the best way to experiment with using different yarns. If a combination of coloured textured yarns taken from a theme, such as shells, is made up in stripes, it will become apparent which width and colour co-ordination works the best. Start by winding the different combinations around pieces of stiff card and securing the yarn at the back with self-adhesive tape. Experiment fully, exploring the creative potential of the yarn. Feel the textures; they may be rough, smooth, matt, or slippery. They may be pliable or springy. Put a hairy yan like mohair next to a 4-ply wool, then put a shiny, smooth yarn next to a slub matt yarn. Try a fine yarn next to a chenille and angora next to a fine gimp yarn. When an interesting combination results then it is time to try knitting it, remembering to adjust the tension with each different yarn used. By a selective and creative process unusual yet original strips can evolve and this will then result in unique garments.

STRIPPERS, PASSAP. These are inserted into the back carriage and automatically push the knitting down, so it is not necessary to use weights.

SUPERBA KNITTING MACHINE, see *Appendix*.

SURFACE DECORATION, see *Beads, Cords, knitted, Embroidery, French knot, Fringes, Mock Aran, Plaiting, Pompon, Ribbons, Sequins, Swiss darning, Tassels*.

SWATCHES, see *Tension Squares*.

SWISS DARNING (see also *Darning and Darning In Loose Ends*). This is embroidery on knitting that is applied after the knitting has been removed from the machine, and the stitches follow the form of the knitted stitch. It can travel vertically or horizontally. Use a tapestry needle threaded with a contrast yarn of the same weight as main knitting. Catch yarn at reverse of knitting. Follow diagram carefully. This is also a good method for correcting mistakes on patterned fabrics, sometimes called applied chain stitch. Can be used vertically with a striped fabric to create a chequered effect.

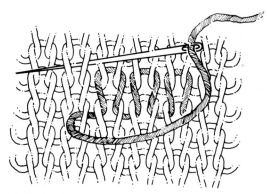

Swiss darning

SYMBOLS, PASSAP (see also *Diagram Patterns*).

AX	=	Tuck.
EX	=	Fisherman's rib.
FX	=	Selected fisherman's rib.
CX	=	Circular or tubular.
BX	=	Selected slip, jacquard and short row knitting.
GX	=	Free move.
N	=	Normal knitting.
HX	=	Tubular Fair Isle.
DX	=	Tubular (loops).

SYNTHETIC YARNS (see also *Fibres, identification, Iron and Ironing, Velcro, Yarn Combinations*). Fibres that are made from coal and oil; nylon, polyester and acrylic are the best known. Nylon was the first synthetic fibre, made in 1938. In early 1941 it was used for parachutes. It is not suitable to be used alone on the knitting machine but can be used when blended with wool, making the yarn hard wearing and pleasant to touch. Velcro is made from nylon. The polyamides are nylon, perlon and celon, the polyesters are terylene, dacron and tetcron and the polyacrylics are orlon, acrilan, courtelle and exlan. Synthetic yarns are best combined with natural yarns, which keeps the quality high and the cost low. The addition of natural yarn also reduces the amount of static electricity, which can be very annoying in pure synthetic yarns, causing the garment to cling to the body and crackle when removed. It is very important that synthetic fibres are not overpressed. They should be ironed with a cool iron and with a dry cloth on the wrong side. If yarns are pressed wrongly and too much heat is applied it will partly melt the yarn; the flat looking fabric that results cannot be rectified.

TABLE, KNITTING (see also *Appendix*). It is important that the knitting machine is clamped to a flat, stable surface. Knitting machine dealers sell a table that is long and narrow and leaves room for the yarn to stand at the back of the machine. It is very important that the table is the correct height so that a slight downward pressure can be exerted on the carriage. Never knit with legs crossed as this pulls on the back when knitting and can be painful. Cabinets to house knitting machines can be bought. Toyota sell a tilting knitting machine table that is made to give the correct angle for the double bed machine. A one-screw adjustment enables the table to be tilted to take the machine back for single bed knitting. This is available either from Toyota dealers or from Toyota direct.

TACKING OR BASTING (see also *Cut and Sew*). Large, even running stitches about 0.75 cm (¼ in) long and the same apart. Used initially to hold garment pieces in place to avoid movement during the final stitching. Garments are tacked and tried on for size, and any adjustments necessary are finished before the final stitching. Tacking is normally done with a sewing cotton of a contrasting colour. Back stitch every so often and make sure to work on a flat table. Remove the tacking as soon as the final stitching is finished or after pressing, according to where it has been used on the garment.

Pin basting. Use pins approximately every 5 cm (2 in) on seam allowance pointing towards the edge. Use a hinged presser foot to stitch over the pins or remove them while hand sewing.

Machine basting. A quick method of putting a garment together, but must only be used on knits that will not slip or show needle marks. Pin first, set machine to the longest stitch and loosen the upper tension slightly. To remove, clip the top thread every so many centimetres and pull out the bottom thread.

TAILOR'S TACKS. Useful for marking textured knits prior to construction. A single layer or double layer may be marked at a time. Working with a long double strand of thread without a knot, take a small stitch through both the tissue of the paper pattern (use a second pattern for these tacks, holding the original pattern back for further use — see *Paper Patterns*) and the knitting at the symbol shown for the tacks. Take a second stitch directly over the first and pull the thread until a loop is formed. Move on to the next symbol with the same needle and thread, leaving a loose thread behind.

Once all the symbols have been marked, clip the joining threads and pull the tissues gently from the fabric. Roll back the first layer of knitting if working double and clip the threads connecting the two pieces.

Pins and chalk are used where only a few symbols are needed. Pin through the tissue and fabric layers at the symbols. Turn knitting over and mark chalk marks using tailor's chalk, where the pins emerge on the bottom of the knitting. With pattern side up pull pin heads through the paper pattern and chalk the top of the pin heads. Remove the pins; mark with thread if not sewing straight away. When chalking do so lightly as it may prove hard in some cases to remove.

A tracing wheel and dressmaker's tracing paper can be used for marking but is seldom needed. It should never be used on light, delicate fabrics as the marks are hard to remove; it is really only suitable for more stable knits. Use only a wheel with

TAPESTRY NEEDLE

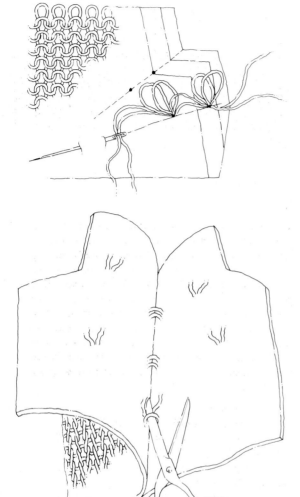

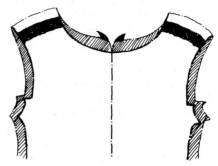

TASSELS. Decide on the required length and cut a square of thick card according to this measurement. Wind the yarn round the card to the thickness required. Pass a length of wool under the strands at the top of the card and tie these strands firmly together. Cut the strands at the bottom of the card and remove the tassel. Wrap wool tightly round the tassel a little way down from the top and sew in the ends. Trim neatly and it is ready to be applied to the garment. A bead can be put into the top part of the tassel. Tassels can be attached to knitted garments by making two holes, either by transferring by hand or using the lace carriage. Then thread the tassel through the holes.

Making a tassel. (©Stanley Paul and Company Ltd, 1978)

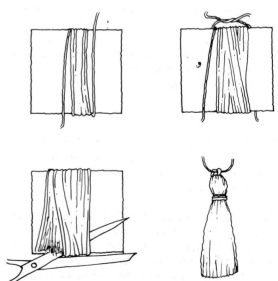

Tailor's tacks

round edges and follow instructions on the tracing paper packet.

TAPESTRY NEEDLE. A large blunt-ended needle with a long eye hole.

TAPING. Tape knitted garments at shoulders where stability needs to be retained. Either catch the tape down during machining if using the cut and sew method, or stitch on by hand after or during construction. Seams that are rather unsightly can be taped, but only on more stable knits. Uneven hemlines can be turned up and taped and a row of crochet worked along the bottom edge.

TEASEL. A flowerhead of a plant that is covered in hooked spikes. Used in raising a nap on cloth, it opens up the fibres and the fabric becomes bulkier. A metal spiked substitute is used in lengths by the cloth industry.

TECHNICAL FACE. The front of the knitting which is away from the knitter when it is being knitted on the machine. It is given this name because both sides of some knitted fabrics can be used for the front.

TECHNICAL REVERSE. Name given to the back of the knitting, which faces the knitter while it is on the machine. The reverse of the fabric with some stitches is the right side of the fabric.

TECHNIQUES, SURFACE (see also *Surface Decoration*). It is possible to apply patterning on knitting once it has been removed from the machine. Batik: wax resist method (see *Batik*). Tie and Dye, silkscreen, paint on dyes, fabric crayons, transfer printing: see *Printing*.

TENSION (see also *Tension Squares, Yarn Combinations*). The number of rows and stitches to a given measurement. Finding the correct tension for a piece of knitting is the most important aspect in garment-making after the choice of yarn and colour. Experience comes with practice and knowledge of the yarns being used (see *Sampling*). However, there are basic guidelines that help at first. A 2-ply yarn should produce approximately 9 stitches and 13 rows to 2.5 cm (1 in). A 3-ply tension square should have 8 stitches and 11 rows per 2.5 cm (1 in). A 4-ply should measure in the region of 7 stitches and 10 rows per 2.5 cm (1 in). Some manufacturers give the tension necessary, but on the whole it is a matter of practice. The knitting should have elasticity, and when pulled gently should jump back into shape. The knitting should not feel tough and hard.

TENSION DIAL, see *Stitch Size*.

TENSION DISC (see also *Automatic Yarn Tension Unit, Mistakes, Threading the Machine*). Tightens or slackens the flow of the yarn on the automatic yarn tension unit.

TENSION SQUARES/SWATCHES (see also *Carriage Jams, Garment Distortion, Lining, Mistakes, Sampling*). Before knitting a garment it is essential to produce a tension square on the machine to check the construction of the knitting.

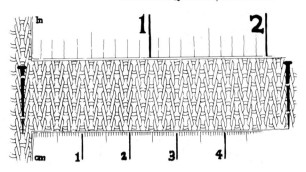

Measuring a tension swatch

The tension varies according to the type of yarn, the stitch and the setting of the stitch dial. A tension measurement should be calculated centrally over 10 cm (4 in) square. The knitted sample should be at least 25 cm (10 in) square. If a pattern is being followed then knit the sample according to the tension and yarn stated. The higher the number on the knitting machine the bigger the stitch, and there are 30 stitch sizes to work from. It is important that the yarn brake tension disc is also set correctly; the following is a general guide.

Lightweight yarn
    2-ply tension dial 1-4   yarn brake 4-5
    3-ply tension dial 4-6   yarn brake 3-4
Medium weight yarn
    4-ply tension dial 5-8   yarn brake 2-3
Heavy weight yarn
    D.K. tension dial 9-10   yarn brake 2-1

Having knitted the sample, remove from the machine and leave, press the swatch with a warm iron over a damp cloth, (with plain acrylic a dry cloth should be used). When dry, put a pin in each corner without stretching it to let the knitting relax, then place a ruler over the square and mark off 10 cm (4 in) in the centre of the knitting with pins. Count the number of stitches and rows and check to see if it is the same as the pattern. If there are too many stitches then the tension is too tight and the stitch dial needs to be altered to increase the tension. If there are too few stitches then the tension needs to be lowered. If a substitute yarn is used in a pattern then make sure that the tension is correct. A skirt is knitted two tensions tighter than a sweater. It needs less stretch to avoid garment distortion and seating. A skirt can also be lined to take a certain amount of stress away from the knitting. If the tension is too tight then it will be hard to knit and more yarn will be used. If the tension is too loose the garment will have little shape. An incorrect tension can also result in a jammed carriage, faulty patterns and knitting that is too hard to handle. If your machine provides a gauge scale, use it to measure a tension swatch. Knitting that thas been knitted on two beds is a little harder to measure. The work should not be pulled but left to relax; most swatches will decrease in size as they have been stretched by the weights. To measure the swatch decide how much the knitting will be stretched when worn and measure with it under stretch. As the swatch is pulled it will shorten in the length so it is important to measure accurately.

TERYLENE (see also *Synthetic Yarns*). In the United Kingdom polyester is called terylene, and is simply a trade name for this fibre. It is very strong, hard-wearing and drip-dry. It is also quite often blended with wool and, because it handles well, a large proportion can be used in the blend than is the case with nylon.

TEXTURE (see also *Lace, Sampling, Tuck Stitch, Weave, Yarn Combinations*). This is the quality conveyed to the touch and is achieved by the use of certain patterns and yarns. The most important part of the attractiveness of finished knitting is in the handling qualities. The combination of the correct tension and colour plus a selective use of yarns makes the garment a pleasure to wear.

THREADING THE MACHINE (see also *Automatic Yarn Tension Unit, Mistakes, Yarn Feeder*). Most machines are threaded in a similar way. A steel rod is fitted into the back of the needlebed and lays a little backwards, just off the vertical position. The yarn is placed behind this rod on the table. Halfway up the rod is a rear yarn guide with two holes. The yarn tension unit (the steel rod) takes two yarns feeding separately up the rod. The yarn on the right is threaded through the right-hand hole. It is then taken up to the top of the rod to the tension disc. Pass the yarn carefully through the right hand disc; it makes a tiny click when in place. Fine yarns can be taken around this disc twice. The yarn is then taken down the front guide arm which points towards the knitter and through the eyehole on the right. The antenna or take-up spring consists of two fine wires with eyeholes at the ends. The yarn is then passed through this hole at the end of the spring on the right-hand side. The yarn is pulled so that the spring bends forward and then the yarn is taken to the carriage (on some models it has to go through a third hole before

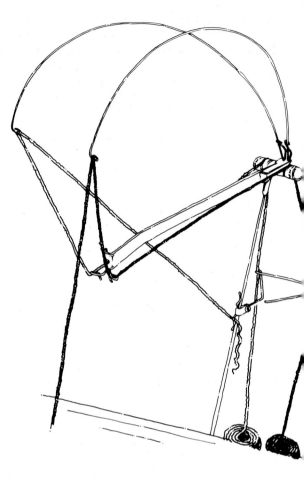

Threading the knitting machine through the automatic yarn tension unit

going on to the carriage) and threaded through the yarn feeder to the rear hole ready for knitting. The second yarn is placed next to the other yarn on the table and is threaded in exactly the same way, in this instance through the left-hand side of the yarn tensioner. If it is to be used for patterning, the yarn is passed into the second yarn feeder. If it is to be used for stripes then it is secured to the side of the carriage or table clamp ready for use — or to the colour changer if being used. The tension disc is altered according to the yarn used. The take-up springs should be pulled approximately halfway down by the yarn when knitting. If it comes down further then it is feeding the machine too tightly. If it keeps jumping back then it is feeding the yarn through too quickly. Adjust the discs accordingly.

THREADS (see also *Yarn Types*). Twisted or drawn-out fibres.

THREE-DIMENSIONAL KNITTING (see also *Beads, Embroidery, French Knots, Mock Aran, Pipe Cleaners, Smocking, Swiss Darning*). Effects can be achieved on the knitting machine to give knitting a three-dimensional quality. Knitting can of course be used to knit armchairs and fun sculptures. On the knitted surface several hems can be knitted one on top of the other. Bobbles, knitted cords and embroidery can be applied. Beads can be inserted into circular pockets knitted on the double bed. Smocking and quilting can give depth to a fabric. Separate knitted shapes can be appliquéd onto the garment after knitting, for example, shaped flower petals with embroidery inside the flower, plus beads, French knots, pipe cleaners and Swiss darning!

TIE AND DYE, see *Printing*.

TOGGLES (see also *Fastenings*). Usually made of either wood or plastic in an elongated shape, with a groove in the centre. One is placed either side of a jacket or cardigan opening. They are fastened by a fabric, leather, or a corded loop which slips over the toggle on the opposite side and sits in the groove.

TOILÉ. The name given in dressmaking to a calico sample garment. It is fitted and re-shaped where necessary and then the final garment can be made with the correct shapings and alterations worked out. Because of the lack of elasticity in paper or calico it is of little use to knitters. Instead, knitters can use cut and sew on body blanks for experimentation.

TOOLS (see also *Accessories, machine, Punchcard Guide Pin*). A selection of the following tools and accessories are supplied with each new single bed machine. The tool box is either built into the back of the carriage or comes in a separate box. Certain models will have extra small items in the tool box; Empisal punchcard machines, for example, have separators.

The needle pushers select needles quickly according to the rib required. 3/1, 1/3, 1/2 and 1/5. 1/1 and a straight edge for every needle welt.

The transfer tools. Used for transferring stitches onto other needles for shaping garments, for patterning and buttonholes. 1/2, 3/2, 3/1.

The crochet and work hook. For crocheting seams together or for an edge where a zip is to be inserted. The hook is used for catching dropped stitches.

Tapestry needle. For sewing in ends, etc.

Spare needles. To replace any bent or damaged needle on the needle bed that impairs the flow of the carriage or the construction of the knitting, where a latch may have bent.

The nylon cord is used for open edge cast on, for hems and sampling. Some machines also supply cast on combs which are better employed over large areas.

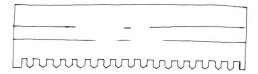

1/1 and straight edge needle pusher

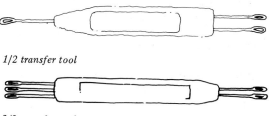

1/2 transfer tool

3/2 transfer tool

3/1 transfer tool

Crochet and work hook

The latch needle

Nylon cord

TOOLS

The latch hook is for picking up dropped stitches, binding an edge, casting off, etc.

The carriage lock plate secures the carriage to the end of the needlebed for transporting the machine in its case.

Bar Pusher, see *Bar Pusher*.

Brush and oil bottle. Oil the machine regularly and remove any dust with a brush after use. (See also *Cleaning Machines*).

Tables clamps secure the machine to the table. The machine should be positioned so that the knitter is sitting slightly higher than the machine, enabling a slight downward pressure to be exerted on the carriage.

Wax. To help the yarn run smoothly it automatically crosses the wax while knitting.

The weights tension the fabric and keep it from jumping up and being caught under the carriage.

Punchcard guide pin keeps the punchcard upright.

Card clamps/snaps. Both ends of punchcard are attached together so that patterning is continuous.

With a *ribbing attachment* a few extra tools are supplied to facilitate the smooth running of the doublebed machine. They are: *Table clamps*, which tilt the machine into a V-bed, so that the ribber can be used too. Extra weight, wire loop and claw type weight hangers, and cast-on cones — one long, one short. *Close knit bar* is used for knitting thinner yarns on tension 0-2. *End stitch presser plate* is used to secure the stitches at the edges. *Spanner* for ribber adjustments. *Double-ended transfer needle* for transferring stitches between the two needle beds (main bed and ribber). *Needle pushers* 1/2 and 2/2 for needle selection.

The tools for Japanese machines are basically the same, but where the gauge of the machine varies the tools are not interchangeable.

Certain accessories can also be included with the knitting machine. These are:

Row counter. Indicates the number of rows knitted and is vital when following a pattern and shaping. Can be positioned at the left or right of the rear cover plate. Sometimes the row counter is built into the machine.

Yarn tension unit (see also *Automatic Yarn Tension Unit*). Regulates the flow of yarn down into the carriage.

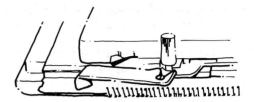

Carriage lock plate

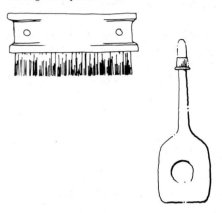

Brush and oil bottle

Table clamps

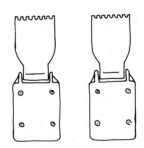

Claw weights for the single bed

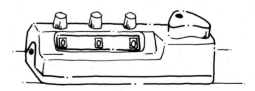

Detachable row counter

The latch hook

Pre-punched pack of cards and single motif pre-punched cards for patterned knitting on punch-card machines.

With a ribber attachment comes *the connecting arm assembly*, to replace the sinker plate assembly, to join the two carriages into one and to hold the yarn when knitting.

If the machine has an in-built charting device then it will usually come with a set of basic patterns.

Passap supply the following tools with their machine (please note that although some Passap tools and accessories are very similar to those of the single bed machines they are called by different names):

Oil
Cleaning brush
Yarn holder cup x 2
Orange stripper x 2
Black stripper x 2
Orange tool (double end, 1 needle 1 spike)
Black tool
1/1 pattern ruler
Deckercomb x 2—20 needles
Tray for stand
Double ended bodkin
Yellow tool (double end, 2 needles, 1 crochet
    hook)
Wax disc x 1
(They also have an extensive list of extra available
    accessories; for details enquire at the nearest
    Passap dealer.)
Every machine comes with an instruction manual.

TOP DYEING. Yarn dyeing on top of other colours.

TOP STITCHING. Used in dressmaking to add a feature to a garment and to ensure that edges stay flat. It is either sewn on the machine or by hand, and is a row of running stitches. Bands in knitting can be applied using this method. The band is folded on to the right side for catching down, instead of the reverse side (so reverse the picking up procedure). Using a contrast yarn and a tapestry needle, top stitch the band very neatly into place with little running stitches. This is obviously best on plain garments, although a colour in a pattern can be picked out and applied in this way.

TOPS. The overdyeing of another colour on to synthetic yarn prior to spinning.

TOYOTA KNITTING MACHINE, see *Appendix*.

TRANSFER STITCHES (see also *Basket Stitch*). To transfer a stitch from the ribber to the knitter with the double eye transfer tool.

Knit 1 Purl 1 rib and 2/2 rib. Push up the empty needles on the main bed opposite the ribber stitches to knitting position and transfer the stitches from the ribber onto the main bed, i.e.

Using the double-eyed transfer tool from ribber to main bed

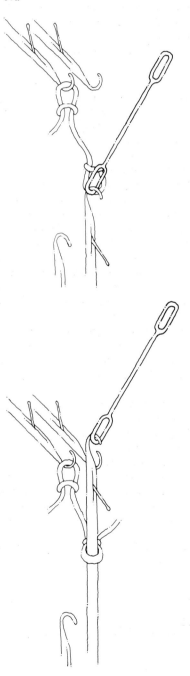

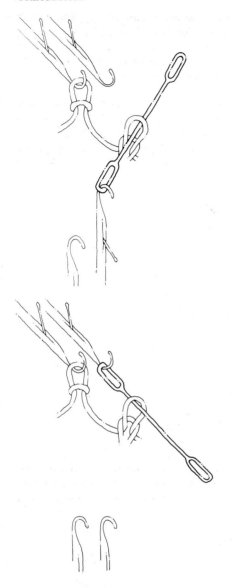

every other stitch, or 2 every 2 stitches. Push the empty needles on the ribber back to non-working position. There are variations on rib transfer; refer to instruction manual.

Double rib. Transfer all stitches to the main bed having set the half pitch lever to P (pitch). Push all needles on ribber back to non-working position.

TRIACETATE. Man-made fibre sold under the names Tricel and Arnel. Has drip-dry qualities and is virtually crease free.

TRICEL, see *Triacetate.*

TRICOT. French word which means 'knitted fabric', used in describing a variety of warp knitted fabrics. It has very little stretch.

TRIMS, see *Edgings.*

TRITIK, see *Printing.*

TRUE LACE, see *Drive Lace, Lace.*

TUBULAR KNITTING (see also *Circular Knitting*). Fabric knitted on both needlebeds in the round. See instruction manuals for settings.

TUCK LACE. Produced by using the relevant punchcards and altering the needle arrangements to achieve different patterns. The tuck needle is left isolated by pushing back the needles on one or both sides of it after removing the stitches. This results in a lacy effect. *To knit tuck lace on non-punchcard machines.* This is done by hand with the help of the needle pusher. The carriage is set so that it does not knit the needles put into holding position. Machines with a locking device on the pattern panel can set the card so that each row of the card knits twice. Tuck lace works well over four rows, on automatic machines as well. *To increase during tuck lace.* Put needle into working position next to the last knitted needle. Knit several rows and place the stitch on the appropriate needle for the lace pattern. *To decrease during tuck lace.* Because of the gap between needles in working position a chain stitch has to be worked for every empty needle. Push the needle forward so that the stitch goes behind the latch, place yarn over the hook and pull the needle back to knitting position; this forms one chain stitch. This is the same method as for casting off.

TUCK STITCH. Formed when the needle does not move forward sufficiently for the stitch to go behind the latch. Therefore the needle returns to knitting position with the old stitch plus the new yarn on the needle. Some patterns can be used both on the front and reverse of the knitting; the reverse is more common. Only one needle at a time will tuck. More raised patterns are achieved by tucking for several rows on the same needles before knitting them in. On the double bed tuck stitch is fisherman's rib. (See *Rib.*)

Fancy tucked ribs can be made by having one bed set for a tuck stitch and the other bed set for a plain rib stitch. As the tucking starts to work, the plain ribbing starts to become distorted and a fancy fabric is produced. This is better produced

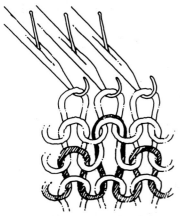

Tuck stitch

with finer yarns as the knitting becomes thicker, with more texture and width. Some textured yarns will not show up to advantage on tuck stitch.

TUITION (see also *Adult Education*). Basic lessons are normally given with each new knitting machine, depending on the price paid. This can be either in the home or shop. Second-hand machines from dealers quite often come with basic lessons too. Adult Education centres run machine knitting courses in some areas and in most towns now there is a knitting club.

TURNING A HEEL (see also *Socks*). This is achieved by knitting short rows. The tension is normally one point lower than main setting. Push forward, to non-knitting position, the needle on the opposite side to the carriage, and knit across. The yarn is passed under the held needle. Push the needle forward to hold on the opposite side of the carriage and knit across. Pass the yarn under the held needle. Continue this until eight needles are held on either edge. Then reverse the procedure by pushing back from the held needles furthest from the carriage to knitting position the needle nearest the carriage. Knit across, passing the yarn under the end held needle. Re-knit a needle at a time, knit a row and continue until all the needles are knitting again. This makes the heel form.

TUSSER SILK (see also *Fibres, identification, Silk*). A fawn coloured silk from wild Indian silk-worms, (*Antheraea mylitta*), the better known being the *antheraea* (or *muga*, as it is also known) and *attacus*. They feed on various leaves and this wild silk is much coarser than cultivated silk, more irregular, has little lustre and less softness. It can be knitted or woven.

TWEED (see also *Wool, Yarn Dyeing, natural*). A rough woollen cloth mainly used for men's suits. Harris, Donegal and Shetland tweeds smell of the boiling lichen, of which there are between forty and fifty kinds which give a dye.

TWIST, S and Z. Yarns that are twisted are either in the direction of S or Z twist. The type of yarn determines the degree of twist. If a yarn is unravelled it can be seen which way it has been twisted. S twist spins anti-clockwise and Z twist spins clockwise.

The twists in yarn

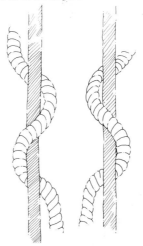

TWISTED CORD. Use two ends of any thickness and twist the strands in a clockwise direction. Knot both ends, leaving a tassel at both ends, and trim.

A twisted cord

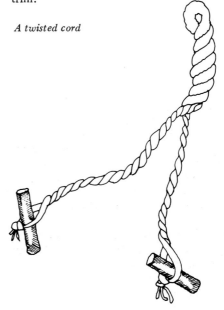

U-NECK (see also *Collars*). A deeper form of round neck. To alter a round neck diagram pattern, extend the front neckline from the inside shoulder line and draw the depth as for a square neck. Gently curve the line so that a U is formed, cutting off the square corner.

UNPICKING (see also *Unravelling*). Old garments can be unpicked and wound into hanks. The hanks should be tied in a figure-of-eight at intervals with pieces of yarn around the hank, and then the yarn can be steamed over a kettle to remove the crimp formed by knitting. Re-wind the hank and the yarn can be used again.

UNRAVELLING. To unravel knitting push the needles back behind the sinker gate so that the needle hooks are holding the stitches securely.

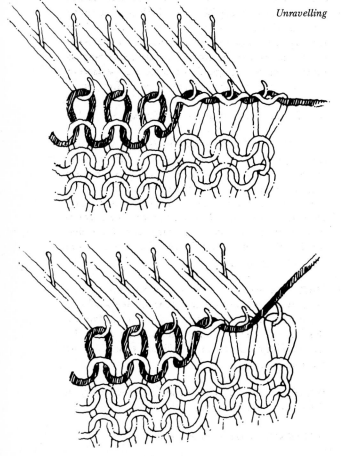

Unravelling

Starting at carriage side remove yarn from carriage and, pulling some slack yarn down, secure the yarn on the clamp underneath; this is to stop any unnecessary tension being put on the stitches. Then, taking the yarn nearest the stitches, pull the yarn tightly and lift it vertically above the needle. The stitch will unpick and the stitch from the row below will be in the needle hook. Continue this until the whole row is unravelled. If more than one row is to be unpicked then push the needles once again between the sinker gate. Count the number of rows unpicked so that any pattern can be re-knitted at this point. If a punchcard is being used set the card feed to hold, disconnect the carriage from the pattern card and set it to slip, passing the carriage across the knitting and back. The needles will not move but the pattern now has been fed into the machine. Connect carriage, reset and continue knitting.

UPHOLSTERY FABRICS, see *Furnishing*.

V-BED MACHINES (see also *Double Bed*). Hand-operated industrial machines are normally referred to as V-bed machines.

VEGETABLE FIBRES (see also *Cotton, Linen*). Natural fibres are either vegetable or animal. Cotton and linen are vegetable fibres.

VELCRO. A touch-and-close fastening that can be used instead of buttonholes or zips. It is bought in a long strip and can be cut to the length required. It consists of a top and bottom strip approximately 2 cm (¾ in) wide that adhere to each other and pull apart for opening. Can be used as a mock opening putting buttons on top, which avoids the problem of buttonholes on fine garments. Available from haberdashery counters.

VELOUR. From the French for velvet, originating from *villosus*, which means hairy. A knitted velour is made so that it has a fine pile surface and is mainly used for sportswear and sweaters.

VICUNA. Fibre from a South American animal in

the Llama family. The fibre is very rarely found in shops for knitters. The vicuna is a wild animal which has to be hunted and killed for its rare hair, of which only the finer is used. Since 1921 the Peruvian government have tried to protect this animal with strict conservation laws.

V-NECK (see also *Collars*). This type of neckline is knitted in two parts. Knit the fabric to the row where the V-neck commences. Carriage at right for these instructions, reverse if carriage is on the left. Place the cam lever on hold and bring forward all needles to furthest point on left of V. The centre 0. These needles do not knit until the right side has been completed. Transfer first stitch on the right of centre to the next needle on its right and return empty needle to non-working position. To fully fashion transfer both first and second stitches onto the second and third needles,and continue transferring two at a time. Then knit two rows and continue the decreasing one stitch every two rows until the required number of stitches remain for the shoulder. Cast off. Put needles at left to knitting position by using the triple transfer tool and putting the stitches onto the needle hooks. Knit this side as the other. For neck band, bring needles to knitting position required for half the neck and back of the garment. Make sure all latches are open on these needles. Set machine for plain knitting. With wrong side facing and using the single transfer tool pick up the stitch nearest the V onto the first needle nearest the carriage. Continue to pick up all the stitches from half the V onto the empty needles. With same yarn as main garment knit one row across making sure that all needles are in knitting position. The bottom end of the band has to be shaped to fit the V-neck by decreasing at the V end until the hem is halfway. Now increase in reverse so that when finished the band has the same number of stitches as at the start. Repeat this process for the other side of the neck starting at the V edge. When casting on for the garment front it is adviseable to add 1 extra stitch for single bed work and 2 extra for double bed. This gives an odd stitch which can be used as a decrease in the centre of the garment to start the V-neck division. A V-neck starts on the first row of the armhole shaping.

VILENE. Type of interfacing used to stiffen areas of knitting. Superdrape is used to give body and firmness to a piece of knitting without stopping the natural stretch quality of the knitting. Wunda-web is useful for hems and pocket tops. Bondaweb is for fusing two fabrics together. These are all applied by heat or sewn in and the manufacturers' directions should be followed carefully.

VISCOSE RAYON (see also *Rayon, viscose*). A man-made fibre originally produced as a substitute for silk. It dyes very well and has a high lustre. It should not be used to knit an entire garment as it tends to drop badly, unless it is a small garment and therefore fairly light. It should be combined in stripes or a pattern with wool or cotton. It is also a good contrast with wool, matt and shiny. It can be used on the edge of plain or picot hems.

WAISTBANDS (see also *Edgings*). Can be knitted and stiffened slightly with an iron-on interfacing, or else petersham can be used, which is attached to the top of the skirt and folded to the inside. If the waistband is to be seen then a feature can be made of it, and it can be treated in the same way as fancy hems or edgings. A mock rib can be used to draw a dress into the waistline, to give a firm fit.

WALE. A single vertical row of stitches.

WALLHANGINGS (see also *Intarsia, Picture Knitting*). Can be knitted on the machine and are most interesting when combined with the intarsia technique of self-selection patterning. Firm constructions are best because the fabric may drop with its own weight. The knitting can have a contrast lining at the back, so that it shows through the knitting, but it should only be joined at the top of the knitting.

WARP. In weaving, the vertical threads on the loom that are lifted up and down by the shafts. If using bought fabrics with machine-knitted fabrics, the threads can be pulled in sections from the woven fabric to match a laddered effect on the machine.

WARP KNITTING. The threads loop vertically in the fabric. Raschel is warp knitting.

WASHING, see *Garment Aftercare*.

WASTE KNITTING. Used where the knitting is not to be cast off; at shoulder seams for example, where the pieces are to be grafted together. It is knitted in a smooth contrast yarn for about 6 rows, the carriage is then taken across the knitting without the yarn, and the knitting drops off the needlebed. Next, the knitting is pressed well to set the stitches, then the waste knitting can be unravelled down to the last row for grafting. It is also used when making welts on the single bed and doesn't show marks from brushes when shaping necklines. The one side of the knitting at the neck in holding position has the carriage crossing it every row and this friction can create a fluffy row or a dirty line across the knitting. Simply knitting several rows of waste yarn and then putting the needles into holding position avoids this problem. The alternative way to solve this is by running a strip of self-adhesive tape across the knitting where the carriage rubs.

Waste knitting is also used where the number of stitches in a row has to be reduced. The knitting is then pressed and unravelled to the last row on waste knitting. Replace the stitches onto the needlebed – one on the first, three on the second, or whatever the pattern requires. If a single rib has been formed by laddering and latching up the loops for a 1/1 rib, waste knitting is used to strip the rib off the machine so that it can be cast off afterwards. The needles holding the latched loops are put forward to holding position. The carriage should be set to slip. Knit one row, making sure that only the reformed stitches have been knitted. The lever is then set to stockinette and waste knitting is knitted for about 6 rows. The knitting is then removed from the needle bed.

WAXING YARN. It is advisable to wax the more hairy yarns to facilitate easier running of the carriage. Some machines have a place to put wax where the yarn automatically passes, before going into the carriage. It is paraffin wax and is available from any machine stockist. The wax (or a candle) can be held in the hand while winding the yarn into balls; the yarn then passes over the wax. Do not press the yarn on to the wax; let it pass lightly over it, otherwise the ball will be too tight. The wax will rub off during knitting, but if some should remain it is removed on the first washing. Brittle yarns that tend to break easily will also benefit from waxing. A wax aerosol spray is available on the market, which can also be sprayed onto the carriage and the needles to assist in easy running.

WAX RESIST, see *Batik*.

WEAVEMASTER. An attachment manufactured for Knitmaster which can be attached to the needlebed of any make of punchcard knitting machine. Simple woven fabrics can be produced with it to co-ordinate with the machine-knitted fabrics. The width of the fabric produced, however, is very limiting.

WEAVING (see also *Weaving Brushes, Yarn Combinations*). Refer to instruction manual for machine settings. The right side is the reverse side of the fabric as the inlay yarn shows on this side. If odd needles are left in non-working position the fancy inlay yarn will be seen on the face side of the knitting. A wide variety of yarns from thick to thin can be used for weave, but beware of floats of fine yarn; restrict them to one or two needle widths, as they can easily be snagged and pulled. However, weaving patterns can be varied by hooking up the weaving floats after several rows. Do not use too thick a yarn for this method. Very stable fabrics are ideal for reversible fabrics and, because they do not unravel easily, are excellent for cut and sew.

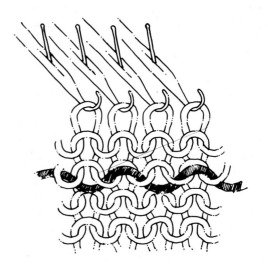

Weaving stitch

WEAVING BRUSHES. Inserted into the sinker plate when knitting a weave pattern to keep the floated yarns from jumping off the needles. Refer to instruction manual for settings. The brushes should be replaced when bristles become ragged as this may impair the flow of the machine.

WEAVING YARNS (see also *Industrial Yarns*). Some weaving yarns can be used for machine knitting. If yarn is so slippery it falls off the cone, cut a section from the ankle of a pair of tights or stockings and place over the cone; this will hold the yarn securely but enable the yarn to flow freely for knitting. Some yarns are twisted too much for the machine and will curl and break or make up with a twist to the left or right. The fine fancy yarns can be run with a wool yarn for strength.

WEFT. The horizontal yarn that is laid across the warp in weaving, either manually or automatically. Either way it is sent across on a shuttle which holds a quantity of the yarn.

WEFT KNITS. Created with a single continuous thread. The threads loop across the fabric horizontally. Jersey fabrics are weft knitted and hand knitted. Two stitches form the basis for all weft knitting: knit stitch and purl stitch. The knit stitch is a loop drawn through the front of the previous one, while the purl stitch is drawn through the back. This knitting has a large amount of stretch.

WEIGHTS (see also *Tools*). On the single bed claw weights are used at either edge of the knitting to keep the knitting from riding up and jamming the carriage by not knitting. They are weights with tiny metal teeth that catch on to the knitting. As the knitting increases, put the weights back into the top of the knitting. When using the cast-on comb on the single or double bed, the knitting is gradually wound around the cast-on comb and the weights which have a metal hook are hung on the comb. Alternatively, remove the comb from the knitting and move it higher up; from the back of the knitting press the teeth carefully through the stitches, replace the wire and the weights. Always make sure the comb is placed centrally on the knitting, otherwise one end will tilt and cause the stitches to pile up at the other end. A good rule is to have two large weights on the small comb and three large ones on the bigger comb. When increasing, side weights need to be used, as the new stitches are not attached to the comb. Tuck stitches may need a little extra weight. The Passap knitting machine does not use weights. (See *Strippers*.)

WEIGHT CONVERSION, see *Metrication*.

WELTS, see *Casting On, Hems, Mock Rib*.

WINDING YARN (see also *Cheeses, Cones, Skein Winder*). Yarn that is bought in balls, skeins or hanks must be rewound on a wool winder ready for the machine. Skein holders are available, either metal ones from a machine knitting supplier or wooden ones from weaving equipment suppliers. The skein is placed onto the holder and it is adjusted so that it is held firmly in place. The ties are then cut and the outside is taken to the wool winder. If rewinding from a ball it is important that the inside end is used, to avoid the ball jumping all over the floor. Two chairs back to back can be used for skeins, or someone can hold it. The ball should not be wound too tightly otherwise it will not be fed onto the knitting machine correctly. Never make the balls too large. Spools of knitting can be used directly if stood on a stand on the floor where it is held upright. Be careful that the yarn does not drop and become caught under the bottom of the tube.

WOOL (see also *Fibres, Fibres, identification, Garment Aftercare, International Wool Secretariat, Iron and Ironing, Medulla, Shoddy, Yarn Combinations*). Comes from the fleece of sheep and varies greatly in quality. For knitting the finest is perhaps Merino wool from the Merino sheep; the fleece contains no coarse, brittle fibres. Wool can also include hair from animals such as the angora goat, cashmere goat, camel, alpaca, llama, etc. The basic raw wool contains grease which is removed and sold as lanolin. Wool fibre, like horns, hooves, our human hair and fingernails, is composed of the protein keratin. Wool is known for its shape retention qualities. All wool has to be graded and cleaned prior to spinning. The fleece bales are sorted and the raw wool is washed to remove the dirt and grease. By using acid, heat and rollers, any straw or vegetable matter is extracted. The wool is then carded by being passed through large machines with rollers covered with spiky wires that separate the fibres and mix them well. The wool is then twisted or spun into yarn. Woollen yarn is very light and bulky. Worsted yarns are made from the longer staple fibres, which are passed through a process called combing, before spinning. This produces stronger yarns with more lustre. Shetland wool comes from sheep in the Orkney and Shetland Islands. They produce some of the finest quality British wool. Shetland and tweed yarns are often spun in oil, so it is important to use a tension higher than normal, making the knitting very open and loose. Before construction the pieces of knitting are washed to remove the oil, the knitting fibres expand and fluff out, and the garment becomes lightweight and soft. Remember to wash the sample swatch before measuring. Lambswool is very soft and is clipped from lambs up to six months old. It is also spun in oil.

Mohair, cashmere, camel hair, llama, alpaca and angora are usually blended with wool because they are more expensive.

Oddments of wool can be used to produce very interesting striped garments and if a small amount of the expensive fibres is included, the handling and quality changes dramatically for very little extra cost.

Woollen cloth, whether woven or knitted, shrinks, and this is technically known as felting, fulling, or milling. Suiting of good quality is shrunk to give the cloth body. For hundreds of years tailors in London used to have their cloth finished by a process called London shrinking. At one time this was done at Bermondsey, in London, on common land, where the cloth was laid on the grass. It was left all night for the dew to settle on it and the next day was walked on to felt it. It was then pressed with very heavy, hot irons. Today the same result is achieved mechanically.

WOOL, HISTORY OF

WOOL, HISTORY OF (see also *History of Knitting*). The word wool comes from the old English word *wull*. (In Latin the word was *lana*.) Wool — sheep's hair — has been used for garments for at least 6,000 years. In A.D. 80 the Romans started weaving wool in Britain, and then took sheep to Spain where the climate was ideal, and developed the Merino sheep through cross-breeding. Only the rich could afford Merino wool. In the latter part of the tenth century wool was being exported from England. In the eleventh century the Flemish weavers developed weaving in England. The Domesday Book, started in 1080, mentions sheep rearing and wool production. Until the eighteenth century the making of cloth had been done by hand but then inventions completely changed the textile industry. James Hargreaves invented the Spinning Jenny in 1764, the water frame spinning machine was invented in 1769 by Richard Arkwright, and Samuel Crompton invented the spinning mule in 1779.

How wool fleece is graded commercially, starting with Number 1 as the best quality

Wool sorting. On arrival at the mill the wool is sorted for length, fineness and other characteristics. This is a very skilled craft which requires years of experience of various types of fleece. There are more than 5,000 different wool qualities in commercial use. (International Wool Secretariat)

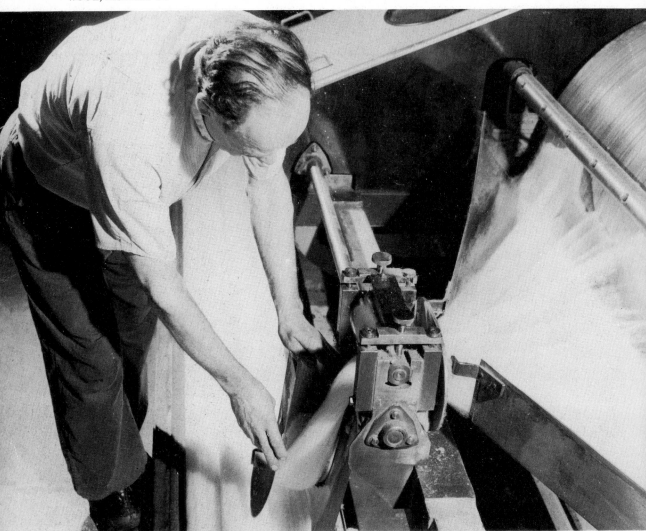

Worsted carding. In scoured wool, the fibres are aggregated in tufts and have to be separated from one another before the wool can be combed. This separation is achieved by the carding machine, which has a series of rollers covered with fine wire teeth which tease out the fibres and remove impurities such as burrs. The photograph shows the machine operator checking the web of wool as it leaves the carding machine. It is gathered together to form a sliver which is carried forward on an automatic conveyor belt for further processing. (International Wool Secretariat)

*Worsted process — drawing and roving. In a continuous process the wool slivers are reduced in thickness by drawing and roving, the final stage before spinning into worsted yarn. (*International Wool Secretariat*)*

Worsted spinning. Detail of a high-speed worsted ring spinning frame. At the top are the rovings. (International Wool Secretariat)

'Haddon Rig', Peppin ram. Warren, New South Wales, Australia. (International Wool Secretariat)

WOOL MARK, see *International Wool Secretariat.*

WOOL; SHEEP BREEDS (see also *International Wool Secretariat, Jacob's Sheep, Merino, Shoddy, Wool*). Sheep are reared in most countries of the world for wool production, but mainly in Australia, New Zealand, South Africa and South America.

Wool from the various breeds of sheep is divided into five groups. Fine, soft, short wool comes from the pure-bred Merino and Rambouillet. The short and medium down wool also comes from pure-bred sheep – Clun Forest, Devon, Closewool Dorset Down, Dorset Horn, Hampshire, Kerry Hill, Oxford, Pool Dorset, Ryeland, Shropshire, Southdown, and Suffolk sheep. The coarse kempy wool from the mountain and hill sheep comes from the Cheviot, Herdwick, Lonk, Scottish Blackface,

Shetland, Spaelsau, Swaledale and Welsh Mountain sheep. The long, lustrous and semi-lustrous wool comes from the pure-bred Border Leicester, Cotswold, Dartmoor, Devon Longwool, Leicester, Lincoln, Romney Marsh or Kent, and Wensleydale sheep. Cross-bred wool from cross-bred and half-bred sheep comes from Columbia (Lincoln and Rambouillet in the U.S.A.), Corriedale (Lincoln and Merino in New Zealand) and Targhee (Lincoln and Rambouillet in the U.S.A.).

WOOL WINDER, see *Rayon, viscose, Skein Winder, Winding Yarn.*

WORK HOOK, see *Crochet/Work Hook.*

WORKING POSITION (see also *Needle Positions*). The position of the needles on the needlebed when they are to knit the yarn when the carriage is passed across them.

WORKROOM, see *Knitting for Profit.*

WORSTED (see also *Wool*). A way of spinning fibres giving a smooth yarn.

YARDAGE. The length or area of fabric measured or estimated in linear or square yards.

YARN (see also *Appendix, Count of Yarn, Roving, Spinning, Wool, history of*). Spun thread. There are thousands of different yarns but they are all spun singly before being plied or folded with another yarn. Beware of calling all yarn 'wool'; either refer to it as yarn or fibre. Originally yarn was spun on a spindle. Home spun yarn can be knitted on the machine providing the yarn is strong. Yarns with less twist and more bulk can be used for weaving in. It is possible to spin the hair from pet animals, particularly Old English sheepdogs, Afghan hounds and Samoyeds.

YARN BRAKE, see *Automatic Yarn Tension Unit.*

YARN COMBINATIONS. The skill lies in experimenting with different yarns and combining them in unusual and experimental ways. There are no particular rules about combining yarns, but a sensitivity is developed the more handling and mixing that is done. Suggestions for yarn combinations: Acrylic 2-, 3- and 4-ply combined with an expensive yarn to keep the cost down. Use in stripes or Fair Isle. If wool is included it will help the garment retain shape better. Angora should be combined with wool to make for easier washing and harder wearing. Never float this yarn or any expensive yarn at the back of the fabrics. This yarn can be teaseled up in areas to make it fluffy. Use in odd stripes over garments and the whole feel of the fabric improves. Use to embroider on a garment. Do not use for very tight-fitting garments, especially under the arms, as it rubs and causes fluff balls, and matts the knitting.

Mohair and mohair loop. The thinner quality mohair will knit over every needle, but the thicker should be knitted over every other needle or every third needle. When removed from the machine it should be teaseled up so that the long hairs make the fabric very thick. It is better, in terms of a firmer fabric, to use it as a laying-in yarn where its texture shows on the reverse side of the fabric, leaving the inside smooth and soft. It can be used for collars and cuffs, and the loop contrasts well with a smooth wool yarn. Textured yarns normally appear on the reverse side of the knitting. Can cause itching if worn next to the skin.

Cashmere, camel and alpaca. Use on its own; superb quality but very expensive. Can be bought mixed with wool or acrylic.

Metallic yarns. Use the smooth, fine yarn that is unsupported (not spun with another yarn). It is very fine and has to be knitted with a rayon, wool, or 2-ply acrylic or thicker. Touches of Lurex can add an extra quality to any weight of garment. It can add a sparkle as a contrast or tonal yarn. Run with a 2-ply yarn for mock lace fabrics. Slub and gimp yarns look good if space dyed. If the yarn is thick then weave it in. Be careful of the fabric becoming too harsh.

Rayon is a fine, shiny yarn that can be knitted alone, although it tends to drop if used in large areas. Use with wool or cotton as a contrast yarn, particularly on the edges of plain or picot hems, or in a variety of stripes. Fancy viscose rayon yarns run well with wool. They do need to be run with another yarn as they are so fine and tend to twist back on themselves.

Bouclé. Use in a stripe or pattern as a contrast yarn. Can be run with a fine wool or fancy viscose.

Chenille. Use in stripes with wool, rayon or acrylic. The finest chenille is best. Use as a laying-in yarn. When knitting stripes do not jump from a fine yarn on a low tension into chenille on a high tension. For example, any thickness of yarn can be combined, but do it carefully; 2-ply wool, 2-ply rayon, 4-ply cotton, 4-ply wool, then chenille, then back to 4-ply wool then on to 2-plys again, and so on.

Because of the change in weight of yarn and tension the edge of the knitting tends to go in and out. This is rectified by simply picking up for bands on the narrowest row; on hems of skirts the edge is turned up and covered with a strip of bias binding. An edge can be picked up on the shortest section before turning up. If a lot of varied strips are used on a garment, it could be plain on the reverse side, or certain stripes every so many centimetres could match at the sides. The remaining rows in between can be random.

YARN COUNT, see *Count of Yarn*.

YARN DYEING (see also *Dyes, natural, history of, Dyes, synthetic, history of, Printing, Space Dyed Yarns*). Dyes come with full instructions for dyeing and printing. For natural and chemical dyes in large and small quantities, and for mordants, see *Appendix*. Use containers that are rust-free, enamel, stainless steel or glass as other materials and metals are likely to react with the mordants and dyes. You will need: one small saucepan for dissolving the dye; one tablespoon; wooden tongs or spoons for removing the wet hanks from the dye pot; weights and scales; supply of water; an apron and rubber gloves; cleaning rags and scourers for cleaning the pots; two clean bowls for rinsing the yarn; a notebook and pencil to keep a record of the yarns dyed and the receipes used. Wind the yarn into hanks (see *Hank Dyeing*) and wet the yarn thoroughly in warm water prior to dyeing. If the yarn is not soaked well patchy dyeing might result. The most common *chemical dyes* are direct dyes which are used on cotton, viscose, rayon and linen. Only salt has to be added with the dye. Acid dyes for wool, silk and nylon require the addition of salt and acid. Acid increases the degree of exhaustion of the dye pot and therefore, with pastel shades, only a small addition of acid is necessary. The dye, salt (and acid where necessary) is dissolved in the small saucepan and then added to the (heated) main dye pot and stirred well. Wool and cotton is gradually brought to the boil and then left to cool. Silk is dyed in the same way but must not boil. Nylon often needs an addition of 2g of ammonium sulphate. Some manufacturers stipulate the use of either acetic acid or sulphuric acid according to the colour of dye. I advise only the use of acetic acid or vinegar in the home, particularly where there are children. (Two-and-a-half per cent acetic acid is equivalent to vinegar.) Various elements can effect natural dyes: the soil it was grown in, fertilizers used for its growth and the effect of the sun and light, especially in the week prior to picking. Twigs make a rusty brown dye bath when soaked, a more orangey bath if put into cold water and boiled, and a yellow if put straight into hot water. Some plants instantly dye one colour, but when dyeing is continued change into a completely different colour. For all these reasons, as well as taking into account the effects of washing and the air, no two dye pots will tally. Make sure to dye enough yarn for the required garment as the exact colour can never be repeated. Start with wool, as it is easier to dye than cotton and linen. There are three ways of dyeing with natural dyes:

1. To use mordant prior to dyeing. 2. To put mordant and dye together in the same pan. 3. To dye the wool first and fix the colour after dyeing. The latter has the effect of making the colours darker and duller. Fine and loose spun wool takes in more dye than coarser wool or tighter spun wool, and wools of different textures will dye differently in the same dye bath. The breed of sheep will also vary the colour, as well as the chemicals used on the wool in sheep dips, etc. and the diet of the sheep.

The following used in small quantities can vary the colour of the dye bath and need experimentation; the colour will also change according to the mordant used. (Use mainly on wool.):

Acids. For example, acetic acid, vinegar and lemon juice;

Alkalis. For example, ammonia, bicarbonate of soda and washing soda. (Use sparingly as wool may become harsh and brittle.):

Salt. Little effect except to make the colour slightly darker or lighter;

Detergent. If added before dyeing can brighten the colours, and darken them with the addition of iron. Do not wash yarn dyed in purple fruit as it tends to turn green!

When test dyeing always record details on a card for each experiment: the yarn dyed, dye bath contents, any additives, date dyestuff picked and date dyed. Be prepared for yarn to fade. Some colours fade a great deal, or sometimes part of the yarn fades. Leave the samples in a sunny position before recording the final result.

Tie-dyeing and over-dyeing with natural dyes. Colour variants can be achieved either with the dye plant or the mordants. Tie up the fabric by binding in areas (see *Printing*) and place in a mordant. Dry it and add more ties, or re-tie the first ties in another position. Then place in another mordant, dry the fabric, remove the ties and place the fabric in the dye.

Alternatively, the fabric can be tied and dyed, and then tied in other places and re-dyed, each time in a stronger dye. This method does not give the same effect that chemical dyes do, as the natural dyes vary and can be completely different in each dye bath.

YARN FEEDER. The yarn is sent through this feeder in the centre of the sinker plate. Where the machine has two sections use the feeder that is nearest to the back of the carriage. The yarn must fit correctly in the feeder or the stitches will not form or, if there is knitting already on the machine and the carriage is passed across the bed, the knitting will drop off the machine.

Feeding two yarns into the yarn feeder for Fair Isle knitting

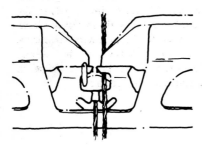

YARNS, RANDOM, see *Space Dyed Yarns*.

YARN SIZES, see *Count of Yarn*.

YARN, SLIPPERY, see *Winding Yarn, Yarn Combinations*.

YARNS, DIP-DYED, see *Space Dyed Yarns, Yarns*.

YARNS, STORAGE. Yarn should be stored in a light-proof place and at a constant temperature that is not too high. Beware of using plastic bags as, firstly, it is difficult to see the yarn and, secondly, it may sweat. Most wool yarns are now mothproofed and this lasts through several washings. Be careful that yarn is not leaning against a damp wall as this will rot the fibres.

YARN SUBSTITUTING (see also *Iron and Ironing*). Yarns that are recommended on a pattern can be substituted provided they are of the same type,

not just 4-ply for example; a 4-ply wool and a 4-ply crepe are completely different. The amount of twist will also change the size and shape of the stitch. Finer yarns offer less of a problem because several can be run together to achieve the right weight, but forethought is needed as different yarns require different pressing procedures.

YARN SUPPLIERS, see *Appendix*.

YARN TENSION (see also *Count of Yarn, Swatches, Tension, Tension Squares*). Sampling is of course essential, but a basic guide for the stitch tension is:

Very fine yarn	0/1
Fine yarn	1
2-ply yarn	1-4
Medium yarn	5-8
Thick yarn	9-10
Heavy yarn on every other needle	8-10

YARN TENSION UNIT, see *Automatic Yarn Tension Unit, Threading*.

YARN, TEXTURED, see *Yarn Combinations*.

YARN, THICK (see also *Gauge*). Most domestic machines are 6-gauge and have difficulty taking thick yarns. There are machines available on the market for thicker yarns. If the yarn is difficult to knit on every needle then it can be knitted on selected needles, for example on every other needle, as long as the yarn will fit into the hook of the needle. Thicker yarns should be used for the laying in method; roving is ideal.

YARN TWISTER. Hand-operated accessory for twisting yarns together.

YARN TYPES (see also *Acetate, Acrylic, Fancy Yarns, Rayon, viscose, Synthetic Yarn, Wool*). *Natural fibres* are animal and vegetable. The main fibres in this class are cotton and linen, which are cellulosic fibres, and wool and silk, which are polypeptides or protein fibres. *Man-made fibres*. There are a very large number of fibres in this category. Some manufacturers use a trademark to describe their products. Dictionaries are available which show the trademarks and their chemical types. They are, however, broken down into basic headings. Viscose rayons, cellulose acetate and triacetate, polyamide fibres, polyester fibres, acrylic fibres, elastomeric fibres and blended fibres.

YARNS, WEAVING, see *Weaving Yarns*.

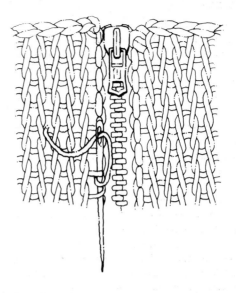

YOKES (see also *Collars, Darts*). Can be knitted by using darts.

Z

ZIGZAG STITCH. Seams can be sewn on the sewing machine, and zigzag stitch gives more elasticity to the seam than a straight stitch. This stitch is used in the cut-and-sew method of garment construction.

ZIPS (see also *Metrication*). Use the type of zipper suitable for the weight of the garment. Always wash the zipper before inserting it, or dry clean it is your garment is to be dry cleaned. This avoids shrinkage and puckering on the first wash. On lightweight garments an invisible zip can be used and a knitted edge running over the opening. False buttons can be put on the edge if so desired. Follow instructions for zip insertions carefully by tacking into place before stitching. Be careful not to stretch the knitting when the zip is put into place as this is very hard to rectify, and results in puckered fabric that will not lie flat and neat. If no other instructions are given, the following are the basic steps for insertion. Before insertion make sure the depth of the opening matches the length of the zipper. When knitting, divide for the back opening by using the centre 0. Knit up the left side of the knitting; use waste knitting and then remove from the machine. The stitches on the right of centre 0 increase 5 stitches using a closed edge method. Make a fold line at the first stitch by reforming stitches. Replace the section removed from the machine originally and complete as above. Fold the edge onto the wrong side and sew up 5 rows at the bottom of the opening. On the wrong side position the zip into place over the opening and tack with cotton thread.

With right side facing sew the zip onto the fabric. Sew the edges of the zip on the wrong side to the folded back knitted edge with hemming stitch. Unravel the tacking.

Some garments may need a zipper length that cannot be bought. To shorten a zip at the bottom, stitch zipper to garment and then sew several stitches over the teeth just below the end of the

Inserting a zip

opening. (This is to keep teeth together). Then cut off the excess zipper. To shorten at the top, stitch zip to within 2.5 cm (1 in) of where the zipper teeth should end. Open zip to top of stitching, cutting off extra teeth. to make new stops, bind straight eyes (of hook and eye) in half and put over the zipper tape above the teeth and stitch well. Make sure ends are sewn securely.

Appendix

KNITTING MACHINE MANUFACTURERS

Brother   Manufactured in Japan by Brother. Known as Jones + Brother in the United Kingdom, but as Brother International elsewhere.

Empisal   Silver manufacture the machine in Japan under the name Empisal. In the United Kingdom it is known as Empisal/Knitmaster, as Studio in the U.S.A. and as Empisal in other countries of the world. In Australia and New Zealand Empisal Electronic is known as Singer Electronic. In South Africa the machines manufactured by Silver are distributed by Brother and Empisal and sold under the Empisal name.

Passap   Manufactured in Switzerland and known as Passap throughout the world.

Singer   The Singer Electronic is known as the Memo II range of electronic knitters. (There are two models at present, and they are sold only in Europe.) In the U.S., Canada, and parts of Asia, Africa, and Latin America, the electronic model SK-560 is sold. The SK-560 is made by Silver-Seiko, Japan.

Superba   Manufactured in France by Superba and sold on the European continent under the names Singer and Phildar.

Toyota   Manufactured by parent company Aisin Seiki in Japan, which is part of the Toyota Motor Group. It is known as Toyota throughout the World, except in South Africa where Toyota call it Singer.

This information comes from the United Kingdom distributors of the various machines. I would like to point out that the franchise for selling machines can change. Check the model number of the knitting machine to verify the brand.

ADDRESSES OF KNITTING MACHINE MANUFACTURERS AND IMPORTERS

U.K.
Empisal/Knitmaster
30-40 Elcho Street
London
SW11 4AX

Jones + Brother
Shepley Street
Guide Bridge
Audenshaw
Manchester
M34 5JD

(Passap) Bogod Machine Co. Ltd
50-52 Great Sutton Street
London
EC1V 0DJ

Singer (U.K.) Ltd
255 High Street
Guildford
Surrey
GU1 3DH

Barry Bryant Ltd (Superba)
Walk Mills
The Walk
Coney Lane
Keighley
West Yorkshire

Aisin U.K. Ltd (Toyota)
34 High Street
Bromley
Kent
BR1 1EA

U.S.A.

Studio Yarn Farms Inc.
10024 14th Avenue S.W.
Seattle
Washington 98146

Brother Corporation
8 Corporate Place
Piscataway
New Jersey 08854

Passap Swiss Knitting Machines
555 5th Avenue
Suite 1500A
New York
N.Y. 10017

Singer Company
The American headquarters for Singer is located at:
10 Stamford Forum
P.O. Box 10151
Stamford, Connecticut 06904
However, queries regarding knitting products
should be directed to the North American
headquarters:
Singer Company of Canada, Ltd.

P.O. Box 1014
St Jean, Quebec J3B 7A6
Canada

Aisin U.S.A. Incorporated (Toyota)
333 Sylvan Avenue
1st Floor
Englewood Cliffs
New Jersey 07632

PUBLICATIONS FOR PARTICULAR MACHINES

Brother Home Knitting Patterns Vol. 1, 2, 3.
Stitch Pattern Book Vol. 3.
Stitchin' Time magazine, printed six times per year.

Empisal Bible for Machine Knitting (in two parts).
Stitch Pattern Books.

Passap Stitch Pattern Book.
Three small books on how to knit basic garments in 3-ply, 4-ply and double knitting.
ABC of Knitting. (How to make own garment patterns.)
Publication twice yearly of International Model Book (of garment patterns).

Singer At their distribution shops they have a selection of garment patterns. The pattern is selected and the pattern is bought singly.

Toyota Basic Pattern Book 1 — for raglan jumpers and cardigans in 3-ply, 4-ply and double knitting.
Family Pattern Books. These have five garments per issue and are published at various times throughout the year.
Punchcard Pattern Book — Fair Isle.
2,000 Stitch Pattern Book.
Knitting Pattern Drafting by Charts.

EQUIPMENT AND ACCESSORIES

U.K.
Combined Optical Industries Ltd
Slough
Bucks
Easi-view magnifying glass that leaves both hands free. (Can be used for a variety of handicrafts.)

Companies Registration Office
Companies House
Crown Way
Maindy
Cardiff
For registration of business names and registration of a company

Creative Beadcraft Ltd
Unit 26
Chiltern Trading Estate
Earl Howe Road
High Wycombe
Bucks
For mail order of beads, sequins and trims

Dryad Ltd
P.O. Box 38
Northgates
Leicester
LE1 9BU
Suppliers of general art and craft materials including wooden beads, equipment for fabric printing, marbling inks, weaving equipment, wax for batik, etc.

Eliza Leadbeater
Rookery Cottage
Dalefords Lane
Whitegate
Cheshire
Fleeces, silk, goat hair, dyes, etc.

Ells and Farrier Ltd
5 Princes Street
Hanover Square
London
W1R 8PH
For beads, sequins and trims. Vast selection, large and small quantity

Handweavers Studio and Gallery Ltd
29 Haroldstone Road
London E.17
Weaving and spinning supplies

R.D. Franks Ltd
Market Place
Oxford Circus
London W.1.
Large haberdashery selection, padded dressmaking dummies, etc.

Laura Ashley Ltd
Carno
Powys
(Branches in Surrey and several in London.)
Fabric for patchwork and interesting, inexpensive cotton prints

Lowe and Carr Ltd
Liberty Works
Eastern Boulevard
Leicester
LE2 7BG
Transfer printing paints

McCulloch and Wallis
25/26 Dering Street
London
W1R 0BH
Specialists in supplies of all haberdashery. They print labels for garments, and also sell braille labels

Marlborough Organisation
Victoria House
Victoria Street
West Houghton
BL5 3AR
Knitting machine cabinet

Matheson Dyes and Chemicals
Marcon Place
London
E8 1LP
For mordants, etc.

Muswell Hill Weavers
65 Roseberry Rd
London
N10 2LE
For natural dyes, mordants, cotton and wool dyes in small quantities. They sell the Russell Dye System for wool, and run courses on dyeing

Nelly's Knitting Machine
236 Main Road
Gidea Park
Romford
Essex
Ooslum attachment

APPENDIX

Pentel Stationery Ltd
Unit 1
Wyvern Estate
Kingston Byepass
New Malden
Surrey
Pentel pastels

Uni-Dye
P.O. Box No.10
Ilkley
West Yorkshire
Chemical dyes in large and small quantities

Value House
349A Whitehorse Road
Croydon
Surrey
Sewing machine specialists; haberdashery selection

Worldwide Machine Knitter's Club
Springvale Estate
Cwmbran
Gwent
Wales
NP44 5YQ

U.S.A.

J.T. Baker Chemical Co.
Have outlets in many of the major cities for dye products

Colonial Woolen Mills Inc.
6501 Berberton Ave.
Cleveland
Ohio 44102
Wool and wool blends, acrylics

Frederick J. Fawcett
129 South St
Boston
Ma 02130
Large selection of yarns and threads

Fibre Yarn Company Inc.
48 West 38 St
New York
Wide variety of yarns

Lilly Mills Company
POB 88
Shelby
North Carolina, 28150
Synthetics, cottons and linens

Mary Maxim Inc.
2001 Holland Avenue
Port Huron
Michigan
Angora, mohairs and wools

Naturalcraft
2199 Bancroft Way
Berkeley
California 94704
Cashmere, chenille silk

YARN MANUFACTURERS AND SUPPLIERS

U.K.

Cambrian Factory
Llanwrtyd Wells
Powys
Wales
LD54 D5
Pure wools

Foster Textile Co.
Market Street West
Preston
Lancashire
Fine wool and acrylics

Hilary Chetwynd
Kipping Cottage
Cheriton
Alresford
Hants
Pure silk

Jamieson and Smith Ltd
90 North Road
Lerwick
Shetland Isles
ZE1 0PQ
Shetland wools

Yarncraft
112A Westbourne Grove
London
W2 5RU
Natural yarns

Silverknit Yarns
The Old Mill
Epperstone Bypass
Woodborough
Nottingham
NG14 6DH
Wool, acrylic, fancy natural and man-made

Texere Yarns
College Mill
Berkerend Road
Bradford
Yorks
BD3 9AQ
Good selection of yarns, mainly for weaving but suitable for knitting

The Direct Wool Group
P.O. Box 46
Bradford
BD1 2AN
Hand knitting yarns

The Spinning Wheel (Hersey) Ltd
8-10 Colomberie Parade
Colomberie
St. Helier
Jersey
Channel Islands
Traditional Guernsey wool

William Hall and Co. Ltd
177 Standley Road
Cheadle Hulme
Cheadle
Cheshire
SK8 6RF
Cottons, fancy and plain, rayon and chenille

U.S.A.

American Needlewoman
2946 50 S.E. Loop 820
Fort Worth,
Texas 76140

Cones Unlimited Inc.
Close Rd
Salisbury Mills,
NY 12577

The Mannings
RD2, Easter Berlin,
Penn 17316

The Niddy Noddy
416 Albany Post Rd
Croton-on-Hudson,
NY 10520

Periwinkle
Box 426
Drexel Hill,
PA 19026

School Products
1201 Broadway
New York, NY 10001

Further Reading

U.K.

Armes, Alice, *English Smocks*, Dryad Press, 1961

Butler, Anne, *The Batsford Encyclopedia of Embroidery Stitches*, Batsford, 1979

The Collins Complete Book of Needlecraft, Collins, 1981

Complete Guide to Sewing, Readers' Digest, 1978

Crafts, published every two months by the Crafts Council, 8 Waterloo Place, London SW1Y 4AT

Dawson, Pam, *A Complete Guide to Knitting*, Marshall Cavendish, 1976

Durands, Dianne, *Complete Book of Smocking*, Van Nostrand Reinhold, 1982

Dryer, Anne, *Dyes from Natural Sources*, Bell & Hyman, 1976

Finkel, Norma and Leslie, *Kaleidoscope Designs and How to Create Them*, Dover Publications, 1980

Good Housekeeping – Knitting, Ebury Press, 1981

Guide to Good Craft Suppliers, Popular Crafts magazine, Hemel Hempstead

Ladbury, Ann, *Sewing*, Mitchell Beazley, 1978

Lenor Larsen, Jack, and Weeks, Jeanne, *Fabrics for Interiors* Van Nostrand Reinhold, 1975

Nichols, Marion (Ed.), *Designs and Patterns for Embroiderers and Craftsmen*, Dover, 1974

O'Connor, Kaori, *Creative Dressing*, Routledge & Kegan Paul, 1980

Pearson, Michael, *Traditional Knitting of the British Isles*, Esteem Press, 1980

Petersen, Grete, and Svennas, Elsie, *Handbook of Stitches (Embroidery)*, Batsford, 1970

Ryan, Mildred Graves, *The Complete Encyclopedia of Stitchcraft*, Robert Hale, 1981

Snook, Barbara, *Embroidery Stitches*, Batsford, 1981

Weaver, Mary, *The Passap Duomatic, The Ribbing Attachment – Part I, The Ribbing Attachment – Part II, Machine Knitting Technology and Patterns, 1979*, Weaverknits Limited, Dartford

U.S.A.

Gartshore, Linda, *The Craft of Machine Knitting*, Merrimack Book Service, 1978.

Holbourne, David, *The Basic Book of Machine Knitting*, Van Nostrand Reinhold, 1979.

Holbourne, David, *Book of Machine Knitting*, David & Charles, 1979.

Lorant, Tessa, *Hand & Machine Knitting*, Scribner, 1981.

Ratcliffe, Hazel, *Machine Knitting*, State Mutual, 1982.